D0139444

Handbook of Scenery, Properties, and Lighting

Handbook of Scenery, Properties, and Lighting

Volume 1
Scenery and Props
Second Edition

Harvey Sweet

ALLYN AND BACON
Boston London Toronto Sydney Tokyo Singapore

Copyright © 1995, 1989 by Allyn & Bacon
A Simon & Schuster Company
Needham Heights, Massachusetts 02194

All rights reserved. No part of the material protected by this copyright notice may
be reproduced or utilized in any form or by any means, electronic or mechanical,
including photocopying, recording, or by any information storage and retrieval
system, without written permission from the copyright owner.

Library of Congress Cataloging-in-Publication Data
Sweet, Harvey.
      Handbook of scenery, properties, and lighting / Harvey Sweet. --
2nd ed.
        p.   cm.
      Contents: v. 1. Scenery and props
      ISBN 0-205-14878-6 (v. 1)
      1. Theaters--Stage-setting and scenery.   2. Stage lighting.
   3. Stage props.   4. Amateur theater--Production and direction.
   I. Title.
IN PROCESS   94-10989
792'.025--dc20   CIP

Printed in the United States of America
10 9 8 7 6 5 4 3 2 1   98 97 96 95 94

Color Plate C–1 courtesy of Rosco-Iddings Paint Company.
Color Plates C–2 through C–9 courtesy of M. Grumbacher, Inc.
Color Compass is a registered trademark of M. Grumbacher, Inc.

Contents

Preface

A play, opera, ballet, or variety show may be performed anywhere. All that is needed are performers and an audience, but the addition of scenery, properties, and lighting enriches the event for both the performers and the viewers. The setting for a production may be quite elaborate or very simple. Sometimes a single platform is adequate to make a performance special; at other times a complete room may best communicate the sense of place or the dramatic feel for a production.

Traditional methods have been developed to create scenery, properties, and lighting for the theatre. Many of these processes are especially practical; however, they may require time, materials, and specialized skills not available to everyone who wishes to mount a show. Alternative techniques and materials may be used to simplify construction or minimize costs or time demands.

This second edition of *Handbook of Scenery, Properties, and Lighting* is devoted to the worker in modest production circumstances who has a keen interest in production but is limited by time, budget, experience, or the physical resources to mount a production.

The only assumption made in this book is that the reader is interested in practical ways to create scenery and properties for a staged event. Chapter 1 begins with a discussion of the physical elements that compose a performance space and ways to adapt any room for these purposes. Approaches to designing a setting are presented in Chapter 2, with a strategy about how to determine what should be included in the setting based not only on the needs of the production but also on the resources of the production company. The remainder of the book is devoted to detailed explanations of ways of constructing, handling, and painting scenery and properties. The basics of materials, tools, and hardware are explained. Traditional means of scenic construction are presented, followed by descriptions of shortcuts. Each process is presented cookbook fashion, with a list of tools and materials followed by step-by-step instructions with sketches or photos. This text should serve the novice well and will also be a handy resource for more experienced technicians seeking economical solutions for restrictive production situations.

This book has grown out of numerous questions and experiences of teachers and community theatre people seeking ways to enjoy the experience of mounting plays within restrictive limits. Their questions have challenged me to seek practical solutions for traditional problems. The book is dedicated to all of those devoted, enthusiastic, warm people.

I have been assisted in many ways in the preparation of this text. I am grateful to Marilyn Shaw, who provided critical reading and comment throughout preparation of the first edition of the manuscript. Others who have contributed to this book include Julia Tribe, whose hand and torso appear in some of the photos; Theatre UNI, University of Northern Iowa, which permitted the use of production photos throughout the book; and Becky Burns of the University of Northern Iowa. Special thanks to Lynda Griffiths and TKM Productions for production services and to Alice Nichka for the cover design.

I am especially grateful to my teachers who have taught me how to think in a creative way.

Introduction

People participate in theatre because it is fun—it is also a major commitment of time, energy, and resources. The director and cast spend long hours in advance of the performance developing character, learning lines, and rehearsing the play. The crews invest endless hours building and painting scenery, finding and making props, and focusing and cuing the lights. The goal of all of these people is to move, stimulate, and entertain an audience. Whether the cast and crews work in commercial, regional, community, or educational theatre, each person involved in the production aims toward opening night and the joyful sound of applause and laughter that makes the effort worthwhile. The director, performers, and crews, in bringing a script to life, enrich themselves and enhance the quality of life of the community. They provide artistic experiences that share great literature, stimulating ideas, and a great deal of fun with an audience.

Professional directors, actors, and technicians work full time at the creation of effective productions. These artists in commercial and regional theatre usually have financial and material resources, established performance spaces, time, budget, and training to invest in their art. On the other hand, participants in community and school theatre are often volunteers who must make do with limited resources, restricted budgets, unique performance spaces, and limited materials, time, and talent. These differences not withstanding, similar ideals of artistic endeavor pervade the work of both groups. Participants in community and school theatre simply must be more adaptable when staging a play.

Once the choice has been made to mount a production, whether it is a classical drama, musical comedy, opera, ballet, or a concert, a number of details must be considered. They fall into three categories: money, people, and things. Money is always a concern, since few organizations are sufficiently endowed or achieve adequate ticket sales that they may be extravagant. As a result, careful management of budget and utilization of resources are imperative. People are essential to a production: someone must be in charge, others are needed to perform the roles, and still others are needed to turn on the lights and shift the scenery. Finally, there must be a place for the production to rehearse, for scenery and props to be constructed, and for the production to be performed.

Some organizations are fortunate to have fully equipped, functional theatres complete with shop and wing space, drapes, and lighting and sound equipment. Many organizations, however, must adapt existing spaces, such as cafeterias, gymnasiums, warehouses, old stores, or even factories, to present plays, ballets, and concerts. Any location will do, so long as there is adequate space that also allows the audience to see and hear the performance comfortably.

Creation of the performance space and pulling together all the technical elements needed to mount a play are major undertakings. Traditional processes and uses of materials have evolved to deal with these things. These have been adapted to take advantage of new materials and modern technology that often require sophisticated equipment, special materials, and unique skills—all of which can be quite expensive. In many situations, reasonable trade-offs can be made between traditional methods and easier, faster, more economical approaches. Many of these variations produce results similar to those of traditional techniques; however, some alternatives affect the strength, durability, or final appearance of props or scenery. It is practical to combine traditional and alternative means to achieve the most artistic yet economical scenery, props, and lighting.

Whether a production is mounted in educational, community, regional, or commercial theatre, the purpose consistently is to entertain the audience. The time and energy invested in rehearsal and construction are always directed toward this goal. Although budget and facilities may be limited in educational and community theatre, the quality of work should not be. Creativity, imagination, and commitment can result in effective performances, beautiful settings, and wonderful lighting, even under the most restrictive conditions.

Handbook of Scenery, Properties, and Lighting

CHAPTER 1

Planning the Production Space

INTRODUCTION

After the choice has been made to produce a play, musical, opera, ballet, variety show, or concert, the first problem encountered is where to stage the event. Some organizations have a complete, well-equipped theatre or auditorium; however, many school and community theatre groups must use multipurpose rooms or found spaces for performance. Whether a production is mounted on an established stage, in a gym, or at a park, specific needs must be met to facilitate the performance. The design of a typical proscenium theatre meets these needs and establishes standards for all performance spaces.

THE PROSCENIUM THEATRE

The proscenium theatre divides a large room into two distinct spaces: one for the audience and another for the performance. Occasionally the performance may spill into the area occupied by the audience, but generally the areas are kept distinct. The line of demarcation between the spaces is the **proscenium arch**, the large opening that frames the stage and hides the backstage area. Figure 1–1 is an overhead view of a typical proscenium theatre, and Figure 1–2 is a view of a typical proscenium theatre sliced through the center.

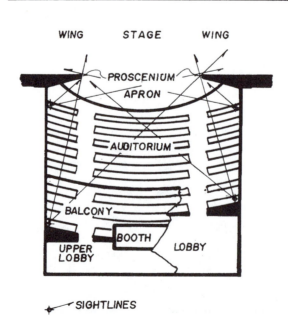

FIGURE 1–1

Overhead (plan) view of a typical proscenium theatre.

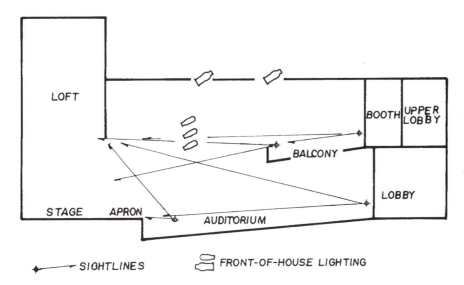

FIGURE 1–2
*View through the center
(centerline section) of a typical
proscenium theatre.*

The Auditorium and Front-of-House

The theatre experience begins for the audience when they decide to attend the performance. This means that every contact with the production must be planned to make members of the audience feel welcome, comfortable, and safe. A well-planned facility, whether temporary or permanent, will address several concerns about the audience from the moment they enter the lobby until they leave at the end of the performance. Not every facility or production situation permits treatment of all these concerns, but awareness of these needs will contribute to a more pleasing experience for the audience.

The entrance to the performance area needs to be obvious from outside the building. If a play is being produced at a school or in a large public facility, signs should direct the audience to the performance. On arrival, people may need a secure place to store coats and will seek restrooms before the entertainment begins and during intermission. The ticket booth, whether a table or window, should be obvious and located so that lines forming to pick up tickets do not conflict with people waiting to enter the auditorium. Ticket-takers should be located to direct the public to the appropriate entrance and ushers should be present to guide people to their seats. The 1991 Americans with Disabilities Act (ADA) requires that all public facilities be accessible to people with physical disabilities. If a facility is not accessible to the physically disabled, accommodations should be made to meet their needs. This may require the addition of ramps or other means to move wheelchairs up stairs as well as provisions to locate wheelchairs in the auditorium without obstructing aisles or exits.

Once seated, all members of the audience should be able to see and hear the performance comfortably. In a typical proscenium theatre this is accomplished by raising the stage 2'-6" to 3'-0" above the front row of seats and arranging the seating in the auditorium on a slope or on steps so that each succeeding row away from the stage has a clear view of the performance. Seats may be staggered between rows so that the people in row 2 look over the shoulders and between the heads of the people sitting in row 1, and the people in row 3 look over the shoulders of the people sitting in row 2. The ability to see the stage is called **sightlines**. Generally, sightlines are checked from the worst seats in the theatre—those furthest to the outside, to the back, and to the front of the seating area—to determine what is visible to the entire audience (Figures 1–1 and 1–2). In an auditorium with balconies, vertical sightlines may be cut off by the underside of the balcony for people on the lower level or by the railing at the front edge of the balcony for the people sitting on the upper level. All of these obstacles must be considered when planning a performance.

Although it is imperative that the audience see the production, it is equally important that they are able to hear what is occurring on the stage. The acoustics of a performance space are a product of all of the architectural characteristics of the stage and auditorium, including the shape of the walls, ceiling, and floor; the materials used for decoration; the layout of the scenery on stage; and the presence of people in the auditorium. Modifying the acoustical quality of a performance space is a difficult task.

In addition to the audience, some production equipment may occupy a portion of the auditorium. Facilities constructed or remodeled in recent years locate lighting and sound control equipment in a booth at the rear of the seating. This permits the board operators to see and hear what is happening during the performance. Often the stage manager will also work from this booth, and if the space is large enough, follow spots may be placed there as well. To be effective, the booth must have intercommunication equipment that allows anyone working backstage to be in contact with the booth personnel.

Another very important group of elements in the auditorium consists of the **front-of-house lighting positions**. These are locations where theatrical lighting instruments may be mounted to focus light on the front third of the stage. The positions may include bare pipes suspended over the audience, pipes mounted in false beams in the ceiling or on catwalks overhead, lights mounted on the front of the balcony, and vertical pipes mounted on the side walls of the auditorium. Each of these positions needs electrical wiring to distribute power to the lighting fixtures. Without front-of-house lighting, it is impossible to illuminate performers adequately near the front of the stage. Since this is the most heavily used portion of the stage, the front-of-house lighting positions are critical.

The Stage

The proscenium stage can be a very simple or quite complex machine. Figure 1–3 shows the "geography" of a typical proscenium stage. In its simplest form, the stage is a bare platform behind an arch that hides offstage spaces: the wings and loft. The **wings** are the areas at the sides of the stage behind the proscenium arch where performers prepare to go on stage and where scenery and properties are stored.

Overhead is the **loft** or **stagehouse**. In smaller facilities with limited space above the stage, immobile rigging is installed on which to mount drapes, scenery, and lighting. This rigging consists of pipes chained to the underside of beams over the stage. When mounted in

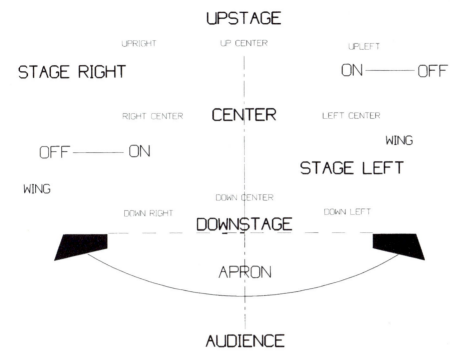

FIGURE 1–3
Geography of a typical proscenium theatre stage. Stage directions are established from the actor's point of view looking toward the audience. Generally, there are nine acting areas: down right, down center, down left, right center, center, left center, up right, up center, and up left. The wings are offstage and anything within the view of the audience is considered to be onstage

this way, properly sized grade-8 chain rated for overhead lifting and connecting links or shackles of adequate strength must be used to secure the pipes. The chains should be placed 6'-0" to *no more* than 12'-0" apart. A pipe hanger should be used to attach the chain to the pipe. In the absence of a pipe hanger, the chain can be wrapped around the pipe, as in (Figure 1–4).

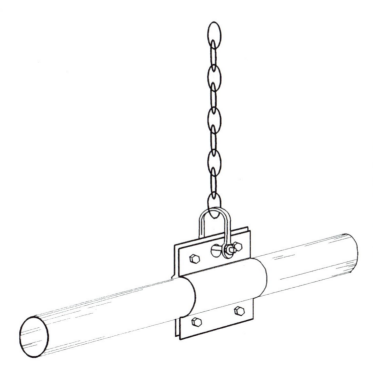

FIGURE 1–4
A heavy ($^3/_{16}$") grade 8 or grade 80 proofcoil chain may be used for stationary rigging. The chain should be attached to a pipe hanger clamp with a shackle or similar chain hardware.

In more functional theatres, rigging equipment is installed in the loft to raise and lower scenery and drapes and to mount lighting instruments. The parts of that equipment are shown in Figures 1–5 and 1–6.

FIGURE 1–5

Hemp set rigging. Scenery is hung on a pipe batten (A). Hemp ropes (B) pass over single pulleys (loft blocks) (C) and then gather together to pass over a multiple pulley (the headblock) (D). All the ropes are tied together at a rope clew or trim clamp (E) to which sandbags (F) are attached. A single working line (the purchase line) (G) is attached to the bottom of the clew or trim clamp. The working line is tied off securely at the pin rail (H).

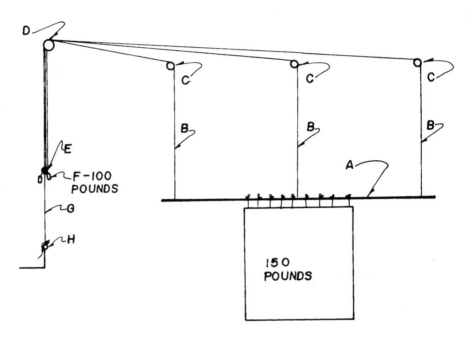

A **hemp set** is a simple pulley system that is permanently installed over the stage. To help raise or lower scenery, a **trim clamp** is incorporated in the system to keep the suspended scenery level, **in trim**, and to allow sandbags to be tied onto the lines to partially balance the load over the stage. Although hemp sets are handy ways to move scenery, *they are very dangerous* and require strong, skilled operators. The scenery must always remain out of balance, with extra weight hanging over the stage, or it will be impossible to bring the scenery to the stage floor. This means that there must always be some way to keep the scenery from falling down. When the lines from the hemp system are tied off at the pin rail, this is not a problem; however, when the scenery is moving, great care must be taken not to lose control of it.

The **counterweight system** is a vast improvement over the hemp set. With this system, the hardware that allows weight to be attached to the hemp set is replaced with more elaborate equipment. When properly used, the counterweight system permits a balanced load, so there is less danger of scenery falling out of control.

Rules for Operating Counterweight Systems

1. **Always keep excess weight at the floor.** When it is possible to load scenery and weight at the same time, load the scenery first, then add the weights to the arbor. When unloading, always remove the excess weight from the arbor first, then unload the scenery.

2. **For rigging only, use ropes and cables that are in good condition.** Inspect them regularly for fraying, kinks, and wear.

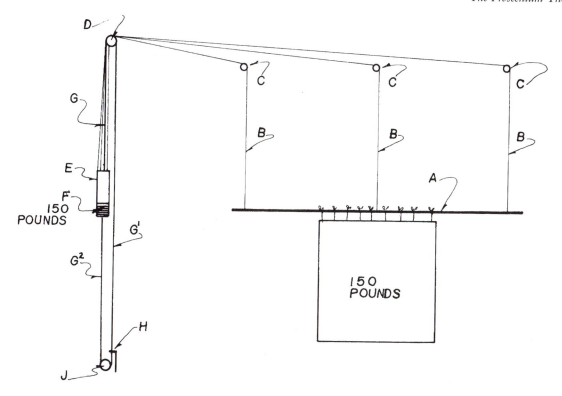

FIGURE 1–6

*Counterweight system. Scenery is hung on a pipe batten (A).
Wire rope (B) supports the batten. Each wire rope is passed over a single pulley (loft block) (C) and then all lines gather together to pass over a multiple pulley (headblock) at (D). All the cables are connected to the top of an arbor (E), a metal cage that moves up and down in a track and carries heavy weights (F) to counteract the weight of the scenery. The arbor, and therefore the pipe batten, is moved up and down by pulling on a rope (G) that passes through a rope lock (H) and around a pulley (J) mounted on the floor and the multiple pulley (D) overhead. When an operator pulls down on G^1, the weights will be raised and the scenery will move toward the floor. When an operator pulls down on G^2, the weights will be lowered, causing the scenery to be raised.*

3. **Always plan a safety factor**. Professional theatre riggers use a minimum safety factor of 8—that is, they use hardware rated eight times stronger than the designed maximum load on a line.

4. **Only move counterweight lines when someone is able to watch the pipe move, preferably the operator of the line**. If this is not possible, someone with a loud voice and a keen eye for potential problems should watch the pipe while it is moving.

5. **Hang scenery and lights on pipes with the proper hardware**. Hangers, ropes, chains, and cables of the appropriate size must be installed properly and securely so anything overhead will not fall off of the rigging.

Some facilities are equipped with **manual winches** (Figure 1–7) to raise and lower heavy loads, such as lighting pipes. These systems may include or replace the counterweights. Only special

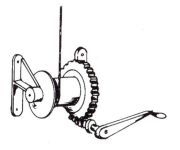

FIGURE 1–7

A manual winch can replace the trim clamp, sandbags, and pin rail on a hemp set or the arbor, rope lock, and floor pulley on a counterweight system.

winches with brakes designed and labeled to hold heavy loads safely above the heads of people should be used in these systems. More modern than hemp or counterweight systems, **Motorized Winch Systems** incorporate the counterweights or replace them with a motor-driven drum specifically designed for lifting and holding loads above the heads of people.

The most common motor-driven system consists of a motor, gear box, brake, controls and sensors, and a grooved drum on which several cables or wire ropes wrap and unwrap to lift and lower a batten (Figure 1–8). Some of these systems, especially those designed to support lighting equipment, operate at a single speed; more sophisticated systems (intended to move scenery or drapes) are usually designed as variable speed systems. All systems allow the batten to stop safely at any location within the normal range of travel.

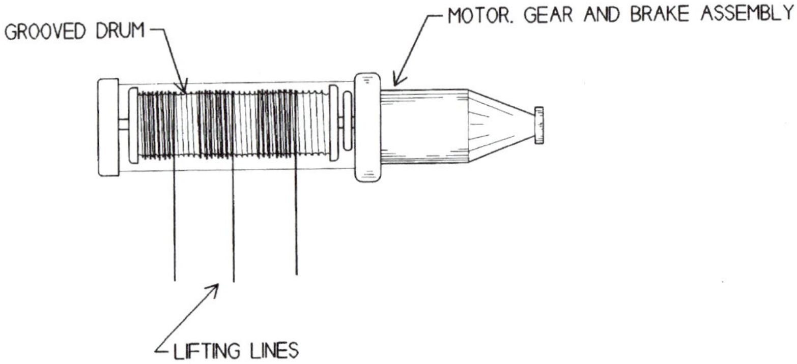

FIGURE 1–8

A typical multiple-line motorized winch. This winch would normally be mounted at the gridiron and operated by remote control from stage level.

GROOVED DRUM

MOTOR. GEAR AND BRAKE ASSEMBLY

LIFTING LINES

An alternative to the multicable winch is the single-cable winch. This system allows a line to be placed anywhere on stage for lifting. Several of these winches can be connected to the same pipe or piece of scenery. When this is done, the control system must coordinate the movement of each of the cables to prevent damaging or dropping the load. This is called a **Synchronous Winch System** (Figure 1–9). A third type of motorized system is the shaft and drum system (Figure 1–10). This system uses a single motor to drive a long shaft on which

FIGURE 1–9

A single-line motorized winch. This can be used to raise an item such as a chandelier that only requires a single support point or several single-line winches can be attached to a batten. This would require synchronous control of the winches to move the lines at the exact same speed and direction.

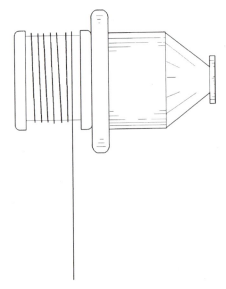

is mounted several drums, one over each lifting point on a batten. A cable is suspended from each drum to lift and support the batten.

A facility with several motorized winches, whether a multicable drum system, a synchronous winch system, or a shaft and drum

FIGURE 1–10
A shaft and drum-rigging system. This system is usually installed below gridirons or on stages where there are no gridirons but there is space and sufficient structure to mount the equipment on the ceiling above the stage. All the drums are connected to a single motor by a shaft. The motor and shaft causes each drum to move at exactly the same speed.

system, often will use a computer to control the winches. These computers can be programmed to automatically select the pipes to move, the direction and speed of movement, and the stopping position for the pipe. Very sophisticated controllers can adjust the rate of travel for different parts of the movement. The controllers can even be programmed so several winches follow exactly the same pattern of movement.

Although motorized equipment is usually significantly more expensive then manually operated systems, it is usually much safer to use than any manual system. There is less likelihood of human error, and most winches are built with failure sensors to shut the system down immediately in the event of a problem. Brakes are normally designed to be engaged unless the system is actually moving.

Drapes are used to hide or **mask** the wings and loft. A complete set of stage curtains (Figure 1–11) consists of legs, borders, an upstage drape, and an act curtain. **Legs** (Figure 1-11E, G, I) are narrow, vertical drapes placed 5'-0" to 8'-0" apart downstage to upstage along each side of the acting area. Each leg may be in a fixed position or mounted on a track that allows it to be towed on or off stage. A leg can also be rigged to rotate 90° on a swivel. Legs are accompanied by **borders** (Figure 1–11D, F, H, J). These are narrow, horizontal curtains placed just in front of each pair of legs. Legs mask the wings and borders mask the loft. A full-width curtain (Figure 1–11K) may

FIGURE 1–11
Drapes are used for masking the wings and loft above the stage. A typical arrangement consists of: (A) valance, (B) act curtain, (C) olio, (D) border, (E) leg, (F) border, (G) leg, (H) border, (I) leg, (J) border, (K) upstage traveller.

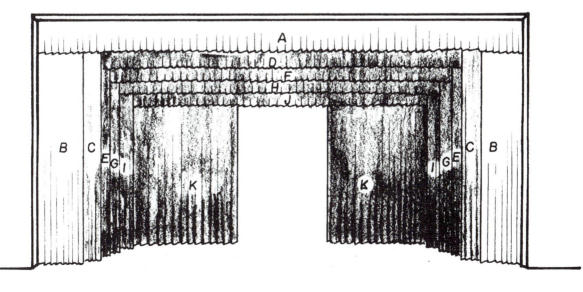

be hung far upstage to enclose the back of the acting area. This drape, when mounted on a track that allows it to open and close from the center, is called a **traveller curtain**. An act curtain or main curtain is usually rigged as a traveller curtain also. Accompanied by a valance, the **act curtain** (Figure 1–11B) usually hangs directly behind the proscenium arch to cover the acting area between scenes and to hide scene changes. The **valance** (Figure 1–11A) helps make a visual transition from the architecture of the proscenium arch to the scenery within the proscenium opening. It also may be used to reduce the height of the proscenium opening. Some stages are equipped with an **olio** curtain (Figure 1–11C), another traveller curtain placed a few feet upstage from the act curtain. This is a full-width decorative drape that covers the backstage area but allows greater stage depth in front of the curtain for between-scene acts.

Stage curtains may be manufactured from almost any material, but the most practical drapes are made of heavy velour or repp. **Velour** is a heavily napped cotton fabric that drapes beautifully and does not reflect light. **Repp** is a less expensive substitute for velour. It has a harder finish and is more light reflective than velour but still drapes well. Legs and borders usually are made of black fabric, but the main curtain, valance, and olio are usually of a colored material.

Stage drapes may be sewn flat or may be built with sewn-in **fullness**, or pleats. Fullness of 50 percent creates pleats in the fabric by using one and one-half times as much fabric as the area to be covered. If a drape must cover a space 10'-0" wide, it will be made from a 15'-0" width of material. The most practical fullness is 50 percent; 100 percent fullness is luxurious.

Curtains that are sewn without fullness may be hung flat or with fullness tied in. This is done by hanging the drape in a space less than the width of the fabric. Each end of the curtain is tied in place, forming a loop between the ties (Figure 1–12A). The center of the loop is tied to the center of the space to form two new loops. The center of each new loop is tied at the center of the remaining spaces and this pattern is repeated until all of the drape is tied in place and the loops are evenly spaced. This is similar to the sewing technique of easing a sleeve. When two sections of drapes come together, they should overlap by at least two tielines (Figure 1–12B).

The proscenium theatre is the most traditional arrangement of the performance space because it offers several advantages:

1. There is a definite visual focus to the performance: the audience faces the stage; the stage is usually the only illuminated area in the room; and only scenery serves as background to the performance.
2. The audience only views the show from one side, so directing, acting, lighting, and scenic construction are easier.
3. It is possible to hide all backstage operations completely, so the audience is never distracted with peripheral activities.
4. There usually are storage spaces adjacent to the acting area to facilitate scene shifts.
5. Scene shifts can be completely hidden.
6. More elaborate scene shifts are possible.

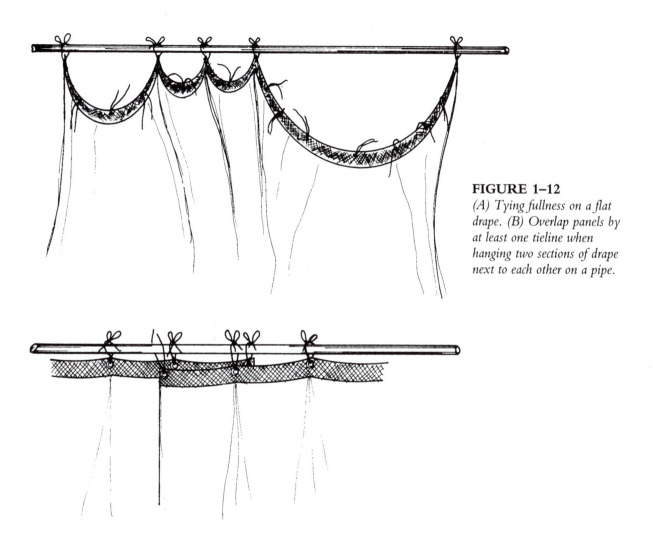

FIGURE 1–12
*(A) Tying fullness on a flat
drape. (B) Overlap panels by
at least one tieline when
hanging two sections of drape
next to each other on a pipe.*

OTHER TRADITIONAL SHAPES FOR THE PERFORMANCE SPACE

A fully equipped proscenium theatre is a highly efficient and flexible machine that can facilitate mounting any play, musical, or concert. However, many school or community theatres are not equipped with such complete facilities, so many productions are mounted in multi-purpose rooms or found spaces that are devoid of all theatrical equipment. This review of the typical proscenium theatre identifies needs that must be considered when planning any performance space:

1. **Actor-audience relationship**:   the proximity and physical arrangement of the audience to the performance.
2. **Sightlines**:   the ability of the audience to see the performance comfortably.
3. **Acoustics**:   the ability of the audience to hear the performance comfortably.
4. **Wing space**:   offstage storage space for scenery, props, and costumes, and a place for actors to prepare to go on stage.

11

5. **Scene-shifting capabilities**: includes places to move and store scenery on the floor and overhead.
6. **Lighting**: a place to locate lights and a means to control lighting.
7. **Sound**: the ability to project sound effects and recorded music.
8. **Intercommunication**: communication among the production staff.
9. **Orchestra**: a place for musicians during musical productions that allows an adequate blending of instrumental and vocal music without damaging other production values.

Depending on the production, budget, and talent, stage and seating arrangements other than the proscenium type are practical for many productions. A permanent stage may be built in any of these layouts or a temporary one may be set up.

Traditional Shapes

Most similar to the proscenium theatre is the **apron stage** (Figure 1–13A). This format places a large acting area immediately in front of the proscenium arch. This arrangement, whether permanent or a temporary modification of a proscenium theatre, creates greater intimacy between the actors and the audience and makes it easier for the audience to see and hear the performers. Adding an apron to a proscenium stage is also a practical way to enlarge the acting area when there is inadequate stage depth or wing space to mount a show. An apron extension may be built using any of the platform techniques described in Chapter 3. It is imperative that front-of-house lighting positions allow illumination to strike the faces of the actors when they are far ahead of the proscenium arch.

A **caliper stage** (Figure 1–13B) extends the apron far to the right and left of the proscenium arch, providing acting areas on either side of the audience as well as directly in front of them. Once again, this extends the acting area, bringing the production closer to the audience but now surrounding them with the performance. This design also creates challenging directing, scenic, and lighting problems.

An **end stage** (Figure 1–13C) is essentially a proscenium theatre without the proscenium arch: there are no wings and often no loft. An area or platform at the end of the room is identified as the stage, and the audience sits in rows facing it. The stage is used in essentially the same way as the proscenium theatre. However, all backstage operations are exposed, and there is no place on stage to store scenery, props, or costumes, or for actors to prepare for entrances. This arrangement offers some of the features of the proscenium theatre but does not establish the formal barrier of the proscenium arch to separate the performers and the audience.

A **corner stage** (Figure 1–13D) places a square or rectangular acting area in a corner against two walls where scenery might be mounted and locates the audience on the other two sides of the square. This adds some complications to the acting, directing, scenic con-

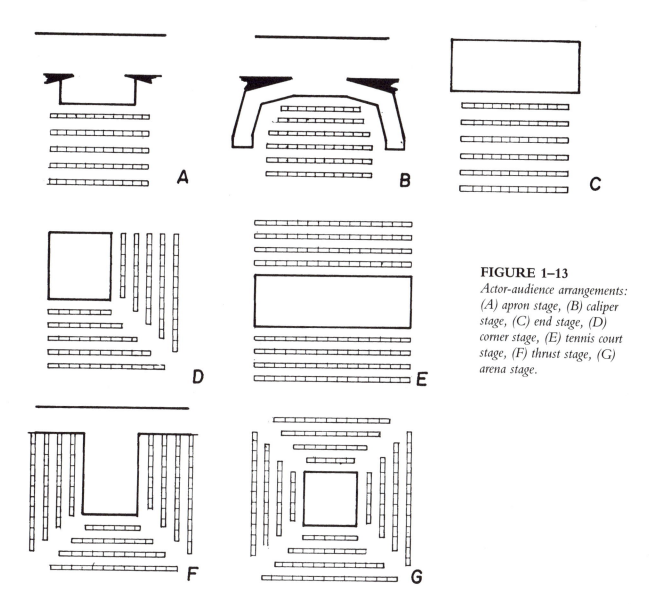

FIGURE 1–13
*Actor-audience arrangements:
(A) apron stage, (B) caliper
stage, (C) end stage, (D)
corner stage, (E) tennis court
stage, (F) thrust stage, (G)
arena stage.*

struction, and lighting because the audience views the show from two directions rather than just one. This arrangement permits an offstage area behind the two scenic walls.

A **tennis court stage** (Figure 1–13E) places the audience on either side of a central strip, which becomes the acting area. This stage is open on the sides to the audience but enclosed with scenery at each end. This provides two scenic walls to help create the locale while allowing the performers to be close to the two groups of audience. Acting, directing, and lighting for this arrangement are challenging. (1) There are two separate and distinct audience groups seeing opposite sides of the performance. As a result, the two groups will not react at the same speed or in the same manner to any moment of the performance. Actors must be carefully placed during critical moments to ensure adequate sightlines for both groups. (2) Entrances may be through the scenic walls at either end of the stage or through aisles in the audience. (3) Lighting must be from at least two, and preferably three, sides of the stage. (4) Each section of audience sees the audience seated on the opposite side of the stage as a background to the performance.

The **thrust** or **three-quarters stage** (Figure 1–13F) is a peninsula thrust into the middle of the audience. Seating is arranged so that all members of the audience face the stage. This brings the actors and the audience close together. Actors may enter from upstage and additional entrances are usually placed within the seating. The upstage wall is used for scenery. This arrangement establishes directing, scenic, and lighting challenges as well. (1) All properties and scenic units downstage must be kept low enough so as not to interrupt sightlines. (2) The actors and scenery are visible from three sides of the stage. (3) Scene changes are completely exposed. (4) Lighting must be from at least three sides of the stage. (5) Two-thirds of the audience see other members of the audience as a background to the performance.

An **arena stage** (Figure 1–13G) places the acting area at the center of the seating with the audience on all sides facing the stage. The arena is similar to a thrust stage in many ways. (1) Once again, the audience is very close to the performance, and now the actors always enter through the seating. (2) All scenery must be kept low so it does not interrupt sightlines. (3) Scenery is usually restricted to very well-chosen properties and set dressings that must be carried through the audience or stored within the acting area for scene changes. (4) Lighting must originate from a minimum of three sides of the stage to illuminate the performers adequately. (5) All members of the audience see other audience members as a background to the performance.

DEFINING THE STAGE

When dealing with temporary or multipurpose production facilities, it is usually necessary to create the performance space. In its simplest form, this consists of setting up seats and defining the stage. A stage may be defined in numerous ways. In part, it is a matter of use, and in part, it is a matter of creating some kind of physical identification to create the acting area.

Seating arrangements are the simplest way to define a stage. By arranging chairs around and facing an open space, a place where the audience will not be sitting—the stage—is defined. The area can remain bare, or scenery, properties, and lighting can be added to adorn the performance space. It is, of course, always better to arrange the seating in rows on platforms to help sightlines, but in the worst circumstance the simple arrangement of chairs will create the performance space.

It is imperative to check local building codes whenever setting up temporary seating for an audience. Most communities restrict the number of seats in a row to 13 or 14 chairs, with an aisle at each end of the row, and allow no more than 7 seats when one end of the row is against the wall. It is usually necessary for chairs in a row to be attached to each other. There is a requirement for a minimum distance between rows of seats, usually 21" to 24" from seat back to seat back. There are additional codes that establish the width of aisles (usually no less than 42" wide) and the number, size, identification, and location of exits.

The location of the stage can be more clearly defined by either painting the floor of the acting area or laying a carpet or ground cloth in that area. A **ground cloth** is a piece of muslin or canvas that is painted and then temporarily stretched over the floor. It may be attached with staples, nails, or tape, or it may be held in place with weights. A combination of the seating arrangement, scenery, and properties and a ground cloth clearly distinguish the acting area from the audience space. In place of the ground cloth or carpet, it may be possible to coat the floor with a paint that can be washed off after the production. This approach should be taken *only with advance permission* and *only after testing the paint* in a small area of the floor. Paint or subsequent cleaning may damage some floor materials.

Light alone may be used to define a performance space. This is especially effective if the light can be kept very sharply focused on the performance area without stray beams spilling onto the audience. This is a very simple way to define a stage. Although details about lighting are discussed in Volume II, it is suggested that hard-edged lights, such as ellipsoidal reflector spotlights, be hung directly above the acting area and aimed straight down to define the stage. The shutters will allow the edges of the stage to be given a precise shape.

The most effective way to define an acting area is to build a raised platform for the stage. The platform may be constructed to any shape and as high as desired. Several ways to create an elevated platform are described in Chapter 3.

Proscenium apron and caliper stages are the only layouts that require some kind of vertical enclosure. In a temporary production situation, the proscenium arch can be formed with drapes, flats, or even crates stacked up on either side of the stage.

PROBLEM SOLVING

No matter what kind of facility is worked in, whether temporary or permanent, proscenium or thrust, there are always a few problems that must be solved. These may range from dealing with a slippery floor to poor acoustics.

Floors

Many proscenium stages in schools and public buildings have been properly constructed with softwood floors and coated with nonskid, nonglare finishes. Many other stage floors are coated with high-gloss finishes that reflect light into the audience and on the scenery. This mirror-like effect makes walking and dancing very difficult, as well as frustrating when trying to control lighting. Many floor finishes are skid resistant; however, some are not. A slippery floor can be mopped with a nonslip coating available from some custodial and theatrical suppliers. This coating will dull an existing finish and reduce the likelihood of slipping. An inexpensive and handy alternative to the commercial coating is to mop the floor with a bucket of water containing approximately one quart of cola. After the mop solution has dried, both glare and slipperiness should be reduced. It may be necessary to strengthen the concentration of cola on some floors. It is a good idea to wash the floor clean every few days and to reapply the cola solution before each succeeding performance. An excessive build-up of cola will become sticky—it will also attract ants. Both the commercial finish and the cola solution should be tested on a small area of the floor before making a general application to be sure neither mixture damages the permanent floor or finish.

Lights

Often an adapted performance space does not provide a way to mount lighting instruments overhead. **Booms** or **trees** (Figure 1–14) may be used to mount lights. These are free-standing vertical poles set up in heavy steel bases. The booms and trees can be located anywhere they are needed so long as they will not tip over, block aisles, or obstruct sightlines. Extra weight should be added on the bases, and it is imperative to tie the top of the pipes to something rigid overhead.

In facilities where the steel structure supporting the roof or celling is exposed and accessible, a pipe can be suspended from beam hangers attached to the flange of the beams or trusses. Lighting instruments can then be mounted on the pipe. Lighting fixtures should not be clamped directly to beam or truss flanges. This mounting is not sufficiently secure to be safe.

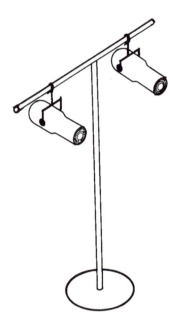

FIGURE 1–14

Lighting boom or tree. Add weights to the base and, tie off the top overhead.

Sound

If a room is too alive with sound, some of the garbled effect can be reduced by covering hard, sound-reflecting surfaces such as plaster, concrete, and stone with thick, soft, sound-absorbent materials such as fiberglass batting or velour drapes. Drapes may simply be suspended in front of the reflective surfaces. The drapes should be as full as possible. Sound-absorption panels can be manufactured to place in front of these surfaces as well. Rectangular frames 3½" deep, 24" wide, and 8'-0" long can be made of wood. The interior of the frame is filled with 3½" × 8'-0" blankets of fiberglass insulation and covered with burlap, corduroy, or velour. These panels may be kept in place permanently or taken down between productions and replaced for the next show.

When a space is large and cavernous, like some gyms, it is also necessary to break up the overhead movement of sound. This may easily be done by hanging panels of absorptive material down from the ceiling to baffle the movement of the sound. Heavy velour drapes or several layers of fire-retarded felt may be used for this application.

Sometimes the acoustical problem is an absence of reflection rather than an excess of sound. If too much sound is trapped backstage, a hard surface such as flats coated with latex paint can be placed behind the performers to bounce some of the sound forward into the audience. Also, if a production is performed in a large space not fully occupied by an audience, flats covered with wood and painted with latex can be placed around the seating area to reflect some sound back to the audience. Caution is necessary, however, since reflected sound can often cause an echo effect. This may distort sounds more than it enhances the ability of the audience to hear the performance.

CONCLUSION

The nature of the performance space contributes significantly to the way an audience perceives a production. A pleasant, comfortable atmosphere will contribute to a positive response from the audience. A safe environment will contribute to the well-being of everyone. Not only must careful consideration be given to the needs of the audience but equal consideration must be given to the needs of the production. This begins with careful planning. An awareness of the limits of the production space and the producing organization and an understanding of the needs of the show are essential. Once the needs and limits of the production have been determined, work can proceed to mount the show.

Designing the Production

INTRODUCTION

Once the decision has been made to do a play and the performance space has been determined, it is necessary to design the setting. The setting is composed of the scenery, properties, and lighting, which work with the costumes and makeup to create a total image that fulfills many important functions for an effective performance. It establishes a place for the actors to perform, defines the mood and style of the play, provides expository information about the characters and situations, and controls where actors move on stage.

FUNCTIONS OF THE SETTING

The setting defines a place to perform by separating the activities of the play from the activities of daily life. This allows the performers to create characters and perform actions that might not be accepted or believed without some indication that the people and the activities, although credible, are not real. For instance, when a character is murdered on stage, the audience must believe in that death as part of the performance, but should not be concerned about the safety of the actor performing the role. By doing a play in a place that clearly distinguishes reality from performance, the audience is able to accept extreme characters, actions, and situations and believe in them as part of the performance.

The setting establishes mood by manipulating the elements of design (line, shape, mass, texture, and color) and by controlling the principles of art (balance, emphasis, rhythm, and proportion). For instance, a setting composed of thick, solid, vertical bars will evoke a completely different mood from one composed of soft, undulating, curvaceous lines or jagged lines crossing at sharply conflicting angles. The way color affects mood is more apparent. People respond negatively to black and gray, describing them as "gloomy." On the other hand, bright colors, such as yellow or turquoise, are usually seen as cheerful, but intense red is considered alarming. By means of careful selection of the colors, textures, shapes, and lines that compose a setting, it is possible to communicate the way a scene or the play as a whole feels. Dynamic control of mood is achieved by changing the color, angle, and intensity of the lights.

The setting defines the style by making a distinctive visual statement. The scenic style should be consistent with the literary style of the script. A realistic style in stage design, as in literature, does not necessarily mean absolute veracity. Normally, there is selection of details included in the design rather than the unselected look of naturalism. If the script is distinguished by obviously artificial characteristics, such as the extremes of a nineteenth-century melodrama, then the setting should be equally artificial. Some examples of scenic styles are shown in Figure 2–1.

The setting provides exposition to introduce the story and characters. In theatre, unlike fiction, it is impractical to include long descriptions in the dialogue to acquaint the audience with the locale, historical period, country, time, and personalities composing the story. Instead, the setting communicates a great deal of this information as soon as the curtain is opened on the performance. Within a moment, the audience is informed of the locale (apartment, living room, forest, bedroom, mountain, or an imaginary world), country, and historical period of the play. As they are able to study details of the setting, the audience can begin to understand the social and

FIGURE 2–1
(A) Realism (When You Comin' Back Red Ryder?), (B) formalism (Hang Onto Your Head), (C) cartoon (The Mandrake); (D) fragmentation (The Dining Room), (E) stylization (The Bacchae), (F) theatricalization (Yankee Doodle). (Courtesy Theatre UNI, University of Northern Iowa.)

A.

B.

C.

D.

E.

F.

economic status of the characters and the situation of the play. For instance, a room assumes one personality when the walls are covered with expensive looking modern art, but projects a different image when the same walls are covered with *Playboy* centerfolds, protest banners, or smears of blood. Different expectations about the inhabitants of the space and the action of the play are established with each of these decors. The impressions created are enhanced with appropriate furniture, such as lacquer and glass benches and a leather sofa to accompany the modern art, or well-worn, tattered, overstuffed furniture, stacks of books, a desk and typewriter, and an old brass lamp with a torn shade to accompany the centerfolds. On the other hand, the effect of one element, for instance the protest banners, can be confused by accompanying it with an unexpected element such as a Louis XIV armoire. Any duality of this vision must be consistent with the characters and actions of the script, or the audience will be confused about the nature of the characters or the situation of the play.

Equally important is a consistency of historical styles. Although furniture styles are eclectic in most periods, a play taking place in Victorian England should not be confused by adding furniture from a later historical period such as Art Deco. Whether or not the audience is familiar with periods of furniture, they will sense the inappropriateness of this mix. Scenery and props can communicate a lot of information, but the messages must be stated clearly.

The setting is a plan of action that forces the actors to move to certain places by means of specific paths. This plan of action is created by placing doors, windows, stairs, ramps, furniture, and other obstacles and islands on the set. The doors restrict where an actor may enter or exit and the furniture forces the actor to move around the set in specific patterns and sit or stand in definite locations. The furniture functions as islands for the actors to work around, sit on, and come to. By placing interesting properties and set dressings on tables, mantels, or chairs, an actor has reasons to move to a location—perhaps to pick something up or just to look at it. In addition, the location of entrances, stairs, ramps, and platforms tend to force certain scenes to be played in specific areas of the stage. Decisions about each of these elements must relate to the script.

With all of these important functions, the setting makes a major contribution to the way an audience perceives, understands, and enjoys a play. The level of achievement for the production as a whole is heightened when the scenery, properties, and lighting are planned as a cohesive part of the overall experience. An appropriate design for the show has been achieved when the setting supports and enhances the characters, the action, and the ideas expressed in the script. Although modern audiences want the setting to be exciting, they usually are most satisfied when the performance as a whole, including the setting, makes a total unified impact on them.

DESIGN ELEMENTS

When planning the setting, objects are selected and arranged to define the space. Reduced to the most basic level, it is the elements of design— line, shape, mass, color, and texture—that are manipulated to affect contrast, balance, and rhythm for the purpose of creating an appropriate visual composition that will support the action of the play.

Line, whether actual or implied, indicates position and direction. In addition, the shape and quality of a line may evoke psychological or emotional responses that should be considered in the design of a setting (Figure 2–2).

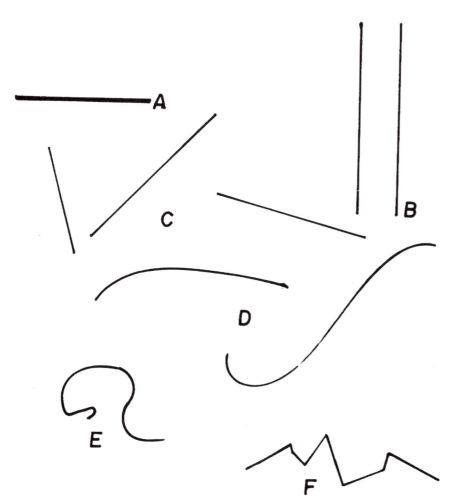

FIGURE 2–2
The psychological effect of lines. (A) Horizontal lines are restful and stable. (B) Vertical lines suggest dignity and tallness. (C) Diagonal and sloping lines are lines of action, transition, and unbalance, suggesting dramatic and powerful movement indicating a dynamism of unresolved tendencies. (D) Slow curves are sensuous and sophisticated, whereas (E) sharp curves are comic and (F) jagged lines are exciting, nervous, and irritable.

Shape is delineated by actual or implied lines that state the boundaries of a flat plane. **Mass** is actual or implied three-dimensional shape. It frequently has some geometric form such as a cube, triangle, or oval.

The location of a form is referred to as **position**. It is commonly believed that certain positions on the stage cause a stronger psychological impact on an audience than other locations. Each of the nine major acting areas of the proscenium stage are rated by psychological weight in Figure 2–3. Height also adds emphasis. Elevating a performer has the effect of strengthening the psychological impact of that person without regard to location in a specific acting area.

Proportion is the term used to describe the relationships of height, width, depth, and surrounding space. These relationships are often referred to as **scale**. An object or an entire setting may be just the right size or may appear too large or too small for the stage, the actors, or the play—in which case it is "out of scale."

FIGURE 2–3
Acting areas on a proscenium stage rated by their psychological strength.

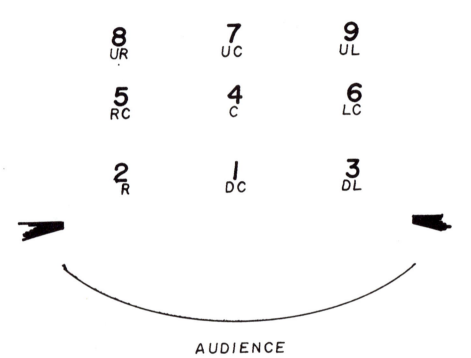

Every surface has **texture**—that real or implied physical quality that gives a plane its own apparent feel and that appeals to the sense of touch. The texture may be smooth, rough, slippery, granular, hard, soft, shiny, dull, or bright.

Color is the combination of hue, value, and chroma. By controlling each of these components, several thousand colors can be created, each imbuing its own sense of appropriateness and its own psychological effect. This is discussed in Chapter 5. Color can control focus as well as suggest actuality or unreality.

These elements affect the rhythm, contrast, and balance of a setting.

Rhythm (Figure 2–4) visually creates a sense of movement and direction by repeating patterns with accents.

Contrast refers to the differences in the field of vision that reveal form. Contrasts may be the result of subtle or gross differences of one or several of the elements of design within an object, between objects, or between an object and its backround. Too little contrast in a composition will result in monotony and an inability to distinguish form; too much contrast will result in visual chaos.

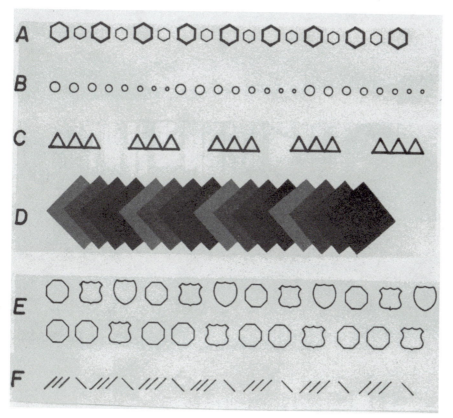

FIGURE 2–4
Examples of rhythm. (A) Parts of a pattern might be placed alternately—big, little, big, little. (B) They might occur in sequence such as big, medium, small. (C) A pattern may be created by the proximity of shapes separated by spaces. (D) The repetition might be created in color or value, (E) shape, or (F) direction of objects or lines.

Visual **balance** occurs when objects that demand equal attention are placed so that none is dominant. There are two types of balance: symmetrical and asymmetrical. **Symmetrical balance** (Figure 2–5A) occurs when matching objects are placed equidistant from each other, creating a static, rigid picture that suggests great dignity. **Asymmetrical balance** (Figure 2–5B) occurs when dissimilar objects or forms are given qualities that make them demand equal attention. These special qualities may increase or decrease proportion, color, or contrast; modify position; or make an adjustment in some other manner that will alter the emphasis on a form. Asymmetrical balance is dynamic, exciting, and comfortable.

A.

FIGURE 2–5
(A) Symmetrical balance
(The Mikado), *(B)*
asymmetrical balance (A Flea
in Her Ear). *(Courtesy*
University of Northern Iowa.)

B.

PREPARING TO DESIGN

The setting for a performance should support and enhance it. Achievement of this goal begins with careful study of the script to determine (1) what the play is about, (2) how the play feels, and (3) what the physical requirements of the production are. This information contributes to formation of a **design idea**, an image based on research of period and style and an understanding of the script that leads to the actual design.

Analysis of the Script

Studying a script to determine what a play is about is a typical directorial function. This analysis usually considers who the characters are, what they do, how and why they do it, and what the results of their action are. This may lead to a thematic statement about the effects of ego for a play like *Oedipus The King* or a simple statement about life as an early teenager for a script such as Lillian Hellman's *A Member of the Wedding*.

Understanding what the play is about will also help develop an emotional response to it. When the play is read—and when an audience sees it—what emotional response should be elicited? How does the play feel? Does it evoke a sense of happiness, sadness, depression, warmth, joy, conflict, hate, fear, excitement, anticipation, love? These responses should influence the look and feel of the performance. A happy play should occur in a bright environment, whereas a conflict-ridden script would be out of place in a cheerful, daisy-filled drawing room. However, the feelings stimulated by a play may change during the course of the action. A script that is primarily happy may have an ironical twist causing sadness and depression during the last few moments when, for instance, an unexpected death occurs. Depending on the show, the setting may stand in ironic contrast to the end of the play or the setting could foreshadow the twist of fate by subtly suggesting impending doom through manipulation of the design elements.

Finally, it is necessary to determine the physical requirements of the production. Two categories of information are needed: what is *requested* and what is *required*.

Most plays are published with a brief description of each setting. These statements may have been prepared by the playwright or they may be notes from the original production of the script. They are *suggestions* of the location and appearance of architectural features, furniture, and set dressings that *might* compose the setting. Very seldom is it necessary to include exactly what is described in these notes, nor is it necessary to place things precisely where they are called for in the descriptions. Usually these instructions should be considered as requests for a *kind* of place rather than a requirement for doors, windows, furniture, and set dressings. *The Odd Couple* by Neil Simon exemplifies this well.

TIME: *A warm summer night.*

SCENE: *The apartment of Oscar Madison. This is one of those large eight-room affairs on Riverside Drive in the upper eighties. The building is about 35 years old and still has vestiges of its glorious past. High ceilings, walk-in closets, and thick walls. We are in the living room with doors leading off to a kitchen, bedrooms, and a bathroom, and a hallway to other bedrooms. Although the furnishings have been chosen with extreme good taste, the room itself, without the touch and care of a woman these past few months, is now a study in slovenliness. Dirty dishes, discarded clothes, old newspapers, empty bottles, glasses filled and unfilled, opened and unopened laundry packages, mail, and disarrayed furniture abound. The only cheerful note left in this room is the lovely view of the New Jersey Palisades through its twelfth-floor window. Three months ago, this was a lovely apartment.*

AT RISE: *The room is filled with smoke. A poker game is in progress. There are six chairs around the table but only four men are sitting....* [*]

This set description primarily describes the quality of this apartment: an older building in an expensive neighborhood in upper Manhattan. The apartment is well furnished but covered with trash. Several doors are called for as well as a window. There must be a table on which to play poker and six chairs. No other specifics about the furniture or the architecture are stated here. When the dialogue begins, it is discovered that there must be a nonfunctioning air conditioner in the window, another window that opens, a telephone that rings, and several other specific items. These are required by the dialogue and the actions of the characters. They have been omitted in the set description but are absolutely necessary for the play to progress.

A quick count reveals that at least five doors are required in the stage directions: one to the kitchen, two to bedrooms (the dialogue indicates that two bedroom doors should be on the set), one to the bathroom, and one as the apartment entrance, plus a hallway to additional bedrooms. Although several pieces of business in the play require all of these entrances, the bedroom and bathroom doors can be eliminated by having all of these entrances down a hallway that is not visible to the audience. Stage directions referring to each of the bedrooms and the bathroom would simply be played at the entrance to the hallway. Although this reduces some of the humor of the play, it also eliminates a lot of scenic construction. It is a matter of choice to include everything called for in stage directions and set descriptions. The choices must be made on the basis of the practical production decisions as well as the dialogue and actions of the play.

At the back of this script is a props list that requires eight chairs, seven tables, a sofa, a love seat, several lamps, and a few other pieces of furniture, plus two additional pages of text listing set dressings. This is a list of props used in an earlier production of the play—probably the original Broadway production. Simply because the list calls for all this furniture plus a red and black diamond tie, two pots of dead ivy, a paisley pillow, a toy airplane, and dozens of other items does not mean these specific articles are required for the show. Although furniture and set dressings are needed, none of these specific items are required by any action nor are they referred to in the dialogue. Most of the furniture and set dressings called for in this list may be replaced or eliminated without affecting the play. The props list at the back of most scripts should be considered as a guide, a place to begin; the dialogue in the script and the action worked out in rehearsals will establish the actual scenic and properties requirements. The script must be read carefully and rehearsals monitored to determine the real needs of the show.

The objective of this analysis is not to strip the setting to the minimum, but to discern what is absolutely required by the play and then to figure out what other things would be helpful to the performance to complete the visual image and to aid the actors. This under-

[*] From The Odd Couple, by Neil Simon. Copyright © 1966 by Nancy Enterprises, Inc. Reprinted by permission of Random House, Inc.

standing allows greater flexibility in planning the setting and in seeking the props for the production.

The analysis of the text should also consider the historical period in which to mount the play. Some scripts may be easily modernized to make them more understandable by a contemporary audience. Also, updating can simplify the design task by placing a show clearly within the experience of the production company. It can also ease the work of the properties crew by allowing the use of contemporary furniture and set dressings. Not all plays, however, may be updated. In some instances, the actions, values, or social mores of the play restrict the production to an earlier historical period. In some of these, it may be possible to make an adjustment of historical period without bringing a play all the way into a contemporary setting. For instance, a play written about medieval England might be placed in a Victorian setting. If the setting is updated, the dialogue and costumes must be modified as well.

Analysis of the Production Situation

Once the needs established by the script have been determined, it is important to identify the limits and restrictions that may exist as a result of the production situation. Each of the following should be considered and should be kept in mind while completing plans for the production:

1. Budget
2. Existing scenery and properties available
3. Raw materials in stock
4. Schedule
   a. Rehearsal time
   b. Scenic construction time
   c. Dress rehearsal time
   d. Performance time
   e. Strike (tear-down and clean-up) time
5. Space
   a. Availability
   b. Condition
   c. Sightlines
   d. Acoustics
   e. Lighting capabilities
   f. Orchestra requirements
   g. Size of stage
   h. Wing space
   i. Scene-shifting capabilities
   j. Rigging capabilities
   k. Relationship of stage to audience
   l. Possible modifications to the space
6. Talent available
   a. Carpenters
   b. Painters
   c. Properties people
   d. Stagehands

  e. Lighting people
  f. Sound people
  g. Designers

Research

Designing a setting is a matter of selecting and assembling the proper details. Decisions about what is to be included and where things are to be placed are made on the basis of the analysis of the text and the production situation. After that analysis, some settings can be planned based on personal experience, but many plays occur in locales or time periods that require study to obtain the appropriate sense of place. This research need not be extensive or difficult: what is sought are several examples of the kinds of places to be represented on stage to acquire a familiarity with the form and style of the historical period and the locale. Ultimately, the research saves time by simplifying and clarifying the choices about scenery and properties.

The sources of information on which to base a design are virtually endless. They include pictures in old family albums, magazines, period paintings and photographs, art books, old catalogs, or any other visual source that might be helpful. The researcher is looking for distinctive architectural and decorative treatments and a feeling for the uses of line, form, mass, color, and texture typical of a style or period.

This research should evoke feelings and ideas about the appearance of the setting tempered by a consideration of the requirements of the script and the limits of the production situation.

THE DESIGN PROCESS

In many situations, budget, time, or talent restricts the production process to setting up existing scenery and perhaps refreshing it with a coat of paint. Other production situations allow more variety in assembling settings by permitting flats and platforms to be placed in several different arrangements. When budget and time allow, the scenic stock may be expanded to increase the variety possible. The ideal production situation allows the use of existing scenery supplemented with new pieces or items built especially for the show currently being mounted.

Within each of these situations, scenery can simply be set up and moved around until the desired arrangement is achieved. However, it is usually more efficient to do some advance planning in preparation for mounting the scenery. This may consist of simply sketching a floor plan and thumbnail or may include painting a rendering or constructing a model.

A **floor plan** is a drawing of the setting as it appears (more or less) from overhead (Figure 2–6). Most scenic designs begin with this sketch, which is drawn in **scale** as a miniature representation of the actual setting. The handiest scale for this work is to make ¼" on the drawing represent 1'-0" in actuality, so that a line ¼" long represents 1'-0", a line ½" long represents 2'-0", and a line ⅞" long represents 3'-6". Using a ruler and pencil, the exact placement of walls, doors, windows, arches, stairs, railings, and bookshelves is indicated, and all

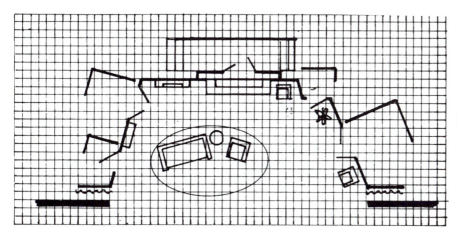

FIGURE 2–6
Typical floor plan of a setting.

architectural detail and all furniture are drawn to the proper size to be sure of the relationship of parts to each other and to the stage as a whole. It usually takes several tries to get all of the scenery and props to fit exactly where desired. (See *The Complete Book of Drawing for the Theatre* for detailed instructions about these drawing precesses.)

The floor plan only represents the location of furniture and architectural parts; it does not help very much with planning the appearance of walls or the shape of trees for an exterior setting. Although it is not requisite that these details be designed on paper, communication, budgeting, planning, and the work process are eased when some kind of graphic representation of the setting is made. This may be a thumbnail sketch, a rendering, or a three-dimensional model.

A **thumbnail sketch** (Figure 2–7) is a miniature drawing that shows the approximate appearance of the setting from the front of the stage. Although it is best to do the sketch more or less in scale, just getting a rough view of the setting will help solidify thinking about the design.

FIGURE 2–7
Thumbnail sketch of the scenic design in development.

A **rendering** (Figure 2–8) is a well-done, properly scaled perspective drawing of the setting complete with all details and colors. Most of the design decisions are made while the rendering is in process so that the only decisions about the appearance of the show that must be made while the scenery is being constructed are minor details or adaptations to accommodate changes. Renderings are extremely helpful in planning a show but they require training and practice to paint or draw.

FIGURE 2–8

Watercolor rendering of the scenic design.

A **three-dimensional model** (Figure 2–9) can be constructed to show the exact placement of each of the elements of the setting. The model may be constructed from balsa wood, cardboard, illustration board, or almost any other material. The model may be left unpainted or may be painted a neutral color so that it represents only the physical arrangement of the setting, or it may be fully painted and decorated with all of the details of the setting. Once again, the model can be extremely helpful in planning a show because it identifies the exact use of space and all other design decisions.

FIGURE 2–9

One style of a three-dimensional model of a scenic design. Furniture has been painted on the wall to indicate the style of the furniture and the space it will fill on the wall. The space the items are to occupy on the floor is indicated by outlines of the furniture. Three-dimensional furniture could be constructed to fit the model and show the placement, size, and relationship of the pieces.

CONCLUSION

Once the design has been developed, whether it is held in mind or committed to a floor plan and thumbnail sketch, rendering, or model, it will provide a basis for planning the construction and painting of the scenery, development of the props list, and planning the lighting. By being able to identify the content of the set at the beginning of work on the show, meaningful plans regarding time, budget, and materials can be made. From that point on, it is simply a matter of utilizing resources in the best possible way to mount the production.

CHAPTER 3

Constructing and Handling Scenery

INTRODUCTION

Scenery is intended for temporary use on stage. Its purpose is to create the impression of a location, such as an apartment or a garden, or to establish an appropriate theatrical environment for performance that evokes an effective mood. Whether the setting is realistic or theatricalized in style, reality itself is left to Mother Nature. Actual rooms are the province of the construction industry and pure abstract expression is the realm of the easel painter and sculptor.

People who build scenery are concerned with economy, strength, weight durability, ease of construction, and ease of handling. To accommodate these needs, a variety of standard construction practices have evolved as traditional techniques and uses of materials. The materials are readily available in most locales and may be easily worked with common tools. The combination of standard techniques and standard materials yields strong, economical, adaptable scenic pieces. When sizes are standardized, these scenic units may be treated as interchangeable parts that can be combined and recombined in infinite variety to form a vast array of settings from just a few pieces. These traditional methods save time and money but do not solve all design and construction problems, nor are they always the most appropriate choice for all theatres or all production situations. New design challenges and unforeseeable problems often lead to the need for creative solutions. New materials and techniques are often found to solve these problems. No solution should be discarded simply because it has not been used before or does not exist in a book. If an idea, technique, or material seems practical and safe, it should be tested; if it works, it should be used. The methods described in this chapter should provide a foundation for basic scenic construction as well as creative thinking to solve problems. These practices are a beginning; they are not the sole solutions.

Throughout this chapter, traditional construction methods are presented. These are followed by explanations of some alternative ways to create the same or similar effects at less cost or using alternative techniques. Each theatre practitioner should explore these methods along with other techniques to create scenery that is practical for his or her own production situation.

CONSTRUCTION MATERIALS

Many standard supplies used to build scenery are readily available from lumberyards and building supply dealers. It is helpful to know the names and characteristics of these materials for the purpose of placing orders or selecting alternative approaches.

Lumber

The construction material most commonly used for scenery is lumber. It is readily available, moderately inexpensive, easily worked with both hand and power tools, and it meets the basic needs of weight, strength, economy, durability, and workability. Softwoods, especially firs and pines, are used for scenic construction because they meet these criteria and are relatively inexpensive.

Softwoods are graded at the lumber mill just as meat is graded at the butcher shop. This grading system describes the quality of the lumber, indicating the presence and tightness of knots, straightness of grain, quality of drying and milling, and other characteristics. The system divides woods into two categories. The first category is called *finish* or *select* and is graded A through D, A being the best. This wood is virtually knot-free and very straight grained. It is very expensive and is usually reserved for moldings, fine construction, and furniture. The second category of wood is identified as *common* or *construction* lumber. It is graded #1 through #4, #1 being the best. A great deal of scenery is constructed from #2 pine, although most commercial scene shops build scenery from finish lumber. The cost of select grades of wood is prohibitive for general use. Lumber grades #3 and #4 are usually too poor in quality for scenic construction.

Lumberyards maintain a stock of standard-size boards. The material is identified by **nominal dimensions**. That is, the name of a board, for instance a *one by three* (1 × 3), does not describe the actual dimensions of the lumber: the actual dimensions are somewhat less because of the milling and finishing processes (Figure 3–1). Table 3–1 lists commonly available board sizes. The first column gives the name or nominal dimension of the lumber, and the second column lists the actual dimensions for each size board. When purchasing lumber, the pieces are ordered by *nominal* thickness, *nominal* width, and *actual* length. The lengths of boards usually stocked are 8'-0", 10'-0", 12'-0", 14'-0", and 16'-0", although some yards will cut wood to other specific lengths. Lumber for special use is often stocked in lengths up to 24'-0". The actual length of boards received is usually ⅛" to ½" longer than the dimensions ordered, so all wood must be trimmed to the exact length needed. This allows a worker to be sure that each end of a board is cut square without shortening the board to less then its possible maximum length.

A typical lumber order would be stated in this way: "Ten pieces of #2 pine one by three 12-feet long." Ten pieces of lumber measuring ¾" × 2¾" × 12'-¼" or slightly longer would be delivered. The lumber would probably have several knots that are tight in the wood; it would be smooth and straight, with a slight wave in the grain. The lumber would not be sanded. If the lumberyard had to cut the wood to size, it might have a rough end or edge.

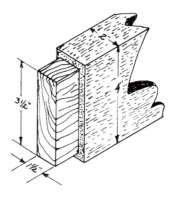

FIGURE 3–1

The nominal dimensions for lumber are determined when a board is first cut to size. During milling, the lumber is planed smooth, reducing its actual dimension to somewhat less than the nominal dimensions.

TABLE 3–1
Standard lumber dimensions.

Nominal	Actual
1 × 2	¾ × 1¾
1 × 3	¾ × 2⅝
1 × 4	¾ × 3½
1 × 6	¾ × 5½
1 × 8	¾ × 7¼
1 × 10	¾ × 9¼
1 × 12	¾ × 11¼
2 × 4	1½ × 3½
2 × 6	1½ × 5½
2 × 8	1½ × 7¼
2 × 10	1½ × 9¼
2 × 12	1½ × 11¼
4 × 4	3½ × 3½

Another type of wood used for scenic construction is called **plywood**. This is a manufactured lumber composed of several thin layers of wood, The grain of each layer, called a *ply,* is placed in opposing directions (Figure 3–2) for maximum strength and then glued together under pressure to create a large sheet of wood, most often measuring 4'-0" wide × 8'-0" long. Plywood is made in thicknesses from as thin as ⅛" to as thick as 1½". The most common thicknesses used for scenic construction are ¼" 3 ply (which is three layers thick) and ¾" 9 ply (which is nine layers thick). The plywood used in the theatre is usually made from pine or fir. As with other lumber, plywood is also graded. In this case, the material is rated on each surface, so one side might be very good, smooth, and free of blemishes (grade A) and the other might have several knots, scrapes, voids, and other flaws (grade D). The kind of glue used to laminate the plys also determines some characteristics of the material. Normally plywood is made with "interior" glue; however, it is possible to buy "exterior" plywood, which has been manufactured with an adhesive that will resist weathering. A typical plywood order might be "one sheet of ¼" AD plywood four feet by eight feet." The ¼" indicates the thickness of the sheet, and AD indicates that one side is the best grade and the other is the worst. Since no other specifications are given, interior grade fir or pine would be supplied.

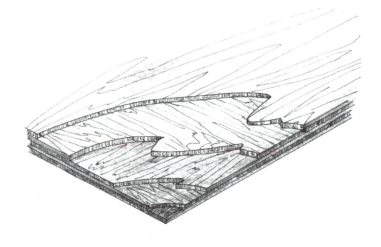

FIGURE 3–2
Plywood. The grain of each layer of a sheet of plywood is at a right angle to the next layer.

Luan is a thin (usually ⅛" thick) plywood material that is used in the construction industry as the outer surface of hollow core doors. It is available from lumberyards in 4 foot by 8 foot sheets. Luan can be used for a variety of purposes in scenic construction because it is thin, lightweight, and quite strong and damage resistant. It is easily worked with woodworking tools and can be bent to large radius curves with relative ease. It takes paint very well. Luan is less likely to warp than cardboard or foam core materials and is much more resistant to surface damage than either of those materials. In commercial theatre, television and motion pictures luan is often used to build "hard flats" (also known as "Hollywood flats").

Particle board is an inexpensive material that can often be substituted for plywood. It is manufactured from sawdust impregnated with plastic resins to form a heavy, smooth sheet of material that makes excellent platform tops when properly supported. Although it is significantly less expensive than plywood of equal thickness, particle board is not quite as strong. Because it is brittle, some care must be taken while working with it: when dropped on its side, the edge of particle board will crumble; it is hard to nail; and it is very wearing on saw blades, dulling them rapidly. Particle board is available in 4'-0" × 8'-0" sheets, just like plywood, and in thicknesses from 3/8" to 3/4".

Another common construction material is **hardboard**, often sold under the brand name of Masonite. This is a thin, hard, fibrous sheet that is usually colored light or dark brown. It is sold in 4'-0" × 8'-0" sheets in thicknesses from 1/8" to 1/2". Significantly less expensive than plywood or particle board, it is used extensively for trim and other nonstructural applications. It is available in two varieties: tempered, which is quite stiff and has a hard surface that is very resistant to damage; and untempered, which is softer and bends and tears more easily. The advantages of hardboard are not only its low cost and the self-supporting strength of thicker sheets but also the ease with which thinner sheets can be curved around forms to create columns or the inside of arches. It can be used to create a great deal of inexpensive and highly detailed trim, cut into precise patterns with a saber or band saw, and used as a thin laminate of three-dimensional detail.

In addition to having an oily quality that seems to resist many water-based paints, a disadvantage of hardboard is that it has no grain and thus lacks the structural strength of plywood or lumber. Although it differs among manufacturers, the material is sometimes supplied with one smooth surface and one textured surface; this has no significant effect on the quality of the material or its strength. Either side of the sheet may be turned toward the audience; however, the smooth surface tends to be easier to paint.

Metal

Steel and **aluminum** are often used as framing and structural materials in scenic construction. Both materials are available in an enormous array of shapes and thicknesses. Local suppliers can provide sourcebooks that detail the variety of steel and aluminum materials available.

Both steel and aluminum can easily be cut and drilled with commonly available tools. They can be screwed or bolted to themselves or other materials and they can be welded to themselves. It is relatively easy to learn and become skilled at steel welding; aluminum welding, however, is much more difficult and requires a great deal more training and practice.

Normally, mild steel is used for most theatre applications. The most commonly used shapes for scenic construction are square and rectangular tubes, which provide excellent strength-to-weight ratios. Black steel pipe is also commonly used for battens in counterweight systems. Steel is relatively inexpensive compared to aluminum. Although aluminum is lighter weight and easier to cut, drill, and bend, it is difficult to weld and very difficult to paint satisfactorily.

Fabric

Canvas is often thought of as *the* scenic material; however, it has become so costly that few theatres are able to afford it; instead, muslin is used. **Muslin** is a lightweight, relatively inexpensive cotton fabric. Wide, unbleached, nonflameproofed, all-cotton muslin is used for scenery so that the material *will shrink* into a smooth, even surface when it is painted. (Cotton-blend and synthetic "muslin" are available but should not be used for scenic construction because of unpredictable shrinkage characteristics.) It is sold by the yard in several widths and threadcounts. **Threadcount**, or threads per square inch, indicates the weight of the fabric. Medium-weight muslin at 128 threadcount is one of the most practical fabrics for scenery. It is strong enough and dense enough for most uses, yet moderately inexpensive. When building scenery intended for a very long life or hard use, it is preferable to use the thicker and stronger 140-threadcount (heavy-weight) muslin. In the long run, the difference in cost is compensated for by the extended length of service of the heavier fabric. Very wide muslin is used on flats to avoid seams whenever possible. The specific width of material used depends on several factors: (1) the width of scenery being covered, (2) the necessity to remove the selvage edge from the fabric, and (3) the shrinkage rate of the material. It is always desirable to avoid as much waste as possible in scenery construction, so care must be taken to purchase fabric of the appropriate width. When covering flats around six feet wide, 76" to 81" wide muslin is ideal; however, if only four-foot-wide flats are being covered, then 54" wide muslin would be more practical. If a show uses flats of various widths, then muslin wide enough to cover the maximum width flat should be purchased and the cut-off pieces of fabric saved for smaller flats or other applications. There are occasions when it is necessary to build extremely wide scenery. For those applications, muslin from 108" up to 33'-0" wide is available, but very expensive. To avoid the extreme costs of these materials, narrower fabric can be pieced together on a flat to make a greater width either by sewing strips of muslin into bigger pieces or by joining strips of muslin where they overlap on a board within a flat.

As part of the covering process the selvage edge of the muslin must be removed. The **selvage edge** is the double-woven strip along the side of the fabric that prevents raveling. Because it is thicker than the rest of the material it will be clearly visible from the audience. Also, its added thickness causes the selvage edge to dry and shrink at a different rate than the body of the fabric; if not removed, it will cause wrinkles and lumps after painting.

Muslin is sold by the roll, bolt, or yard. A roll is usually several hundred yards long, and a bolt is around 50 yards long. Suppliers will sell less-than-bolt lengths but add a cutting charge.

Almost any other fabric may be used to cover flats; however, muslin and canvas are still the best for lightweight painting surfaces.

Fasteners

Scenic construction uses most standard hardware and building materials, including nails, screws, bolts, and staples.

Nails are permanent fasteners that are intended to be driven into wood and left forever. They are made in numerous shapes, sizes, and finishes for a variety of uses. There are three major classifications of nails used in the theatre: common, box, and finish nails (Figure 3–3). Common nails are used for rough construction such as building platform frames; box nails are used for heavier construction with thinner woods; and finish nails are used to attach moldings and decorative materials. In addition to a variety of types, there are various sizes of nails. Most nails are sized by their length and diameter. This dimension is called *penny* and is indicated by a *d* adjacent to a number. The larger the nail, the higher the number. Specific uses of nails will be indicated throughout this chapter. Nails are sold by the pound, so a typical purchase might be "three pounds of eight-penny (8d) common nails." Drywall screws are often used in place of nails for modern construction.

Although some may consider it a virtue to drive a "straight nail," joints assembled with nails are stronger when the nails are driven at a slight angle so the metal fastener crosses several grains of wood. Nails should not be placed close together at a joint or on the same plane, for they are likely to split the wood. It is possible to minimize splitting boards in almost all nailing situations by turning the point of the nail up and lightly tapping it with a hammer to blunt the point before turning it back over and driving it into the wood; this slight blunting of the nail point reduces splitting.

As a rule of thumb, 6d nails are used to join two pieces of one-by material to each other, such as a 1 × 3 and a 1 × 6; 8d nails are used to attach one-by material to two-by material, such as a 1 × 6 to a 2 × 4; and 12d or 16d nails are used to join two pieces of two-by stock together, such as two 2 × 4s.

Screws, unlike nails, are intended to be removable. These fasteners may be turned into wood, metal, plastic, or almost any other material. During installation, they cut a matching thread in the material into which they are being inserted. This causes the screw to grip firmly but also allows it be removed without causing significant damage. Many different kinds of screws are manufactured. Figure 3–4 shows the common kinds used in the theatre. Screws are described by the kind of thread, the material for which they are intended, and the shape of head and slot, as well as by their dimensions. Screws are sized by

FIGURE 3–3
(A) Finish nail, (B) box nail, (C) common nail.

TABLE 3–2
Nail sizes.

Name/Size★	Length in Inches
2d	1
3d	1¼
4d	1½
5d	1¾
6d	2
7d	2¼
8d	2½
9d	2¾
10d	3
12d	3¼
16d	3½ × 9¼
20d	3¾

★d = penny

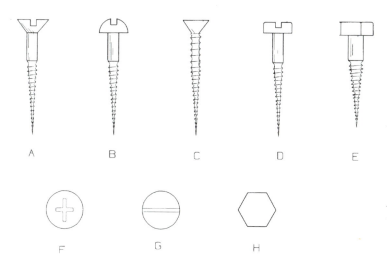

A   B   C   D   E

F   G   H

FIGURE 3–4
(A) Flathead wood screw, (B) roundhead wood screw, (C) plasterboard screw, (D) pan head screw (used in plaster, metal, plastics, and wood), (E) lag screw (for large, heavy assemblies). Screw head patterns: (E) Phillips, (F) slotted, (G) hex.

their length and by a numeral indicating the diameter; the higher the number, the larger the screw. Thus, a screw might be described as "an inch-and-a-half number twelve roundhead wood screw." Most stage hardware is made for use with #8 flathead wood screws.

When putting screws into most materials, it is necessary to drill a small **pilot hole** approximately half the diameter of the screw and two-thirds its length. The pilot hole makes it easier to insert the screw, reduces splitting, and helps the screw enter the material in a straight line. In preparation to insert a $1\frac{1}{2}$" × #8 flathead wood screw, a pilot hole approximately 1" deep should be drilled with a $^3/_{32}$" bit.

Fasteners similar in appearance to a screw but in the price range of nails are **drywall screws**. These fasteners do not need a pilot hole in most materials and, like other screws, are self-tapping, cutting their own matching thread with which to mate. They may be used in place of either screws or nails. Drywall screws can fasten lumber, plastic, and even sheet metal with relative ease. As with standard screws, they may be removed with minimal damage to the material into which they have been inserted. Although they may be installed using a hand screwdriver, they work best when inserted with an electric or cordless screwdriver. Drywall screws are sold by the pound, just like nails. They are not intended to be reused. These have become the standard fastener for most construction.

Bolts are used when a strong fastener is needed to carry a significant amount of weight or to resist stress. They require a predrilled hole large enough for the bolt to slip into without permitting it to move around. Bolts must be joined to a prethreaded mate, such as a nut, or a hole that has been prepared with a matching thread. There are four different kinds of bolts, each with a different style head (Figure 3–5). **Carriage bolts** are most often used for scenic construction due to their low cost and smooth rounded head. When a carriage bolt is used in wood, the square part of the shank just below the head must be seated in the wood with a firm blow from a hammer. The wood will grab the square shank and (usually) will keep the bolt from rotating while the nut is being tightened. Larger bolts are dimensioned by diameter and length in inches.

Prevailing-torque locknuts are designed for use on bolts when it is essential that a joint not loosen due to vibration. These fasteners are

FIGURE 3–5
(A) Carriage bolt, (B) machine bolt or screw, (C) roundhead stove bolt or screw, (D) flathead stove bolt or screw.

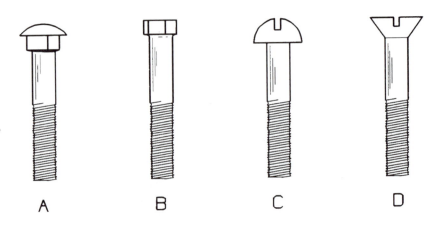

A   B   C   D

available in several styles. Nylon-insert prevailing-torque locknuts are the most common and cause the least damage to bolts.

Nuts and bolts are designed by hardware manufacturers for one-time use. The holding force of the threads is reduced with each retightening. Although one-time use is the "rule," in practice, bolts and nuts should be replaced after the fifth retightening, as a minimum. When a bolt is tightened into place, a minimum of three threads should be exposed beyond the nut. This assures proper strength in the joint.

Anaerobic thread treatments, such as Loctite, are used to chemically bond threaded fasteners together. These liquid "adhesives" are manufactured in varying degrees of strength from semipermanent to absolutely nonremovable bonds.

Adhesives

Adhesives and glues are used extensively in scenic construction. Most gluing is done with one of three different kinds of adhesives available from most lumberyards and hardware stores: white glue, panel adhesive, and hot-melt glue.

One of the most universally used adhesives is **white glue**. There are several varieties of this material available, ranging from very inexpensive weak compositions that look just like a good glue to more expensive and highly concentrated industrial glues. Borden Brand Elmer's Glue-All and Swift's are typical brand names of this kind of glue.

Panel adhesives are also very practical for scenic construction. These glues, such as Contech's PL200, are sold in tubes and are applied with a caulk gun. In the construction industry, they are used to attach interior paneling to walls; however, the adhesive is so strong and so universal in application that it can be used to glue lumber, paper, plastics, and metals to almost any other material. Its disadvantage is that it is rather thick and can create lumps under thinner materials such as fabrics, and if applied too heavily, it will ooze out of the edges of an assembly.

Hot-melt glue is a handy craft glue that is especially useful in props construction. A hot-melt glue gun is needed to use this adhesive. This inexpensive tool gets quite hot, and then glue sticks are pushed into it, causing melted glue to come out of the nozzle. While the glue is hot, it will stick to almost any surface, completing the bond as the adhesive cools. In general, the glue is fairly weak and not intended for heavy construction. It is excellent for attaching trims to upholstery or jewels to a necklace. It can also be used as a temporary means to attach props to furniture and allow the prop to be removed later without damaging most surfaces. Different compositions of hot-melt glue are available for various applications.

These are the most commonly used materials for standard scenic construction. There are many other supplies that might be desirable for specific projects; they will be discussed as appropriate.

TOOLS AND SAFETY

Standard Tools

A well-equipped, spacious scene shop will make scenic and properties construction simpler, easier, and quicker; however, this is sometimes a luxury. It is not uncommon for the stage to be both the performance area as well as the construction space. Sometimes a tool or paint room will be provided somewhere near the stage, and it is hoped that a sink will be within easy access of the work area. These are the minimal requirements to mount a setting practically. In addition, assorted tools are needed for scenic construction and making props. Although almost all scenic construction can be accomplished with the tools shown in Figure 3–6, the work is made much simpler and quicker when the additional pieces of equipment shown in Figure 3–7 are available.

Safety Rules

Most important in any working situation—and especially in the use of both hand and power tools—is an understanding of the safe and proper ways of using them. If improperly held, a hammer can become a dangerous weapon. There is not enough room in this book to provide detailed instructions on how to handle and use each of the tools indicated above. Listed in the bibliography are books that provide clear,

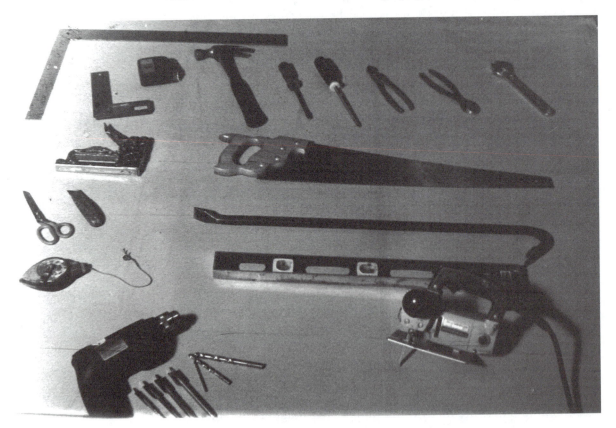

FIGURE 3–6

Minimum assortment of scene shop tools. From top left: framing square, trysquare, tape measure, claw hammer, straight blade screwdriver, Phillips screwdriver, slip-joint pliers, wire cutters, crescent wrench, stapler, hand saw, scissors, matte or utility knife, crow bar, level, electric drill, saber saw.

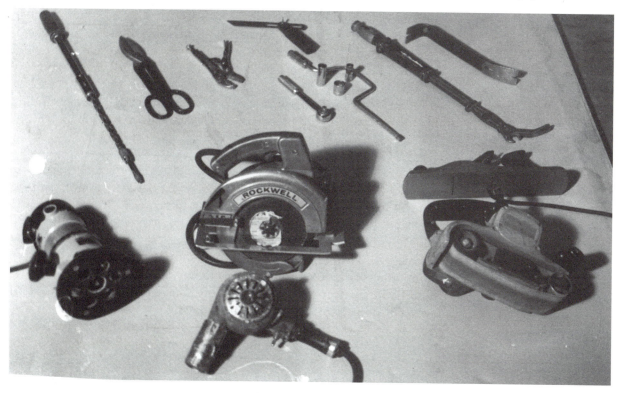

FIGURE 3–7
Additional scene shop tools needed. From top left: ratchet screwdriver, tin snips, locking-grip pliers, bevel square, ratchet wrench and sockets, nail puller, Wonder Bar, router and bits, circular saw, belt sander, hot air gun. Not shown: power screwdriver, hot-melt glue gun, table saw, band saw, drill press, radial arm saw, power miter box.

basic tool-handling instruction. It is imperative, however, that when hand and power tools are used, basic safety instructions are observed:

Read and understand the instruction manual.

Wear a full-face safety shield.

Do not wear loose-fitting clothing that will get caught in the tools.

Pin up long, loose hair.

Do not operate electrical tools in a wet atmosphere or while standing on a wet floor.

Use a grounding plug or double-insulated tools.

Maintain a clean work area.

Use only sharp tools.

Use tool guards designed for the tool.

Disconnect tools when changing blades and bits.

Disconnect tools overnight.

Do not leave tools running while unattended.

Do not distract someone who is working with a power tool.

Wear proper safety equipment.

Protect power cords.

Do not use damaged power cords.

Minimize the use of extension cords.

Safety is a primary concern in any shop or theatre, because such places are filled with potential hazards. On stage there are all kinds of things suspended overhead; in the shop there are tools and equipment that must be treated with respect and understanding. In addition, there are the constant potentials of fire and electrical shock, as well as exposure to airborne irritants, toxic vapors, and fluids. Understanding these hazards and being prepared to deal with them are imperative.

Fire Safety

Most states require that all scenery be treated with fire-retarding chemicals. Although drapes for the stage are always supposed to be protected in this way, many shops neglect to protect scenery with flame retardant. Because of the high temperatures developed by theatrical lighting fixtures, a constant awareness of the potential for a fire must be maintained. The stage and work areas should be equipped with fire extinguishers that are regularly inspected by qualified personnel. Crews should be trained to deal with small fires and know how to behave in the event of catastrophes. Everyone working on a performance or in a shop space should be constantly aware of potential fire hazards and should eliminate them. Smoking should be permitted only when it is a part of the performance. Smoking around scene paints, stage drapes, accumulated sawdust, and many of the modern chemicals and solvents used in the theatre is dangerous and should be prohibited.

Rigging Safety

When something hangs overhead, there must always be real concern for those beneath it. Only qualified personnel should be responsible for hanging scenery or lights above performers and audience. All work, equipment, and materials should be carefully and regularly inspected by qualified experts to ensure the safety of everyone.

Electrical Safety

Electricity is essential for a shop or theatre to function. Its safe use is imperative. All equipment should be properly installed by qualified personnel and it must be grounded. Only properly sized extension cords should be used; extension cords that are too thin will create a fire hazard; extension cords with improper insulation will be easily fractured to expose the wires. In older facilities that still have fuses, the proper size fuse must be used; the fuse should never be bypassed or defeated. Wiring should be inspected regularly. In the event that bare wires or sloppy connections are found, the equipment should be taken out of service immediately and repaired. Once again, only qualified personnel should be allowed to do wiring or electrical maintenance.

Irritants and Toxic Hazards

Many of the materials used in scenic construction are either simple irritants or toxic. It is imperative that each person working with solvents, plastics, paints, dyes, and most other materials read and heed the safety precautions on labels and the product information sheets that sellers must provide. When ventilation is required, be sure there is adequate air movement; when particle or vapor masks or other protective clothing such as face shields or rubber gloves are recommended, be sure to provide and use this protection. High concentrations of many chemicals and particles can cause serious illness that may be totally and permanently disabling. For some people, even the simple irritant of sawdust is debilitating. Before beginning work with any new material, and especially with any plastics, solvents, paints, or aerosol products, *read the label* to understand the directions, hazards, and safety information.

First Aid

All theatres and shops should be equipped with a well-maintained first-aid cabinet. Adhesive bandages, ice packs, tweezers, eye wash, disinfectants, skin washes, and burn ointments are essential. Even more important are personnel trained in first aid. The most basic understanding can sometimes save a life. At least one person in every theatre should be trained in first aid and cardiopulmonary resuscitation (CPR) and should be certified by the Red Cross.

BUILDING SCENERY

Scenery may be roughly classified in two categories: two-dimensional scenery, such as walls and backgrounds, and three-dimensional scenery, such as objects that fill space or can be walked on. The two most basic pieces of scenery are flats and platforms. Not only do these units make up the majority of settings but the methods and materials used to build them are basic to almost all scenic construction. When the techniques for building and covering flats and platforms are mastered, it is possible to construct almost any other scenic piece.

Although much of the scenery used in modern theatre is suggestive or abstract, the construction practices used to build traditional theatrical scenery provide a practical basis for the construction of many nontraditional scenic pieces. In addition, the concept of "interchangeable parts," which establishes many of the formulae for determining standard sizes of scenery used in this book describes an economic concept that may be practical for many regional, academic, and community theatres. These construction practices and sizing formulae have grown out of traditional theatre practice and are often adapted by commercial scenic shops for more abstract projects. These systems of construction should be treated as guides for the theatre practitioner.

Construction Basics

Measuring and marking lumber, using a framing square, and making a few standard joints are techniques that are basic to almost all construction.

Since wood from the lumberyard arrives with rough cuts at each end and is slightly longer than the length ordered, it is almost always necessary to measure, mark, and cut boards square and to the proper length.

Marking and Measuring

Always begin by cutting one end of the board square. To maximize the use of materials, make this cut within ½" from one end of the board. Hold the thick edge of a trysquare firmly against the side of the lumber so there are no gaps (Figure 3–8). Draw a line across the wood against the top or bottom edge of the thin blade of the trysquare. This line will be at a 90° angle to the side of the board. If a wide board must be marked, a framing square can be used in place of the trysquare. Cut the board on that line.

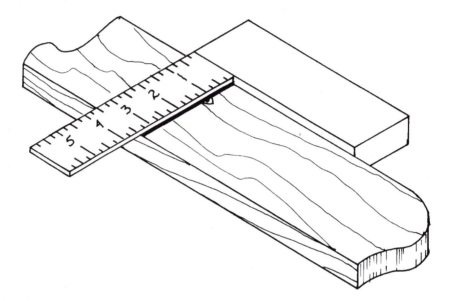

FIGURE 3–8
Placing the trysquare

To measure and mark a board that is to be cut to length, hook the end of a tape measure over the square end of the board (Figure 3–9A). Pull the tape measure beyond the dimension needed. Find the correct measurement on the tape and put a dot inside a carat or circle at that point. Use a trysquare or framing square to draw a line through the dot and perpendicular to the edge of the board.

It is frequently necessary to measure the distance between two objects or surfaces. These inside measurements are made by placing the end of the tape measure against one object and pulling the tape out until the case of the tape measure is against the other object or surface (Figure 3–9B). The dimension visible on the tape is read and the length of the tape measure case is added to that dimension. The length of the tape measure case is usually printed on the side of the case.

Cutting Lumber

It is very important to support lumber properly when making any cuts with a handsaw, circular saw, or saber saw. When trimming the end off a board, generally the cut-off piece does not need to be supported, but when cutting a long board into two long sections, both parts of the board need support. Four sawhorses, crates, or chairs should be used: two sawhorses should be placed under the board on each side of the line being cut. If a large sheet of plywood is to be cut, boards can be placed between the sawhorses for additional support.

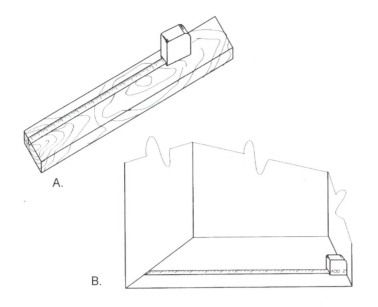

FIGURE 3–9
Using a tape measure.

Wood Joints

There are several different kinds of wood joints but only a few of these are usually needed when making scenery. The most common is a **butt joint** (Figure 3–10A), where two boards are placed against each other and nailed or screwed together. A **miter joint** (Figure 3–10B) joins two boards at an angle. The ends of two boards meeting at a corner may be cut at 45° angles; when assembled, they will make a 90°

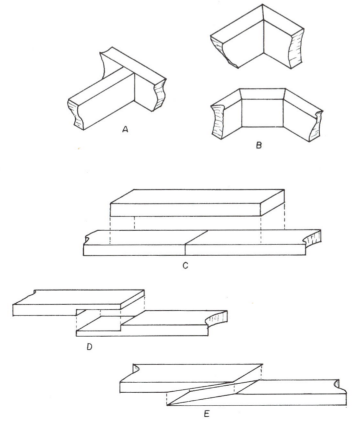

FIGURE 3–10
Wood joints. (A) Butt joint, (B) miter joints, (C) lap joint, (D) half-lap joint, (E) scarf joint.

corner with the joint at the center of the corner. A **lap joint** (Figure 3–10C) places two boards side by side or end to end and a third board is attached (lapped) over the top of them at the joint. A **half-lap joint** (Figure 3–10D) is one method to assemble two boards without increasing their thickness at the joint. Exactly half the width of each board is removed with a router or a dado set or by carefully sawing through half the thickness of each board. Glue is spread in the cut-away sections, which are then lapped over each other and nailed or screwed together. A scarf joint (Figure 3-10E) fulfills the same function as a half-lap joint. To make this joint, two boards are placed on top of each other and they are cut through at the exact same angle. The angled cuts are coated with glue, placed against each other, and then nailed or screwed together.

Two-Dimensional Scenery

Traditional Flats

Flats are lightweight frames on which fabric is stretched and then painted. The purpose of the frame is to allow the fabric to be "free standing" and portable so that settings can be moved, placed in storage, or changed between scenes. The fabric is painted in a particular pattern to represent the walls of a room, a texture, or some other locale. The traditional construction techniques that have evolved for flats are the result of centuries of practice. These methods and uses of materials yield strong, sturdy, durable, lightweight, portable units that can be easily constructed, painted, and stored. Although it takes some practice to get used to the construction materials, tools, and the flats themselves, once mastered, scenery can be constructed rapidly and with ease.

Geography of a Flat

Figure 3–11 shows the "geography" of a standard flat. The entire frame is constructed of 1 × 3. Although other lumber may be used, 1 × 3 is preferred because it is the smallest-size lumber that provides sufficient strength. It is therefore the most economical choice if 1 × 3 of adequate quality can be obtained. Joints are assembled by lapping ¼" plywood keystones and cornerblocks over the seams in the lumber. *It is imperative to orient the top grain of both the cornerblocks and keystones in the proper direction. The strength of this construction is entirely dependent on the direction of the grain of these pieces.* Two other important concerns are the need to keep the cornerblocks and keystones spaced ¾" in from the outside edge of the flat to accommodate joining flats together and to install the appropriate quantity of toggle rails for strength. As taller flats are constructed, additional bracing is necessary and more toggle rails are required.

Construction Process

Standardized flat construction and the concept of "interchangeable parts" not only indicate a specific pattern to the placement of cornerblocks and keystones but also specific dimensioning patterns for flats. One of the more practical standardization systems for flat construction establishes two rules: (1) flats are constructed in even 6" increments in widths between 1'-0" and 6'-0" and (2) flats are constructed in even

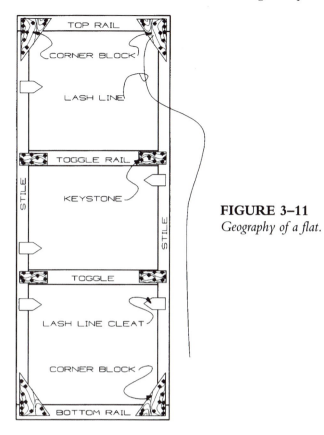

FIGURE 3–11
Geography of a flat.

Standard Widths
1'-0"
1'-6"
2'-0"
2'-6"
3'-0"
3'-6"
4'-0"
4'-6"
5'-0"
5'-6"
6'-0"

TABLE 3–3
Dimensions for standard flats.

Standard Heights	Placement of Toggles From Outside Bottom Rail
8'-0"	4'-0"
10'-0"	5'-0"
12'-0"	4'-0", 8'-0"
14'-0"	3'-6", 7'-0", 10'-6"
16'-0"	4'-0", 8'-0", 12'-0"
18'-0"	4'-6", 9'-0", 13'-6"
20'-0"	5'-0", 10'-0", 15'-0"

2'-0" increments in height. Walls narrower than 1'-0" are cut from lumber of the appropriate width, and walls wider than 6'-0" are made by putting together several flats. Walls that are of an uneven dimension, such as 4'-4" wide, are made by adding a narrow board to a wider flat. This 4'-4" wide wall would consist of a 4'-0" wide flat and a piece of lumber cut 4" wide and attached to the flat (see Batterns on page 123). This system of standardization provides a reliable way to predetermine how units will fit together to achieve the intended effects.

**To Build a Fabric-Covered Wooden Frame 4'-0"
Wide by 12'-0" Tall Flat**

Materials List	*Equipment List*
2 1 × 3 × 12'-0" #2 pine	Pencil
2 1 × 3 × 8'-0" #2 pine	Framing square
¼ sheet ¼" AD plywood	Crosscut saw
White glue	Tape measure
½ pound drywall screws or plasterboard nails	Hammer
	Clinch plate (a piece of steel ¼" × 12" × 12")

1. Make four cornerblocks. Cut two pieces of ¼" plywood into squares that measure 10" on each side. Cut a line from corner to corner of each square to make a total of four 90° triangles.

2. Make four keystones. Cut four pieces of ¼" plywood 3" wide and 8" long. The grain *must* go in the long (8") direction of each piece.

3. Make the top and bottom rails. Each rail must be the full width of the flat, 4'-0" long, and must be cut square at each end. Select a straight 1 × 3 at least 8'-0" long. Place the long side of the framing square against the side of the board so that the short blade of the square crosses the 1 × 3 close to the end. Mark a line along the short blade of the square and carefully cut the board on that line. Now measure the length of the board needed, 4'-0", and make another mark, using the framing square in the same way. Once again, carefully cut the board on the new mark. Check the length of the board. It should be exactly 4'-0" long. Cut a second board in the same manner. Label one 4'-0" board *top rail* and the other *bottom rail*. Lay these boards side by side on the floor touching each other.

4. Cut the stiles. Select two 1 × 3 boards that are at least 12'-0" long and as straight as possible. Cut one end of each board square. Place the square end of each board against the side of the top and bottom rails. Since the stiles fit between the top and bottom rails they must be cut the height of the flat less the width of these boards. Hook a tape measure over the edge of the top and bottom rails and measure the total flat height on the long boards (Figure 3–12). Using a framing square, at that point draw a squared line on each board and cut the stiles to the proper length. The boards will be approximately 5½" shorter than the total flat height; in this case, they will be approximately 11'-6½" long. *Their actual dimension is irrelevant so long as the stiles and rails together equal the total height*

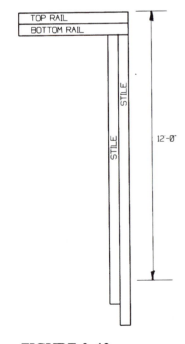

FIGURE 3–12
Measuring stiles to compensate for the width of top and bottom rails.

of the flat. Label each newly cut board *stile* and place them side by side on the floor with an end against the top and bottom rails.

5. Cut the toggles. Select two more 1 × 3 boards each at least 4'-0" long. Be sure that one end of each board is square; if it is not, cut it to be square. Place the square end against the pair of stiles. Measure the width of the flat, 4'-0", from the outside of the stiles along the new 1 × 3s (Figure 3–13). Mark and cut the boards at the 4'-0" measurement. Each board will be approximately 3'-6½" long. Label each board *toggle.*

6. Prepare for assembly. Lay all of the pieces out in the pattern shown in Figure 3–11. Look carefully down the length of each board as it is lying on the floor. If any boards bend (are bowed), turn the bend toward the center of the flat. Draw a line on the stiles and top and bottom rails ¾" in from the outside edge of the frame all the way around the perimeter of the flat. Place the framing square on the outside of a corner. Maneuver the rail and stile so that both boards touch the entire length of the framing square. There should be no gaps at all between the square and the lumber.

7. Assemble the corners. Put some white glue on the underside of one of the cornerblocks. Place the cornerblock over the joint, being sure that the grain on the top of the cornerblock is parallel with the long side of the flat. Adjust the cornerblock so that each edge is on one of the pencil lines ¾" in from the outside edge of the frame. Drive ten plasterboard nails two-thirds of the way into the wood or ten 1" drywall screws all the way into the wood, following the nail pattern shown in Figure 3–14. Repeat this process at each corner.

8. Attach the toggle rails. These will be evenly spaced between the top and bottom rails. In this case, they will be 4'-0" apart, creating three even spaces. If a stile is bowed (bent) and was rotated to turn the bend toward the center of the flat, it may be necessary to force the toggle into place by bending the stile out. Do not shorten the toggle to fit because that would create a permanent warp in the side of the flat. However, forcing the toggle into place will force the bow out of the board and will keep the flat square unless the stile is too badly bent, in which case it should be replaced. Place some glue on the underside of one of the keystones and lay it over the joint between the stile and toggle rail so that it is on the pencil mark ¾" in from the outside edge of the flat. Following the nail pattern in Figure 3–14, drive eight plasterboard nails two-thirds of the way into the wood or 1" drywall screws all the way into it. Repeat at each end of each toggle.

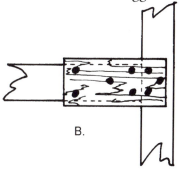

FIGURE 3–13
Measuring toggles to compensate for the width of the stiles.

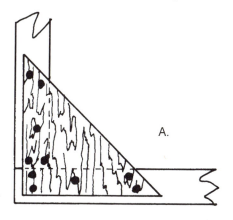

A.

B.

FIGURE 3–14
Nailing pattern for (A) cornerblocks and (B) keystones.

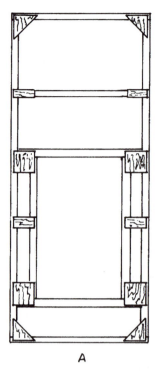

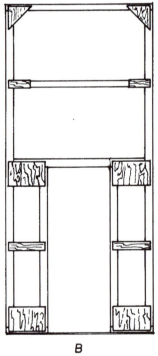

FIGURE 3–15
(A) Typical window flat, (B)
typical door flat.

The flat is now tacked together. Recheck each corner with the framing square to be sure it has remained in square. If one or two corners have gotten out of square, remove the nails or screws on one side of the joint and adjust the boards until they have returned to square; then reattach the corner.

9. If the flat was assembled with nails, place the **clinch plate**, the ¼" × 12" × 12" piece of steel, underneath one of the corners. Holding the flat firmly against the clinch plate, with as few strokes as possible, drive each nail at that corner all the way into the wood. The nail will go through the wood, strike the steel, and bend over to clinch the wood in a manner similar to a staple in a stack of papers. Repeat this procedure at each cornerblock and keystone, being sure to hold the flat firmly against the clinch plate at each location. This will make a strong permanent joint. If the joint is assembled with screws, this won't be necessary.

Door and Window Flats

To build a window or door flat, the same procedures as above are followed, but additional rails are needed to frame the top and bottom edges of the window opening and extra stiles are needed to frame the vertical edges of both window and door openings.

The interior stiles of door flats are placed between the bottom rail of the flat and a toggle rail at the top of the door opening (Figure 3–15B). After the flat is completely constructed and covered, the bottom rail is cut out in the area of the door opening. A sill iron (Figure 3–16) should be attached across the bottom of door flats that will be moved during scene shifts. A **sill iron** is a piece of ¼" × ¾" flat steel drilled with countersunk holes to accept a #8 or #9 flathead wood screw. Sill irons may be purchased from theatrical suppliers or from a steel supplier.

The opening on a window flat is constructed with additional stiles placed vertically between a toggle rail across the bottom of the window

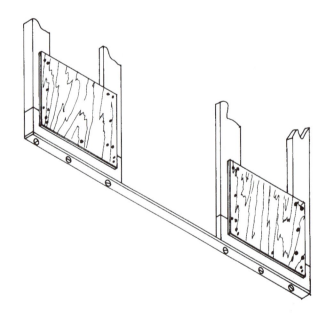

FIGURE 3–16
A sill iron.

opening and another toggle rail across the top of the opening (Figure 3-15A). The toggles span the entire width of the flat between the stiles. Toggle rails on both door and window flats may be adjusted up or down to accommodate the proper size and placement of door and window openings. The actual doors and windows may be constructed as separate units and placed inside these openings in the flats or may be constructed as part of the flat.

Arches

Arches are door openings that have been given a special shape; the arch may be square, round, Gothic, or some other style appropriate to the show. A narrow arch may be formed by cutting the shape of the top of the arch in a piece of ¾" plywood and using that piece as the toggle rail at the top of the door opening in a flat (Figure 3-17A). If the arch is fairly large, excess lumber can be trimmed away within the center areas of the plywood. Long arcs may be cut from a single piece of lumber, such as a 1 × 6 or 1 × 12, and attached in place with keystones within an existing door opening (Figure 3-17B). Very long arcs may be made by piecing several boards together to cut the arc that forms the inside of the arch (Figure 3-17C). These boards are then attached to each other and then finally to the inside edge of the flat

FIGURE 3–17
Forming arches in a flat.

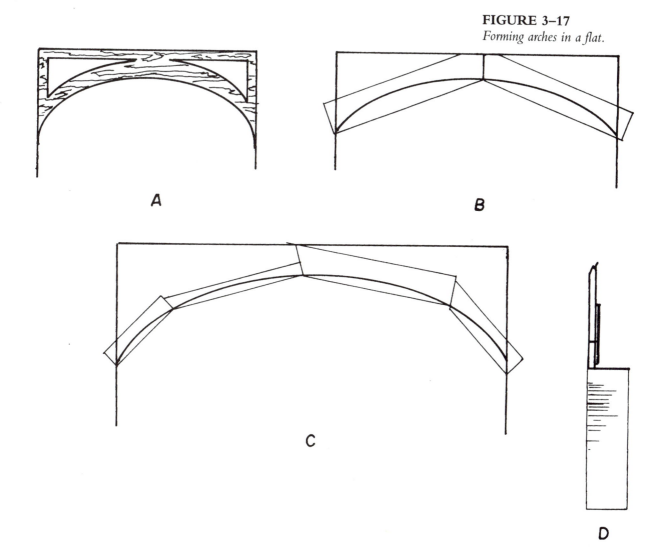

A

B

C

D

with keystones. Extra bracing may be required to support the arch. To create the sense of depth on the arch so that it looks like a real wall instead of a 1" thick piece of scenery, a 3" to 12" wide strip of standard (untempered) hardboard or other thin material may be attached to the inside edge of the arch (Figure 3–17D). If necessary, a dutchman (see page 127) may be placed over the edge of the hardboard to give a more finished appearance.

Covering

No matter what its shape, once a flat has been constructed, the frame must be covered. Almost any material may be used to cover a flat; however, unbleached all-cotton muslin is the preferred fabric because it reliably shrinks to a smooth, flat, tight surface.. The covering process is very specific to achieve the best results.

To Cover a 4'-0" Wide × 12'-0" Tall Flat

Materials List	*Equipment List*
A piece of muslin 54" wide by 12'-6" long	Knife or scissors
	Staple gun
White glue	Paint brush
Water	Bucket
³⁄₈" staples	Stir stick

1. Place the flat face up with the keystones and cornerblocks against the floor. Lay a piece of muslin on the flat that is longer and wider than the frame. Tear off the **selvage edges**, the double-woven band along the side of the muslin. Smooth the fabric out so there are no major wrinkles or twists. The muslin should rest on the floor between the stiles and rails.

2. Attach the fabric to the frame. This is a tricky job because the material must be installed with enough slack in the muslin to allow shrinkage without tearing when it is painted but there must not be so much slack that the fabric is unable to shrink sufficiently smooth and tight. For a flat this size, an area of muslin approximately 3" × 3" should touch the floor between each of the toggles and stiles; larger flats require more slack and smaller flats less. Begin to attach the muslin at the center of a long side of the flat with a partner working directly opposite on the other long side. Keeping the fabric smooth but not too tight, drive a staple through the muslin into the stile ¼" in from the inside edge of the board; space the staples approximately 8" apart (Figure 3–18). The staples must go all the way into the wood and be even with the top of the muslin. Sometimes it may be necessary to finish driving the staples in with a hammer if the staple gun does not put them in completely. After the two long sides have been stapled, fasten the fabric to the top and bottom rails and around any door and window openings. Staples are only put into the toggle rails when they frame a door or window opening. The fabric should be fastened all the way around the perimeter of the flat so that it is smooth but not tight.

3. After stapling, the muslin is glued in place with a solution called **dope**. This is a homemade mixture consisting of white glue

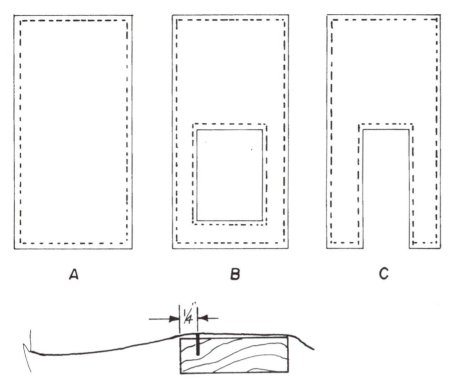

FIGURE 3–18
Stapling the muslin in place to cover a flat.

diluted with only enough water to allow it to be easily brushed onto the muslin. **Whiting**, an inert filler available from theatrical suppliers, may be added to the mixture to give it body.

Dope is placed only on the portion of the fabric that will be in contact with the outside frame of the flat and around door and window openings. Turn the free edges of the fabric back onto the body of the flat. Working quickly, spread a generous amount of dope (1) on the underside of the muslin, then (2) on the exposed portion of the frame (Figure 3–19). Smooth the muslin into place. Be sure there are no bumps, ridges, or threads of fabric caught in the doped area. If desired, a third coat of muslin may be brushed (3) on top of the muslin that was previously glued. This third coating is optional. It assures thorough saturation of the fabric with dope; however, the additional treatment may affect the appearance of paint in contrast to the remainder of the flat. Allow the glue to dry completely before moving or painting the flat.

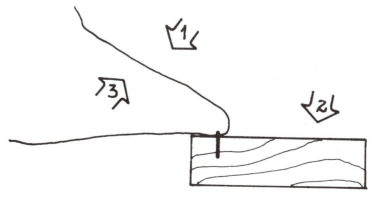

FIGURE 3–19
Apply dope to (1) the underside of the muslin, (2) the outer frame of the flat, and, if desired, (3) the top surface of the muslin around the perimeter of the flat.

4. After the dope has dried thoroughly, trim off the excess muslin hanging over the edge of the frame. The material is trimmed with a matte knife ⅛" in from the outside edge of the flat (Figure 3–20).

FIGURE 3–20
*After the glue has dried
thoroughly, trim the muslin
with a matte knife ⅛" in from
the outside edge of the flat.*

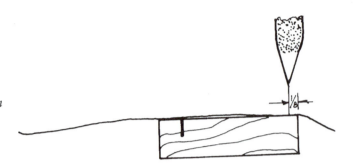

The flat is now ready for the first coat of paint, which will stretch the fabric to a smooth, even surface. The substance used to shrink the muslin is called **size** or **size water** because it adjusts the size or dimensions of the fabric covering the flat. Size water is made by thinning one part white glue with five parts water or one part pastel scenic paint with five to seven parts water. The mixture should be thin but must contain some glue or paint to stretch the fabric effectively. The size water is brushed onto the entire surface of the muslin using a **crosshatched stroke**, that is, moving the brush in a random X pattern. As soon as the size mixture comes in contact with the fabric, the material begins to shrink. Once sizing is started on a flat, the work should continue uninterrupted until all of the fabric on that flat has been coated.

After the size dries, the flat should be a perfectly smooth, even surface ready for painting. If too much slack was left during the covering process, the fabric will not be stretched tightly. In that case, it may be possible to cause additional shrinkage by painting the muslin on the backside of the flat with an additional coating of size. If the fabric is still too loose, the flat should be recovered. If the fabric was stretched too tightly during covering, the material will pull away from the staples and tear, possibly even shrinking completely off of the frame. In that case, the flat must be recovered with a new piece of muslin. If sizing has left an acceptable surface, the flat is ready for further assembly and painting.

The **Hard flat, Hollywood flat,** or **Studio flat** has been used in the movie industry and for television production for quite some time. This style of scenic construction is used in theatre production because construction is fairly easy and the flats are very durable. These flats are framed with 1 × 2 or 1 × 3 and covered with luan. **Luan** is a relatively inexpensive material that is made from thin layers of wood in a manner similar to plywood but not nearly as strong nor as costly. The 1 × 2 or 1 × 3 is placed on edge about 2'-0" on center in both a vertical and horizontal direction (Figure 3–21). Assembly is usually done with two or three 1 ⅝" drywall screws and white carpenters' glue at each joint. After the frame has been constructed, the luan can be attached to the 1 × 2 or 1 × 3 frame with nails, drywall screws, or even long staples. It is a good idea to glue the luan to the frame with either white glue or panel adhesive in addition to the nails, screws, or staples. Figure 3–21 shows a typical layout for the frame of a hard flat.

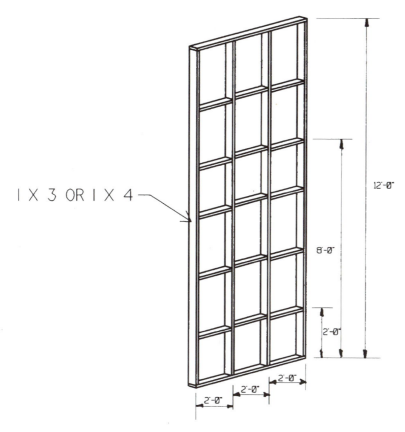

I X 3 OR I X 4

12'-0"

8'-0"

2'-0"

2'-0" 2'-0" 2'-0"

FIGURE 3–21
1 × 4 "on edge" to form a hard-framed or "Hollywood-style" flat. The surface is to be covered with luan.

Since luan is usually limited in size to 4'-0 × 8'-0" sheets, there are often joints between panels of luan composing a scenic wall. The joints must be supported by framing member of the flat. On the front, the joints can be filled with **joint compound**, a material used to fill joints between sheets of drywall in building construction. After the joint compound dries, it is usually sanded smooth. The most consistent smooth finish usually is achieved by covering the luan with muslin, which also makes the most satisfactory painting surface. Flats constructed in this style are easy to join together to make larger units. To assemble a corner or two flats side by side, drywall screws may be inserted between adjoining frame members. If it is necessary to strengthen a wall, stiffeners can be used as well (see page 124).

Steel-framed flats are becoming increasingly popular for scenic construction. Often, steel tubing will provide equal or greater strength than wood at an equal or lesser weight and cost. Steel-framed flats are usually constructed from square steel tube measuring 1" on each side. The walls of the tube may be as thin as 16 gauge steel, which is about $\frac{1}{16}$" thick, or as thick as 11 gauge steel, which is about $\frac{1}{8}$" thick. When greater strength is needed than these materials can provide, square tubes that have a larger profile or rectangular tubes of greater dimensions can be used. This will, of course, increase the price of the materials and the weight of the scenery.

Steel-framed flats usually are constructed to the same general design as flats made with 1 × 3 or 1 × 2 hardface flats (Figure 3–22). The top and bottom rails cross the entire width of the flat; stiles extend between the top and bottom rails; and the toggle rails, placed approximately every 4'-0" on-center, are between the stiles. Assembly is accomplished by welding all four sides of the butt or mitered joints. The welds are then ground smooth. The process of assembly must assure that each completed unit is square and solid. To minimize twisting, it is helpful to add angled corner braces a the top and bottom inside the frame. These braces should be 2'-0" long or longer. Both corner braces will do the most good by occurring on the same side of the flat.

Often, steel-framed flats are covered with luan or a combination of luan topped with muslin, rather than just muslin. The luan is usually attached to the face of the steel frame with panel adhesive such as PL200 and drywall screws.

FIGURE 3–22
A steel-framed flat constructed from welded 1" square tubing.

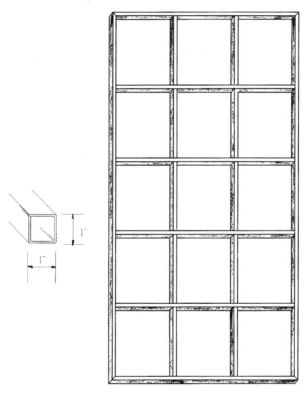

Drops

Drops are another kind of two-dimensional scenery. A drop may be a plain background to represent the sky or painted to represent a specific locale. It may also be a collage of various objects and textures that provide an interesting background but that do not represent a specific place.

Nonrepresentational backdrops can be made from almost any material. Interesting backgrounds have been created with chain link fence, real tree branches, or empty picture frames or by stringing together styrofoam balls, rusty tin cans, or even auto parts. There are no rules about what may be used; it is simply a matter of finding the appropriate materials to create the desired effect.

Cycloramas, sky drops, are usually made for a specific stage. They are normally the full width of the stage and at least the height of the proscenium opening. These large drops are made of light blue or white seamless muslin or lenocloth. **Lenocloth** is a special fabric for the stage that reflects light especially well. Cycloramas, also known as **cycs**, are usually flat but may be curved to surround part or all of the stage. These drops can represent the sky, serve as a neutral background, or be used as a surface on which to project slides or other images.

Another special kind of drop is a **scrim**, which is made from a material called **sharkstooth**. This is a wide, expensive fabric with an open weave that gives it special lighting characteristics: when light is only in front of the drop, it appears mostly opaque; when light is only behind the drop, it appears mostly transparent; and when lit from both the front and behind the drop, a misty quality is created. When using a scrim, it is often necessary to hang an opaque drop or curtain behind it when it is necessary to completely mask the upstage area. Scrims may be left plain or may be painted with dyes to depict a scene that becomes transparent as the lighting changes during the performance.

Drops painted to represent a specific scene may be purchased from some theatrical suppliers, but they are often too costly for most school or community theatres. Some of these drops may be rented, such as a Bali Hai drop for *South Pacific,* the library for *The Music Man,* or a "standard" woods, city scape, countryside, or mountain scene. Unpainted muslin drops that will be painted by the theatre may also be purchased or they may be homemade. As with flats, there are traditional requirements as well as practical alternatives to guide the construction of a drop.

Construction of a Drop to Be Painted

The dimensions of a drop for painting must be considered carefully. A drop may be painted on almost any fabric; the most common material is unbleached muslin. There will be a great deal of shrinkage when this fabric is sized. Sufficient fabric must be allowed to accommodate a shrinkage rate of 10–15 percent, so if a finished drop measuring 20'-0" high by 35'-0" wide is needed, the unpainted drop should be sewn to approximately 22'-0" high by 38'-0" wide.

Although it is possible to purchase muslin over 30'-0" wide to use for a seamless backdrop, the cost is often prohibitive, so most drops for painting are made from widths of narrower fabric sewn horizontally with as few seams as possible. If a theatre uses muslin 81" wide, only two seams would be needed to make a drop 20'-0" high.

Figure 3–23 shows the typical "geography" of a standard drop. The top edge is reinforced with a 3" or 4" wide strip of jute webbing sewn to the back. Holes for tielines are made through the drop, and the webbing is reinforced with brass rings, **grommets**. A grommet set and grommets can be purchased from a hardware store, tent maker, or boating-supply dealer as well as from theatrical suppliers. The bottom hem of the drop is usually 4" deep and reinforced with double stitching to carry a chain or pipe that stretches the drop vertically. The right and left edges of a painted drop are seldom hemmed. A commercially made drop is sewn with flat-feld or double-stitched face-to-face seams. Three or four layers of muslin may be folded into the top hem to replace the jute webbing reinforcement.

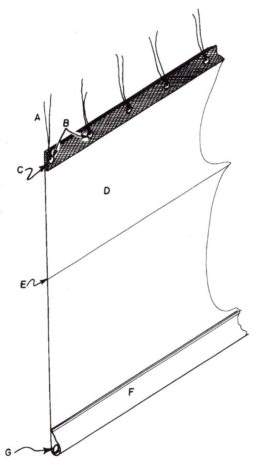

FIGURE 3–23
Geography of a drop. (A) Tielines, (B) brass grommets, (C) 3" or 4" wide jute webbing, (D) muslin or some other fabric, (E) horizontal seam—a flat feld seam is preferred, (F) bottom hem forming a pipe or chain pocket, (G) pipe in pipe pocket.

The bottom edge of a drop must be weighted or stretched. The bottom hem can be stapled to a wooden floor and the suspension lines pulled tight to stretch the drop. It is more satisfactory to use a 1" to 1½" diameter pipe placed in the bottom hem of the entire width of the drop. If there is any kind of break in the pipe, it will create a wrinkle in the drop, so all sections of the pipe must be joined together with either a pipe coupling or an internal batten splice. A **batten splice** (Figure 3–24) can be made by slipping a smaller diameter pipe inside of the bottom batten and inserting bolts through both pipes on each side of the

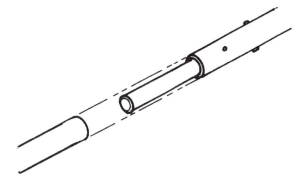

FIGURE 3–24
Batten splice.

joint to hold everything in place. This requires cutting and drilling the pipe and grinding the bolts to be sure they do not tear the hem of the drop. Another simple splice can be made by forcing a large dowel rod or broomstick into the end of each pipe section to be joined and wrapping the joint with duct tape. The internal rod has to be large enough to prevent the joint from sagging.

Drops have several characteristics that make them easy to use. First, they take up very little space. They are mounted by tying them to overhead rigging, usually a pipe or board over the stage or a counterweighted batten if available. As a result, they require no floor space for mounting and do not need braces for support. On a stage with counterweight rigging, several drops can be quickly put into or taken out of the acting area for rapid scene changes. Compared to flats, drops are an easy and inexpensive way to create large backgrounds quickly. The construction only requires several yards of fabric, webbing, grommets, and basic sewing skills. Drops may be folded or rolled for easy transportation and storage.

The large solid sheet of fabric weighted at the bottom is the most common kind of drop. However, it is sometimes difficult to make a painted drop hang smoothly and square. To solve this problem, a drop can be stretched onto a frame. The frame is normally constructed from 1 × 4s or 2 × 4s and the drop is either stapled or laced to it (Figure 3–25A). This technique is occasionally used for touring productions with a frame that can be taken apart for transportation and assembled on stage and the drop laced in place. When a drop is mounted in this manner, it is necessary to hem its right and left edges and insert grommets through which to lace. Care must be taken to get the drop smooth and tight or there will be little value to attaching the fabric to the frame.

Another kind of drop frequently used in the theatre is called a **cut drop** (Figure 3-25B). These drops have sections cut out to create arches, colonnades, or forests. Any design can be used. A cut drop is usually sewn and painted in the same manner as a full drop, but on completion of painting openings are cut in it. Where there is a tendency for cut edges to curl, net is glued to the back of the drop to span the opening and maintain tension on the fabric.

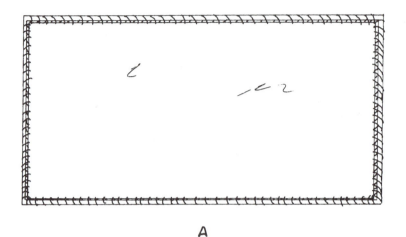

A

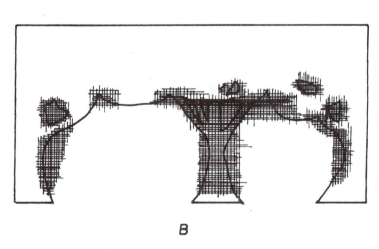

B

Three-Dimensional Scenery

Platforms

Platforms are interchangeable parts used to create stages and raised acting areas, to elevate members of a chorus or band, or to raise scenery above the floor. Directors like to use platforms because they contribute to interesting movement patterns for the actors and create strong acting areas and good entrances that help to solve many blocking problems. These units are as important to a setting as flats and backdrops. The complement to platforms is stairways. Platforms and stairs must meet criteria in four areas. They must be (1) strong enough to support performers walking, dancing, or jumping; (2) quiet so that footsteps do not distract from or drown out the performance; (3) sufficiently flexible to allow them to be placed in a variety of arrangements; and (4) light enough to be carried around.

Standard Platforms

Platforms, like flats, are usually constructed to standardized dimensions. The best formula for these dimensions is: 2 × width = length. In other words, if a platform is 3'-0" wide, it should be 6'-0" long (2 × 3'-0" = 6'-0"); a platform 4'-0" wide should be 8'-0" long. When dimensioned in this way, platforms can easily be assembled side by side and end to end in several patterns (Figure 3–26). Most theatres construct standard platforms measuring 4'-0" × 8'-0" because this is the size of a standard sheet of plywood and a size and weight manageable by workers. Platforms measuring 2'-0" × 4'-0" and 3'-0" × 6'-0" are built for smaller stages. Usually platforms greater than 4'-0" × 8'-0" are not made because they are too large and too heavy to handle. Of course, special needs will sometimes dictate construction of larger units and nonrectangular shapes.

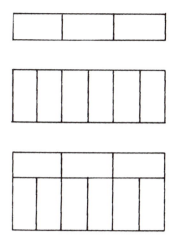

FIGURE 3–26
Typical patterns to arrange 4 × 8 platforms to form large units.

To Construct a Standard 4 × 8 Platform (Figure 3–28)

Materials List	Equipment List
3 pieces of 2 × 4 × 8'-0" long	Hammer
3 pieces of 2 × 4 × 4'-0" long	Trysquare or framing square
1 sheet 3/4" × 4 × 8	Saw
CDX plywood	Pencil
½ pound 12d nails	Matte knife
½ pound 8d common nails	Chalk line
White glue	
A piece of old carpet (not shag) with jute backing	
½ pound 3/4" plasterboard or roofing nails	

1. Cut the sides. To begin construction, cut two 2 × 4s exactly 8'-0" long. Be sure the ends of each board are cut square. Label both boards *side*.

2. Cut the ends. Cut one end of two 2 × 4s exactly square. Starting at the squared end of each board, measure the width of the platform, 4'-0" less the total thickness of the two side boards, 3"; the dimension will be 45". Mark a square line at this point and carefully cut each board on its mark. Label each board *end*.

3. Cut the center rail. Cut one end of a long 2 × 4 exactly square. Starting at the squared end, measure the length of the platform, 8'-0" less the total thickness of the two end boards, 3"; the dimension will be 93". Mark and cut the board. Label it *center*.

4. Lay out the boards for assembly. Draw a line 1½" in from the end of each *side* board and place another mark at the very center of the *side* boards, 4'-0" from each end. On the *end* boards mark the exact center of each board and then draw a line 3/4" to either side of center.

5. Assemble the frame. Turn each *side* board over so the marks 1½" in from the ends are visible. Between the end of the board and each mark drive two 12d nails through the wood until they just start to come out the other side. Be careful not to drive the nails so far through the board that they become embedded in the floor. Put a dab of glue on the end of an *end* board, place the board between the *side* boards, and drive the nails all the way into the ends of the short 2 × 4s. It is not necessary to drive the nails in a straight line so long as the points of the nails do not come out of another part of the board. In fact, the platform will be stronger if the nails are driven at a slight angle. As long as the boards are nailed together to make a tight, neat corner, it is not necessary to check the square of the frame during this step of assembly. Squaring will happen automatically when the plywood top is put on. Assemble all four corners.

Spread some glue on each end of the *center* board and place it between the center marks on each end. Nail through the *end* boards to attach the *center* board to the frame.

6. Cut the short center braces. Inside one end of the platform frame, measure the distance from the inside edge of the outer board to the near side of the *center* board. Do the same thing on the other side of the *center* board (Figure 3–27). These dimensions should be close to 21 ³/₄". Cut 2 × 4s to each of those measurements, and label them *right brace* and *left brace*, as appropriate.

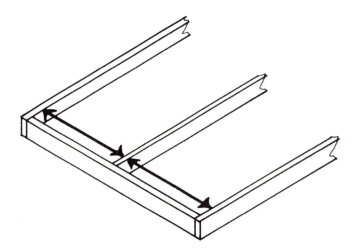

FIGURE 3–27

Measuring for center braces to be cut for a platform.

7. Find the centerline mark on each side board. Put one edge of each brace at the mark on the appropriate side of the frame. The boards can be staggered to each side of the mark for easier nailing (Figure 3-28). Add a dab of glue to the end of each board and nail it in place with 12d nails.

8. Attach the lid. Spread glue all the way around the top edge of the platform frame, including the center boards. With one person at each end or at each corner of a sheet of ³/₄" plywood, place the material best side turned up on top of the 2 × 4 frame. Bring one corner of the frame exactly to the edges of the sheet of plywood (with some pressure the frame will move around under the plywood). Drive an 8d nail through the plywood into the frame at that corner. Go to another corner and force the frame to conform to the edges of the plywood at that location. Drive an 8d nail in at that corner. Repeat this process at each of the remaining corners. The platform should be perfectly square now.

Drive an 8d nail into the lid of the platform approximately every 10" around the perimeter of the frame. If any of the frame members bow in or out from the edge of the plywood, try to force them into alignment while nailing.

At each end of the platform, measure 2'-0" from the edge toward the opposite side of the platform and make a mark. On each long side, measure 4'-0" from the end of the platform toward the center of the platform. With a chalkline, snap a line on each pair of marks. Drive an 8d nail into the lid approximately every 10" on the long line, hitting the long center board. Also drive nails on the appropriate side of the short line to cause the nails to strike the short 2 × 4 braces.

9. Pad the lid. Place a piece of old carpet upside down on top of the platform. Get it as smooth as possible. Along one side of the platform drive a ³/₄" roofing or plasterboard nail every 8" to 10" apart through the carpet into the ³/₄" plywood lid. Working with a helper along the opposite side of the frame, pull the carpet smooth and tight and nail it to the plywood. Stretch each end smooth and tight and nail it in place. While maintaining tension on the carpet, use a matte knife or a saber saw with a knife (toothless) blade to cut the carpet even with the outer edge of the platform. Keep the cut as neat as possible. It is imperative to use a sharp knife blade when doing this trimming. If there is much raveling, use scissors to trim off the threads. Although it will not serve quite as well, corrugated cardboard may be used to pad the platform instead of carpet. The purpose of this padding is to eliminate or reduce the noise of footsteps on the hollow platform construction.

10. Cover the platform. Place a piece of muslin (the heavier the better) or canvas several inches wider and longer than the platform top loosely but smoothly on top of the carpet. Let the fabric hang over the sides and remove the selvage edges. Do not stretch the fabric or pull it tight at all, but be sure it is smooth. Fold back approximately 3" of muslin around the perimeter of the top and apply the same dope mixture used to attach fabric to flats to (1) the underside of the muslin that has been folded back, (2) the exposed portion of the carpet back, and (3) the sides of the platform frame. Smooth the flap of muslin back into place and down the sides of the platform frame, neatly folding the fabric in place and being careful not to create bulky corners where several layers of material overlap. Paint dope on the top of the muslin around the edges of the top and down the sides of the platform frame. Allow the dope to dry thoroughly.

Coat the dried muslin with scene paint or a dilute mixture of latex paint. This will size the fabric and provide slight protection against tears.

Platform Legs

A platform may be used by itself as a low elevation, combined with several other platforms at the same height, stacked in a pile with other platforms to make a higher level, or have legs attached to elevate the unit.

The simplest legging procedure uses 2 × 4s attached inside of the platform with nails or bolts. Care must be taken to ensure that the legs are the proper length. Each leg must be cut to the finished height of the

FIGURE 3–28
One typical layout for a platform frame. Other layouts use additional bracing in both the horizontal and vertical directions.

platform less the thickness of the platform lid. Thus, when a platform is built with a ³/₄" particle board top, the legs for that platform must be ³/₄" less than the finished height of the unit. To make a platform 18" high, legs 17¼" long are needed (18" − ³/₄" = 17¼"); if the platform were to be 30" high, legs 29¼" long would be needed.

Legs should be placed no more than 4'-0" apart, so six legs are necessary for a 4 × 8 platform, one at each corner and one at the center of each long side (Figure 3-29A). Usually six legs are also used on 3 × 6 platforms, but only four legs are needed for a 4 × 4 or smaller platform. When several platforms are bolted together through the side of each frame, legs may be placed only on one side of the joint.

The legs may be attached with three 12d common or duplex nails driven at opposing angles through the legs into the frame. This is a very strong method of assembly; however, it damages both the legs and the platform frame when disassembled. To ensure greater life to platforms, bolted assemblies are preferred, especially if the same bolt holes in the platform are used each time a unit is legged. Each leg is bolted in place with two ³/₈" × 4" carriage bolts. Start by drilling two ³/₈" holes through each leg and into the platform frame (Figure 3–29B). The bolt holes should not be in line with each other but must be offset to reduce the possibility of the boards splitting. Insert a ³/₈" × 4" carriage bolt in each hole, tap the bolt head with a hammer to seat the square shank in the wood, slip a flat ³/₈" washer onto the opposite end of the bolt, and tighten down the nut. Once all six legs have been attached, platforms that are 18" high or taller should be cross-braced. Using 6d nails, or 1⁵/₈" drywall screws attach 1 × 3s in an X pattern all the way around the perimeter of the platform. The boards may be placed both inside and outside of the legs. This bracing stiffens the legs and prevents sway.

FIGURE 3–29

(A) Placement of platform legs, (B) position of bolts through legs. (Note that the bolt closest to the corner is in the high position to allow easier wrench access).

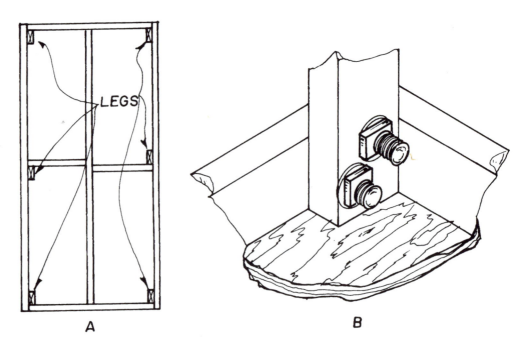

A   B

Another means to attach legs may be used on platforms that will not be moved after they are set up. The 2 × 4 legs are placed directly beneath the frame and attached to it with ³/₄" × 12" cornerblocks with 6d nails or 1⁵/₈" dry wall screws on each side of the joint, as in Figure 3–30. Leg height must be carefully calculated to accommodate the thickness of the platform top (³/₄") and frame member (3¹/₂"). A standard platform legged to a height of 24" in this manner would use legs 19³/₄" long. Legs must be cross-braced with complete Xs.

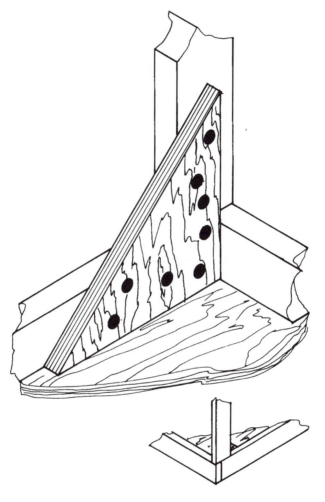

FIGURE 3–30
Platform legs attached with
³/₄" × 12" cornerblocks.

Another kind of leg may be assembled using 1 × 4s. Two pieces of 1 × 4 of the appropriate length are nailed together with 6d nails or 1⁵⁄₈" drywall screws to form a 90° corner. Nails should be placed every 8" to 15" apart. The legs are then placed inside the corners of the platform frame and attached with nails or bolts to the frame. These legs tend to be somewhat sturdier than simple 2 × 4 legs. Once again, cross-bracing is required.

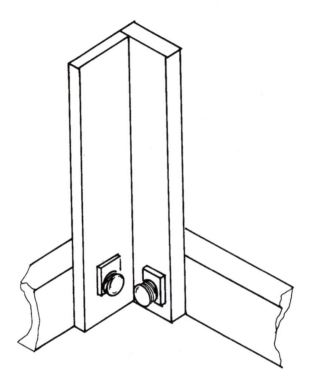

FIGURE 3–31
*Platform leg made of 1 × 4s nailed in an **L** pattern.*

Ramps

Ramps are platforms that have been set up on a slope. A **raked stage**, or a **rake**, is simply a very large ramp. The main body of a ramp consists of standard platforms with legs cut to accommodate the slant. The preferred slope is 1" per foot. In other words, the platform deck rises 1" in every foot of ramp length. Although ramps as steep as 4" per foot have been used on stage, they are very difficult to walk on. The maximum practical slope that is workable for the stage is 2½" of rise per foot of length.

The greatest difficulty with ramp construction is figuring out the height and angle of the legs. An easy method is to set up a board at the same angle that the ramp will be constructed. The position of legs can be found, and each leg measured and cut to fit between the board and floor at those locations. Legs may be made from 2 × 4, or any of the legging systems and means of attachment described above may be used. They are cross-braced in the same manner as platform legs.

The bottom edge of a ramp that tapers to the floor requires some special construction (Figure 3–32). The easiest way to form this portion of the ramp is by cutting 2 × 12 (or narrower) braces about 4'-0" long at an angle consistent with the rest of the rake. Braces need to be placed every 2'-0" apart. Plywood ¾" or thinner is then nailed on top of the braces. Upsidedown carpet can be laid over this section to absorb noise as on standard platforming. However, if the carpet extends onto the floor at the bottom edge of the ramp, it will smooth the transition from the rake to the level floor. The entire assembly is then covered with muslin in the same manner as a platform.

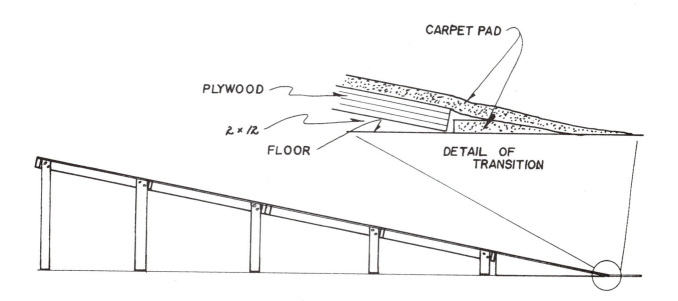

FIGURE 3–32
Sectional view (interior) of a ramp and a detailed view of the transition from the ramp to the stage floor.

Stairs

There are several standard and shortcut methods of stair construction. Each offers either strength, economy, or ease of construction as a primary characteristic. A standard stairway, shown in Figure 3–33, consists of three main parts: treads, risers, and stringers. **Treads**, the part walked on, may be made from any material that will adequately support the necessary weight; often they are cut from ¾" plywood, 1 × 12 or 2 × 12. Treads usually are padded and covered in the same way as platforms. **Risers**, the front, vertical part of each step, may also be made from plywood, pine boards, or hardboard, or they may be eliminated entirely. When present, risers contribute significantly to the stability of the stairway. Standard **stringers**, the side boards that

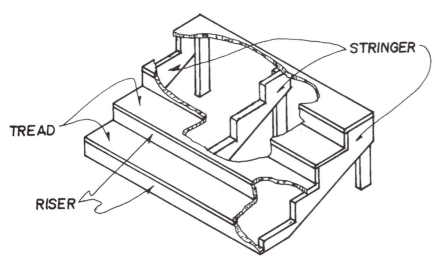

FIGURE 3–33
Geography of a standard stairway. Stairs may be built with or without legs.

71

support treads and risers, are traditionally cut from 1 × 12s or 2 × 12s, although there are several alternatives possible.

Stairs may be independent of adjacent platforms so that they have their own legs or the stairs may be dependent—that is, attached to and supported by the platform. Generally, stock stairways are constructed at the same width as the narrow side of standard platforms. Theatres that have standardized with 4 × 8 platforms usually build stock stairways 4'-0" wide; if platforms are standardized at 3 × 6, stock stairs are 3'-0" wide. In this way a stock stair automatically fits the end of a stock platform and two stock chairs can be put together on the long side of a platform.

The first phase of stairway construction is to determine the height of the risers and the number of steps needed. Design needs may make it necessary to construct stairs in conflict with some of these "rules." These guidelines exist because they produce safer and easier stairways to use. The following rules apply to all standard stairways:

1. All treads must be of equal depth (front to back).
2. No tread should be less than 5" nor more than 15" deep. The preferred tread depth is 12".
3. All risers must be of equal height.
4. No riser should be less than 4" nor more than 10" high. The preferred riser height is between 6" to 8".
5. A stairway should not be constructed with the last step level with the platform. The last step a person takes when climbing stairs should be off of the stairway up onto the platform (Figure 3-34).

FIGURE 3–34
Usually the top tread of a stairway is not level with the platform to which it attaches.

To determine the number of treads and the riser height for a stairway, it is necessary to know the height of the platform to which the stair attaches and the preferred riser height. The formula for determining the number of treads and risers is:

$$\text{Platform height} \div \text{riser height} = X$$

$$X - 1 = \text{number of risers needed}$$

For example, if the platform is 48" high and the preferred riser height is 6", the formula would be applied in this manner:

$$48" \div 6" = 8 \text{ risers}$$

$$8 \text{ risers} - 1 = 7 \text{ risers}$$

This stairway, with each tread 12" deep, will fill an area of the stage measuring 4'-0" wide × 7'-0" long. The amount of floor space occupied can be minimized by reducing the tread depth to 10", 9", or 8", or by using a taller riser and reducing the number of steps. A great deal of stage space can be gained by using an 8" riser:

$$48" \div 8" = 6 \text{ risers}$$

$$6 \text{ risers} - 1 = 5 \text{ risers}$$

Using the taller riser will reduce the overall stairway dimensions to 4'-0" wide × 5'-0" long, saving two feet of stage space.

To Build a Standard Stairway 4'-0" Wide to Go to a Platform 30" High (Figure 3–4)

Materials List	*Equipment List*
3 1 × 12 × 5'-0"	Framing square
5 1 × 12 × 4'-0"	Pencil
5 1 × 6 × 4'-0"	Circular and/or hand saw
3 2 × 4 × 2'-6"	Hammer
6 ³/₈ × 3" carriage bolts with washers and nuts	
½ pound 6d box nails or 2" drywall screws	
White glue	

1. **Calculate dimensions**. This stairway will be constructed with 6" risers and 12" treads to reach a platform 30" high.

$$30" \div 6" = 5 \text{ risers}$$

$$5 \text{ risers} - 1 = 4 \text{ risers}$$

This stairway will be 4'-0" wide and have four steps, each 6" high and 12" deep.

2. **Lay out the first tread on the stringer** (Figure 3–35). Select a 5'-0" long 1 × 12 to become one of the stringers. This should be a very good board (grade #1 or better) with very small knots and absolutely no cracks. Measure 1'-0" down from one end of the board and make a mark at the edge of the wood. Find the 6" mark on the inside of the short arm and the 12" mark on the inside of the long arm of the framing square. Place the 6" measurement at the mark at the edge of the board. Rotate the square until both the 6" and the 12" marks are exactly aligned at the same edge of the 1 × 12. Draw the angle inside the square to form a 90° corner at an oblique angle to the edge of the board.

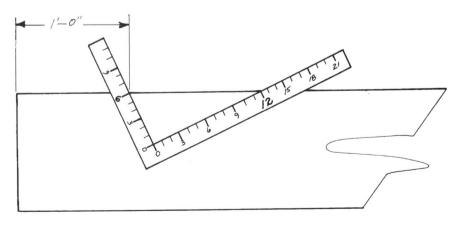

FIGURE 3–35
Marking out the first tread on the stringer.

3. Lay out the middle treads on the stringer (Figure 3–36). Place the 6" mark of the framing square at the intersection of the 12" line and the edge of the board. Rotate the square until both the 6" mark and the 12" mark intersect the edge of the board and once again draw the 90° angle inside the square. Repeat this process once more so there are a total of three steps outlined.

FIGURE 3–36

Marking out the middle treads on the stringer.

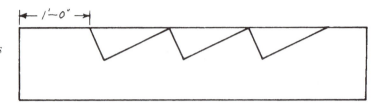

4. The height of the bottom riser and the length of the top tread are critical to the layout of a stringer. Each dimension depends on the materials used for the riser and tread boards. Table 3–4 lists the dimensions of first riser and of tread depth of the top tread for various sizes of materials and riser heights.

Lay out the bottom riser (Figure 3–37A). Place the framing square so that its outside corner is at the intersection of the edge of the board and the last 12" long line. The long arm of the square should be on that line and the short arm pointing down. Draw a line 5¼" long from the outside corner of the square along its short arm.

5. Lay out the bottom edge of the stringer (Figure 3–37B). Align the short arm of the square with the new 5¼" long line so that the outside corner is on the end of the line. Orient the long arm of the square toward the opposite edge of the board and draw a line to the back edge of the board.

TABLE 3–4

Stair dimensions.

Height of Cut on First Riser on a Stair

Riser Height (in Inches)	Thickness of Tread (in Inches)		
	⁵/₈	³/₄	1½
5	4³/₈	4¼	3½
6	5³/₈	5¼	4½
7	6³/₈	6¼	5½
8	7³/₈	7¼	5½
9	8³/₈	8¼	7½
10	9³/₈	9¼	8½

Depth of Cut of Last Tread

Tread Width (in Inches)	Thickness of Riser Material (in Inches)				
	0	⅛	¼	½	³/₄
9	9	8⁷/₈	8³/₄	8½	8¼
10	10	9⁷/₈	9³/₄	9½	9¼
11	11	10⁷/₈	10³/₄	10½	10¼
12	12	11⁷/₈	11³/₄	11½	11¼

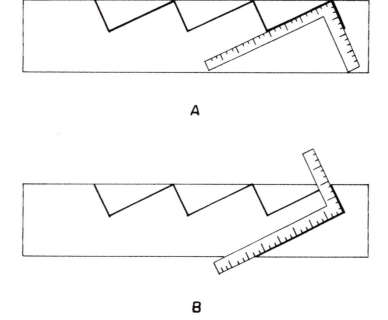

A

B

FIGURE 3–37
Marking out the bottom riser and bottom edge of the stringer.

6. Lay out the top of the stringer (Figure 3–38). Move back to the opposite end of the board at the beginning of the layout. Turn the framing square over so that the short arm is on the first 6" line that was drawn; the outside corner of the square should be at the intersection of the edge of the board and the beginning of the 6" line and the long arm of the square should point toward the opposite edge of the 1 × 12. Draw a line 11¼" long on the outside edge of the square; this is the top tread. Now place the short arm of the square against the new 11¼" line with the outside corner of the square at the end of the new line and the long arm of the square pointing down. Draw a line from

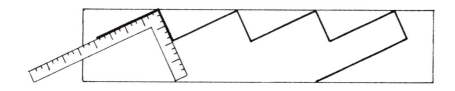

A

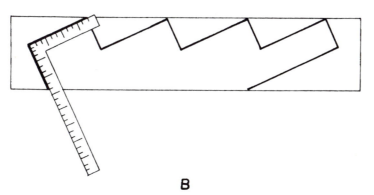

FIGURE 3–38
Marking out the top tread and back of the stringer.

B

this point to the edge of the board. This is the top rear edge of the stringer.

7. Cut out the stringer and trace the pattern on two more boards. (Figure 3–39). Stairs less than 3'-0" wide may use only two stringers, one on each side; stairs 3'-0" and wider should have a stringer on the centerline as well.

FIGURE 3–39

The cut-out stringer.

8. Cut the risers. Cut each 1 × 6 exactly 4'-0" long. Then mark the centerline on one side of each board. Select one of these boards to become the bottom riser and rip it to a width of 5¼"; label it # 1.

9. Assemble risers and stringers (Figure 3–40). Within ¾" of each end and on the centerline of each 1 × 6 including the one ripped to 5¼", drive three 6d nails or 2" drywall screws through the wood until the points show on the opposite side. Put some glue on the face of the 5¼" cut on one of the stringers and hold one end of the board labeled #1 against it. Be sure the board is flush with the top edge of the cut and the outside of the stringer (Figure 3–40). It is sometimes helpful to hold the stringer between the knees while nailing the first riser in place or to have a helper hold the stringer while nailing the riser. Nail the ripped 1 × 6 in place, being sure that all the edges are even. Nail the second stringer flush to the opposite edge of riser #1 and then place the

FIGURE 3–40

Attach the risers to the stringers first.

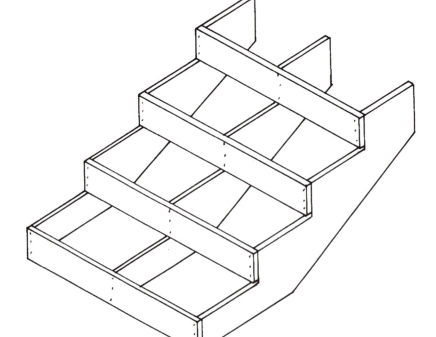

last stringer on the centerline mark and nail it to riser #1. Glue and nail another 1 × 6 in place even with the top edge of the top riser. Once again, check for an even, square fit at the top and outside edges of the riser. Attach each of the remaining 1 × 6s to the riser portion of the stringers, being sure that each board is placed square with the ends and flush with the top of each tread cut on the stringers.

10. Attach treads to stringers (Figure 3–41). Cut each 1 × 12 exactly 4'-0" long, and then mark the centerline on each board; these are the treads for the stairway. Drive four 6d nails or 2" drywall screws through each board on the centerline and within ³/₄" from each end; be careful not to nail the boards to the floor. Working on one step at a time, spread some white glue on the top of each stringer where it awaits a tread and on the top edge of each riser board. Put a 1 × 12 in place for the bottom step. It must be flush with the front of the riser board and with the outside stringers. Drive the nails into the stringers, and then add a nail through the 1 × 12 into the top of the riser between the stringers. Nail a tread in place on each step. There will be a small gap at the rear of each step between the back of the tread and the face of the riser.

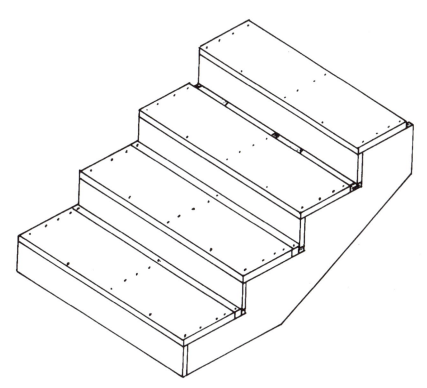

FIGURE 3–41
Attach the treads to the stringers and risers.

11. Fill the gap at the back of each tread. If a 1 × 12 was used for the tread, a ³/₄" gap will remain at the back of each step since the 1 × 12 is only 11¼" wide but the step is 12" deep. Although it is not always necessary to fill this gap, it is usually preferable. Measure the width of the gap on each step and rip a piece of wood to fill the space. Using glue and 6d nails, attach the filler to each step.

12. Install legs and cross-bracing (Figure 3–42). Cut three 2 × 4s 23¼" long. Placed under the 3/4" thickness of the top tread, this will make the top of the stairway 24" high. Place one 2 × 4 at the back of each stringer, drill two 3/8" holes, and bolt the leg in place. Crossbrace the legs with two short 1 × 3s attached with 6d nails.

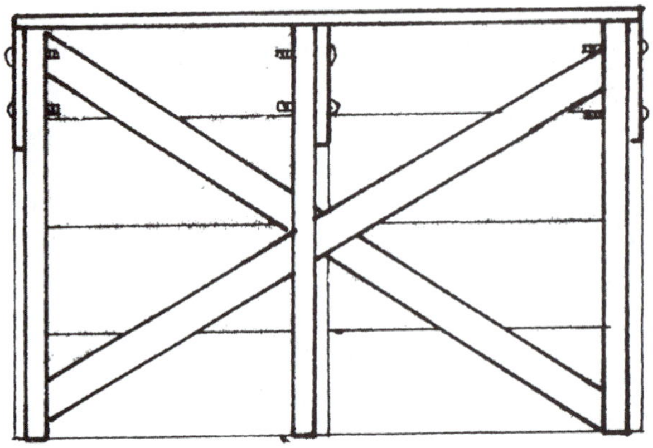

FIGURE 3–42

Rear view of an assembled stair with legs and cross braces for an independent stairway.

13. Supporting dependent stairs (Figure 3–43). Dependent staircases require additional construction on the back of the stairs and sometimes on the platform.

A. (Figure 3–43A) At the bottom edge of each stringer at the top end of the staircase, draw the outline of a 1 × 4 or 2 × 4, whichever shall be used to support the stair. Weight is conserved using a 1 × 4 but strength is increased using a 2 × 4.

B. (Figure 3–43B) Cut a 1 × 4 or 2 × 4 equal in length to the width of the stairway. If the staircase is 4'-0" wide, cut the board 4'-0" long. Using white glue and either nails or drywall screws, attach the board into the notch at each stringer.

C. (Figure 3–43C) Rest the stairway on the bottom edge of the stringers. Using a level, adjust the height of the back end of the stairway so that each tread is perfectly level. Measure the distance from the floor to the bottom of the new 1 × 4 or 2 × 4 at the back of the stringers.

D. At the location where the stairway will be attached to the platform, identify the two nearest supporting legs of the platform. At this point, there are two choices: the stairway may be directly attached to the legs of the platform or the stairway may rest on a board attached to the platform. To directly attach the stairway to the platform, place it against the platform so the bottom of the new 1 × 4 or 2 × 4 just added to the stairway is on the mark on the platform legs (Figure 3–43D). Using at least two ³/₈" carriage bolts or machine screws through each leg, connect the batten on the back of the stairs to the platform legs.

When the legs of the platform do not fall in locations that permit the stairs to be directly supported on the platform legs or if the stairs have to be quickly removed for a scene shift, follow this procedure (Figure 3–43E): Cut a 2 × 4 long enough to span the distance between the out-

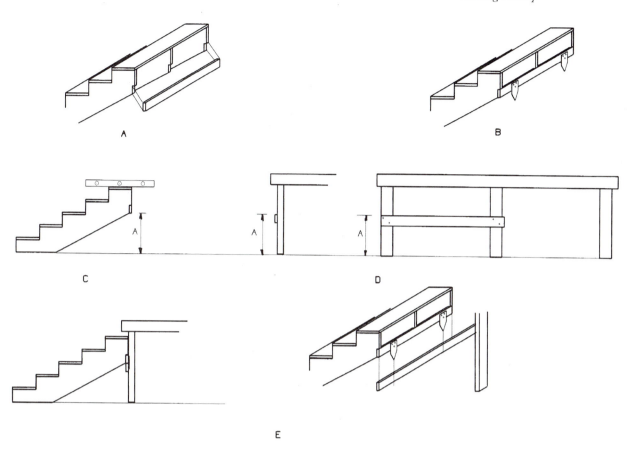

FIGURE 3–43

Supporting a dependent stairway. (A) Notch the stringers to accept a 1 × 4 or 2 × 4 batten. (B) Attach that batten in place. Stop cleats may or may not be installed at this time. (C) Stand the stairway in a normal position, leveling the treads; measure the height to the bottom of the batten on the back of the stringers. (D) Attach a matching batten to the legs of the platform to which the stairway shall be attached. Locate the top of the new batten at the same height as the bottom edge of the batten on the stair when it was leveled (dimension A). (E) Rest the batten on the stair on the batten on the platform. If the installation is permanent, cleats can be attached to both battens. If the stair must be removed for a scene change, stop cleats can be used on the batten on the stair and hooked temporarily over the batten on the platform.

side of the supporting legs on the platform. Using bolts, attach this board to the legs so that the top edge of the new 2 × 4 is exactly on the marks on the legs. Rest the 1 × 4 or 2 × 4 on the back of the stairway on the new 2 × 4 attached to the platform legs.

When the stair shall remain in place during a production, a couple of 1 × 3 cleats can be screwed to the two 2 × 4s to hold the stairway in place. The two 1 × 3s should be placed so the length of the board is more or less vertical. When the stairway must be removed for a scene change or storage, two, three, or four stop cleats can be attached to the back of the 1 × 4 or 2 × 4 on the stairway so that the cleats extend below the upper 2 × 4 and prevent the stairway from sliding forward (Figure 3–43E). To remove the stairway, the back end is lifted high enough for the tips of the stop cleats to clear the lower 2 × 4 and the stairway is carried away.

14. Pad the treads and cover the entire stairway with muslin.

Alternative Stair Construction

Figure 3–44 shows several alternatives to traditional stair construction. The first method (Figure 3–44A) makes use of the angular notches that were cut out of the standard 1 × 12 stringers described above. These triangular blocks are used to make a second set of stringers by attaching these scraps to the edge of a 1 × 6. The cut-offs are fastened in place with cornerblocks cut from ¾" plywood and attached with white glue and 1½" × #8 flathead wood screws or 1⅝" drywall screws. The remainder of the stairway is constructed in the same manner as the traditional stair.

This technique may be most practical when one stringer is cut from a 1 × 12 and its mate is assembled from the cut-offs and a 1 × 6 or when two stairways are constructed, one with 1 × 12 stringers, the other using 1 × 6s and the cut-offs. This construction technique can reduce the cost for stairs significantly since it almost doubles the use of

FIGURE 3–44
Alternative stair constructions.

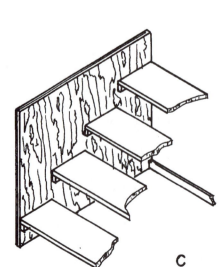

A

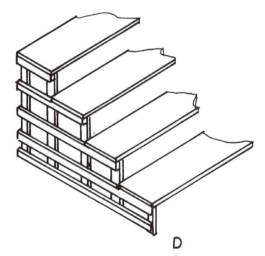

B

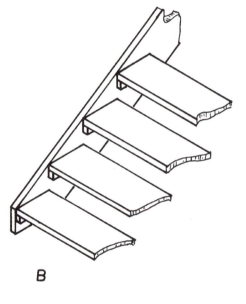

C

D

the lumber for the stringers. Assembly must be done very carefully and the glue must dry thoroughly to attain a sufficiently strong unit.

A second alternative (Figure 3–44B) still uses 1 × 12 stringers laid out as described above, but rather than cutting out the notches for the treads and risers, 11" long pieces of 1 × 2 or 1 × 3 are glued and screwed or nailed ¾" below each line that indicates the placement of a tread. The treads are nailed to these blocks. Alternatively, if 2 × 12 stringers and 2 × 10 or 2 × 12 treads are used, the treads may be attached by simply nailing through the stringers into the ends of the treads. Glue must be used in this construction, and nails must be driven at divergent angles to attain adequate strength. Of course, these techniques will not work for centerline stringers which must be notched to allow the treads to pass over them.

There are a few disadvantages to standard stair construction. Not only are the stairways fairly heavy, when completed the sides remain open and legs must be added to support the top end. By replacing traditional 1 × 12 or 2 × 12 stringers with solid sides cut from ¾" plywood, some of these problems can be solved (Figure 3–44C). The construction process is similar to the stairways described above, with the treads and risers supported on 1 × 2 blocks glued and screwed to the inside of the plywood. The placement of risers and treads is marked out in exactly the same pattern as for a traditional stairway; in addition, the entire bottom edge and the back of the stairway are also drawn on the plywood. The top edge of the stringers may be cut out in the usual stair pattern, cut at a diagonal, or made into a rectangle as shown. A brace from 1 × 3 or similar material must be added at the bottom rear of the plywood to support the bottom back corner of the stair unit.

An economy method for making stairs replaces 1 × 12 stringers or plywood sides with 1 × 2 or 1 × 3 frames, **gates,** that are constructed to the same tread and riser dimensions as a standard stringer (Figure 3–44D). Each gate is built with a 1 × 2 extending to the floor at every vertical edge of the stringer. A 1 × 2 on each horizontal line extends from the face of the riser to the rear of the gate. Although this construction uses a less costly lumber, it does require a great deal of time and manipulation of materials to build the gates. Usually standard tread and riser materials are used for this type of stair. The sides may be covered with muslin or a material-like hard board. The construction process is most easily accomplished by laying out the pattern of the side of the stair, that is, the location of treads, risers, and the bottom and back edges of the stairway, on the floor where the gate will be assembled.

To Build a Gate Stringer from 1 × 2s

Materials List	*Equipment List*
2 1 × 2 × 12'-0"	Framing square
½ pound 6d nails, 50 1½" flathead wood screws, or drywall screws	Saw
	Hammer
	Pencil
White glue	

1. Lay out the pattern of the risers and treads on the floor. Mark the thickness of the risers and treads on the pattern. All parts of the gate fit behind the risers and below the treads.

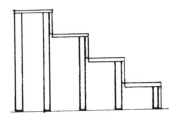

FIGURE 3–45
Vertical members of gate for the side of a straight stairway.

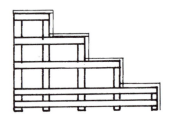

FIGURE 3–46
Stringer constructed from good 1 × 2 as a gate.

2. Cut two 1 × 2s to extend from the bottom of the top tread to the floor. Lay these boards on the pattern on the floor at the front and back of the top tread.

3. At each remaining tread, cut a 1 × 2 to extend from beneath the tread to the floor. Lay each board on the pattern just behind the riser (Figure 3–45).

4. Cut a 1 × 2 equal to the length of the top tread, less the thickness of the material that is to be used as a riser. Lay that board in place.

5. Cut an additional 1 × 2 to extend from the front of each tread (behind the riser) to the rear of the stairway, and lay each board in place beneath its appropriate tread.

6. Cut one more 1 × 2 to extend from the first riser to the back of the stairway. Place this board 2" above the floor line on the pattern.

7. Carefully square each board in place. Spread some glue between the boards at each joint and nail the boards together with 6d nails driven at an angle, or assemble each joint with 1½" flathead wood screws or 1⅝" drywall screws (Figure 3–46).

8. Complete the assembly by attaching risers and treads as needed.

A final technique for stair construction may be used for both straight and curved/circular stairs. This method also uses gates; however, they are located on a plane parallel with the risers instead of the stringers (see Figure 3–53).

To Build a Stairway 4'-0" Wide to a Height of 30" Using Gates

Materials List	*Equipment List*
5 1 × 3 × 16'-0"	Hammer
White glue	Saw
1½" flathead wood screws or 1⅝" drywall screws	Pencil
	Framing square
1 1 × 6 × 4'-0"	Screwdriver
6 1 × 12 × 4'-0"	

1. Figure 3–47. Cut a 1 × 6 exactly 4'-0" long; then rip it to a width of 5¼". This will be the first riser. Label this piece *gate #1*.

2. Figure 3–48. Cut a 1 × 12 and a 1 × 3 each exactly 4'-0" long. Measure 5¼" in from one long side of the 1 × 12 and draw a line all the way across the board. Put some glue on the flat side of the 1 × 3 and place it on the 1 × 12 against the line between the edge and the 5¼" mark. Using four screws, attach the 1 × 3 to the 1 × 12. Label this *gate #2*.

3. Figure 3–49. Cut three more 1 × 3s exactly 4'-0" long. These will be the top, middle, and bottom horizontal rails for the next gate. Cut two 1 × 3s 17¼" long; these will become the legs for gate #3.

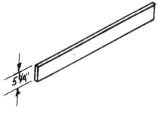

FIGURE 3–47
Gate # 1.

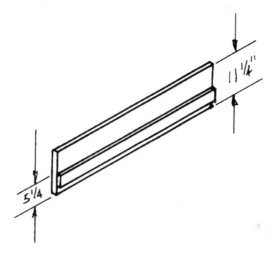

FIGURE 3–48
Gate #2.

Place the legs on a work surface so the flat wide side is facing up. Lay one rail across the top of the legs and square it to one leg. Put a little glue under the rail where it crosses the legs and attach the rail to the leg with two 1½" flathead wood screws or drywall screws. Square the second leg to the top rail and attach the two boards together with glue and screws.

4. Measure 5" up from the bottom of each leg and draw a line across each board. Lay a second rail across the legs with its top edge

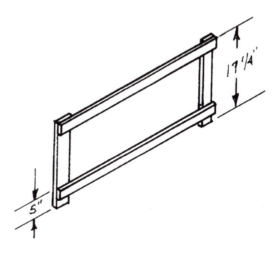

FIGURE 3–49
Assembling the front of gate #3.

against the new lines on each leg. Attach this new rail to the legs with glue and screws, being sure that the entire assembly is square.

5. Figure 3–50. Turn the frame over and measure exactly 11¼" up from the bottom of the legs and draw a line across each leg. Place the top edge of the last rail on the new pencil lines and, using glue and screws, attach this board to the legs. There should be one 1 × 3 on one side of the gate and two 1 × 3s on the opposite side of the frame. Label this piece *gate #3*.

6. The fourth gate looks exactly like gate #3 but is taller. Cut three more 1 × 3s exactly 4'-0" long and two 1 × 3s 23¼" long. Lay out and assemble these five pieces in the same manner as gate #3. That

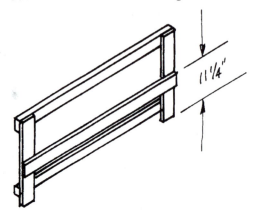

11¼"

FIGURE 3–50

Gate #3 assembled. This is the pattern for all additional gates for this stairway except the last one.

is, attach one rail to the top of the legs, a second rail with its top edge 5" above the bottom of the gate, and the last rail on the opposite side at 17¼" above the bottom of the legs.

7. Gate #5 also resembles gate #3 but is taller than both gates #3 and #4. Cut three more 1 × 3 rails exactly 4'-0" long and two legs exactly 29¼" long. Attach one rail to the top of the legs, one rail 5" above the bottom of the legs on the same side, and the third rail 23¼" above the bottom of the legs on the opposite side of the frame. Label this unit *gate #5*.

8. The last gate, gate #6, only supports the back edge of the last tread; therefore, it will be the same height as gate #5, in this case 29¼", and will have only two rails. Cut two 1 × 3 rails exactly 4'-0" long and two 1 × 3 legs exactly 29¼" long. Attach one rail at the top of the legs, being sure that the frame is exactly square, and attach the second rail 5" above the bottom of the legs on the same side of the frame. Label this unit *gate #6*.

9. Figure 3–52. Cut 1 × 12, ¾" plywood, or particle board to use as the tread for each step. Using nails or screws and white glue, attach a tread to the top of gate #1 and to the 5¼" high rail attached to the 1 × 12 on gate #2.

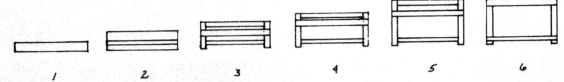

1 *2* *3* *4* *5* *6*

FIGURE 3–51

All of the gates for this stairway.

10. Assemble the remaining gates and treads in order. Glue and nail or screw the front edge of each tread to the top of the preceding gate and the back edge of the tread to the middle rail on the next gate. The back of the last tread will rest on the top rail of the last gate, gate #6.

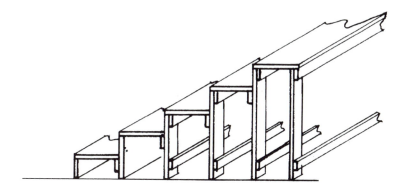

FIGURE 3–52
Assembled stairway.

11. Just above the bottom rail inside each frame, nail or screw a 1 × 3 to each leg to connect the bottom of all of the gates together. Cross-brace the assembly on the inside. Pad and cover the treads, and then, if desired, cover the sides of the stairway and the risers with hardboard or cardboard.

This same method of framing may be used to build **circular stairs**. Simply replace the rectangular treads with plywood cut in wedges of the appropriate shape to form each of the steps of the circular stair (Figure 3–53). This is an easy, fast, economical, and strong method to build a stairway.

When stairway construction is simply impossible for whatever reason, the effect of stairs can be achieved by stacking up platforms stair-step fashion, using choral risers, or putting planks on top of stacks of concrete blocks or any other sturdy modular unit, such as milk cases.

Alternative Platforms, Ramps, and Stairs

Any material that is sturdy enough to support people walking, jumping, or dancing on it can be used as a platform, ramp, or stair. Usually a frame of some kind is needed for rigidity and strength, and some means by which to elevate these surfaces to the proper height is required. Construction techniques discussed above provide some practical ways to build and elevate standard stage platforms; however, there are some less costly techniques that can also be used.

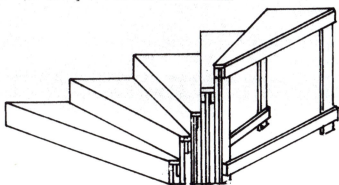

FIGURE 3–53
A circular stairway built from gates.

1. Assemble band risers to create platforms for a stage setting. If it is necessary to raise some of the risers to a greater height, the legs can be placed on concrete blocks, which might be borrowed or rented from a building contractor or supplier. The risers should be fastened together in some way. Most band risers have metal clips that allow them to be joined side to side, end to end, or end to side. If there are no clips, C-clamps can be attached between the risers or, as a last resort, rope may be used to tie the legs together. The open sides of the risers can be covered with cardboard, hardboard, or any other material wedged, taped, or wired in place. Double-faced tape, such as carpet tape, is excellent for holding the facing boards in place.

Band risers are usually quite noisy when walked on. The noise can be deadened by padding the risers with carpeting or cardboard. Turned right side up, the carpet will look good to the audience and will absorb the sound of footsteps. If jute-backed carpet is available, it can be used upsidedown as a coarse surface that may be painted. Cardboard can also be used to cover the risers. It is paintable and will absorb some sound; however, the surface of the cardboard can be easily damaged and will dent and compact from people walking on it. If cardboard is used, it works best when covered with muslin or coated with latex paint. The band director will be very concerned about paint getting on the risers, so care should be taken to protect them from damage.

If band risers are often used as a stage floor or for platforming on stage, an investment in enough ¼" tempered hardboard to cover all of the units might be practical. The hardboard could be placed on top of each riser and held in place with double-faced carpet tape, the seams covered with a dutchman (see page 127), and the floor painted for that show. Although this approach will not provide as much sound absorption as the carpet, the loosely attached sheets of hardboard will reduce noise moderately. Between shows the hardboard could be kept in storage. Glue residue from the tape can be removed from the platforms by spraying the glue with WD40 and rubbling the surface with a cloth.

2. Scaffolds are steel frames used by contractors during construction or building repairs. These sturdy frames are easily transported and assembled and are extremely strong. Many school systems have their own scaffolds, or scaffolds may be rented. They are available in various widths and heights. When set up, most scaffolds create a structure 5'-0" wide by 7'-0" long. Although the most common height for a section of scaffold is 5'-0", the frames are available in 2'-0", 3'-0", 4'-0", and 6'-0" tall sections as well. These may be stacked up for even greater heights, and adjustable legs may be used with the frames to level the units or to adjust them to in-between heights. Boards 2 × 8, 2 × 10, or 2 × 12 are provided as the floors with the frames, or the planks might simply support plywood, particle board, or standard platforms as a floor resting on top of them.

3. Similar arrangements can be created by using sawhorses in place of scaffold. Several sturdy sawhorses can be set up and planks such as 2 × 12s laid across them. Sheets of plywood or particle board can be placed on top of the planks to make a floor, or standard platforms can be laid on top of the sawhorses. If sawhorses are not available, it might be possible to borrow barricades from a construction site, building contractor, or street maintenance department. Whenever possible, the boards and platforms should be fastened to the sawhorses. Nails, screws, bolts or C-clamps can be used to hold all of these parts together. If possible, the sawhorses should be nailed or screwed to the floor.

4. An even sturdier yet more flexible platform can be made by placing stock platforms or table tops with the legs still folded on top of concrete blocks. The blocks can be stacked to different heights to create a variety of levels or they can be kept at one level for a floor at a consistent height. If an intermediate platform height is sought, the stacked blocks can be combined with lumber or other materials to obtain the in-between dimension. The stacks of blocks must be kept rigid. Any size boards of sufficient length can be secured around the stacks as "stays." The boards should be held firmly in place with wire, rope, or even duct tape wrapped tightly around the boards and blocks. Once again, the table tops must be clamped together so they will not move around or separate during the performance. They too can be covered with carpet, cardboard, or hardboard to protect them and to provide a painting surface.

5. Plywood or particle board floors can be replaced with several boards connected together. The boards must be attached by nailing strips of wood across them on the underside. It might be possible to borrow or rent scaffold boards for this use. Although 1" thick lumber such as 1 × 12 can be used, it requires more frequent support than thicker boards. If the lumber is not sufficiently supported, it will be springy and cause performers to bounce up and down when they walk or may even break.

6. A fairly easy and economical alternative to platform construction is to obtain pallets from a local business. They are often available free of charge. **Pallets** are the wooden bases used to load and hold stacks of goods while they are being shipped or stored. Pallets can be stacked up and nailed together to serve as legs for standard platforms or they may be used as a base for sheets of plywood, particle board, or hardboard to create a platform. The gaps in the tops of some pallets can be filled with boards from other pallets to create a solid floor that can be painted or padded and covered. Finally, pallets can be disassembled and the wood used to build platform frames and floors. This lumber is usually very rough and very difficult to nail.

7. Traditional platform legs can be replaced with some unique materials. **Carpet roller tube**, the cardboard core on which carpeting is shipped, can often be obtained free from carpet or furniture stores. These cardboard tubes are very sturdy and have numerous uses for the theatre; short platform legs is one of those uses.

Obtain the sturdiest carpet roller tubes possible. Using a saw, cut the tubes to the desired platform height, less the thickness of the platform lid. In other words, if the platform is to be 12" high and the top will be made from 3/4" plywood, cut several pieces of carpet roller tube 11¼" long. Using white glue or panel adhesive, join three cut lengths of tube together and bind them with two bands of nylon-filament packaging tape (Figure 3–54). Make sure that the ends of the tubes are exactly even. After the glue has dried, place a line of panel adhesive around the rim of each tube. Locate one of these tube-triangles underneath each corner and at the centerline on each long side of a sheet of plywood. If several pieces of plywood are being supported, each tube-triangle should be placed so that it spans the joint

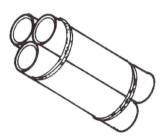

FIGURE 3–54
Carpet roller tube platform legs.

between sheets. Be sure that no single tube is supporting all of the weight at any one point. Additional legs may be needed to attain sufficient support. Allow this assembly to dry overnight and then attach cross-braces. This may be done by using drywall screws to attach 1 × 3s in an X-pattern between each leg assembly. This system may be used for platforms up to 12" high.

8. In the section on page 80, which discusses alternatives to standard stair construction, gates were described as a means of building a stairway. A **truss** is a kind of gate. These are easily built 1 × 3 or 1 × 4 assemblies that can quickly and inexpensively provide support for a walking surface. They can be constructed to any desired shape to form the base for platforms, ramps, a sloped stage, stairways, or asymmetrical platforms. If there is fear that the load will be too great, the trusses can be built from 2 × 4s for greater strength. Trusses may be built as long and as high as desired.

A 14'-0" Long 2'-0" High Platform on Trusses

Construct three trusses following this procedure for each:

Materials List	Equipment List
2 1 × 4 × 14'-0"	Framing square
5 1 × 4 × 2'-0"	Pencil
30 1½" flathead wood screws	Hammer
or 1⅝" drywall screws	Saw
White glue	

1. Cut two 1 × 4s exactly 14'-0" long. These will be the top and bottom rails. Lay them on the floor. Starting at the same end of each board, place marks 4'-0" apart; there will be a mark at 4'-0", 8'-0", and 12'-0".

2. Cut five 1 × 4s exactly 23¼" long; these will be the legs. Draw a line 3" from one end of each leg. Keep this mark toward the bottom during assembly.

3. Figure 3–55. Put a little white glue on one of the legs and place it at one end of the top rail. Square the leg to the rail and fasten it in place with three screws.

4. Adjust the bottom edge of the bottom rail to line up with the 3" mark on the leg attached to the top rail. Make the rail fit squarely to the leg. Assemble the leg and bottom rail with glue and three screws.

5. Attach a leg at the opposite end of the rail and on each 4'-0" mark, repeating the assembly procedure at each point being sure all joints are squared.

6. Figure 3–56. Place a 1 × 3 on a diagonal across the opening between the first two legs and mark a line where the diagonal crosses each of the legs and the top and bottom rails. Cut the 1 × 3 on those diagonal marks so the board will be against each leg and resting on the top and bottom rails. Attach the 1 × 3 to the top and bottom rails of the truss with glue and two screws at each end.

7. Place a second piece of 1 × 3 on the opposite diagonal between the second and third leg. Mark and cut the diagonal lines at each leg and glue and screw the 1 × 3 in place.

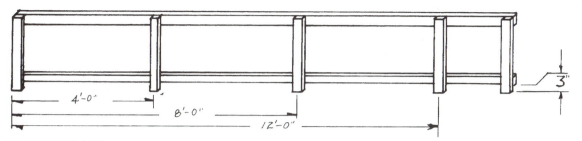

FIGURE 3–55
Assembling the legs on a truss.

8. Repeat placement of the 1 × 3s between each leg, reversing the direction of the diagonal each time.

9. Figure 3–57. Place the three trusses on their feet spaced 2'-0" apart. Using 1 × 3s, cross-brace between the frames at each end and at the middle. Lay a sheet of ³/₄" plywood or particle board on top of the trusses and align it with each edge and the ends of the frames. Drill pilot holes and insert screws about 18" to 24" apart through the plywood into the top edge of the trusses.

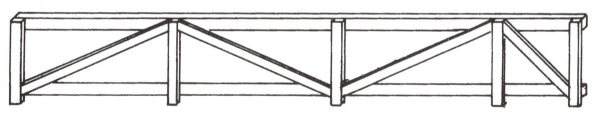

FIGURE 3–56
Attaching cross-braces to the truss.

10. Attach a 1 × 3 or 2 × 4 directly underneath each end of the plywood. The boards at the ends of the trusses should be flush with the ends of the frames. The 2 × 4s placed within the frames should be centered beneath the edge of the plywood. Cut a second sheet of plywood 6'-0" long, lay it in place, attach it with screws, and add the 2 × 4 braces at the end of the frames.

All of these designs can also be built using square or rectangular steel tubing for the framing as well as angle iron or channel iron. Once again, weight, cost, and strength must be analyzed to determine the best choice for the application. In addition, almost any other means of

FIGURE 3–57
Assembling trusses to make a platform.

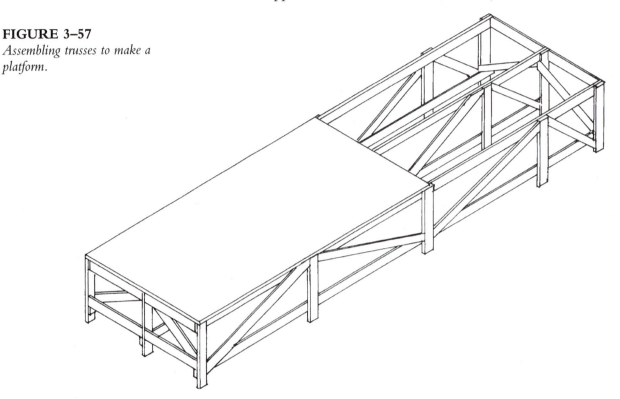

framing that can be thought of will work as a platform base so long as the assembly is solid, well braced, and able to carry the weight and activity planned for it. Bracing is very important and must not be neglected in any of these arrangements.

Doors

It is seldom possible to create a realistic interior setting without doors or windows. These important scenic elements, in addition to being necessary, contribute to the appearance of a setting and help to establish the period and style of a production. Several decisions must be made about a door on stage. Not only must size, style, and shape be determined but choices must also be made about the direction in which a door moves, whether it slides or swings, whether it is a single or double door, and whether the door should be integral to the flats or an independent, discrete unit.

It is practical to construct a few standard independent door frames with interchangeable sashes for permanent stock that can be placed in settings as needed. As with most standard scenery, a significant investment of time and materials is needed to do the initial construction; however, well-built standard units are a worthwhile, long-term investment.

Because of their weight and strength, commercially manufactured **hollow-core doors**, often found in the interior of modern homes, are frequently used on stage. These plain, lightweight doors are usually 6'-8" tall and are available in numerous widths. Good sizes for single doors on stage are 2'-6" or 3'-0" wide and double doors 4'-0" or 5'-0" wide. Occasionally single doors as narrow as 1'-6" and double doors as wide as 6'-0" might be desirable. Since stage doors are usually painted rather than stained or varnished, it is practical to purchase the least expensive hollow-core doors available. Even seconds and damaged doors can be used when they are covered with muslin to hide serious flaws.

The period and style of a doorway are defined by the shape of the door opening and the style of the molding on and around the door. It is handy to have a couple of different style door frames in stock, such as Victorian, Gothic, and Modern. This assortment could provide a base for several other periods and styles.

Independent Doors

Door frames constructed as units separate from flats are called **independent doors**. These are designed to be placed within over-sized openings in flats. The casing masks the space between the opening in the flat and the edges of the door frame. In productions where there is a lot of door slamming, an independent door frame can be set up with sturdy bracing so that the door frame does not come in contact with the flat. This arrangement keeps the walls from wiggling when the door is slammed.

To Construct an Independent Door 2'-6" Wide × 6'-8" High

Materials List		Equipment List
1	1 × 6 × 10'-0"	Hammer
1	1 × 6 × 7'-0"	Saw
2	1 × 4 × 10'-0"	Screwdriver
1	1 × 1 × 7'-0"	Drill
	2'-6" × 6'-8" hollow-core door	Framing square
		Pencil
2	¼" plywood cornerblocks	
2	6" metal corner braces	
2	1½" tight-pin backflap hinges	
¼ pound 6d common nails		
50	1½" flathead wood screws or 1⅝" drywall screws	
24	¾" flathead wood screws	
White glue		

Figure 3–58 shows the anatomy of a door. Although any lumber may be used to construct a door frame, for this example the casing is made from 1 × 4s, the reveal from 1 × 6s, and the doorstop is a 1 × 1. The door itself will be a hollow-core door purchased from the lumberyard. Inside dimensions of the door frame must be large enough to allow the door to fit easily without excessive gaps around the edges.

1. Figure 3–59. To construct the reveal, cut two pieces of 1 × 6 exactly 6'-8½" long and two pieces of 1 × 6 exactly 2'-7¾" long. Place these four boards on edge and assemble them into a rectangle with the long boards placed between the two short ones. Use three screws and white glue at each corner. Using a framing square, check all corners of the reveal and adjust the frame to make it square if necessary.

2. The casing will attach to the reveal. Cut two 1 × 4s 6'- 9¼" long. Lay a line of glue on the edge of the two long 1 × 6s of the reveal. Place the 1 × 4s on the edge of the long 1 × 6s flush with the inside edge of the frame and even with the bottom of the frame. Attach the

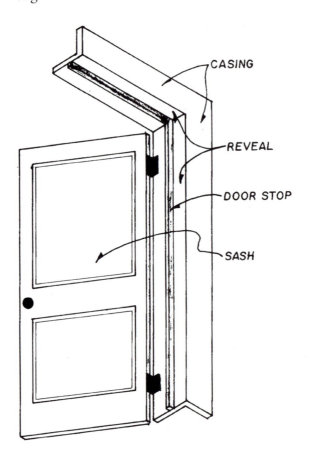

FIGURE 3–58
Anatomy of a door.

1 × 4s with 6d nails or drywall screws. If necessary, bend the 1 × 6 reveals to match the edge of the 1 × 4 casings.

3. The top of the casing spans the distance between the outside of the two long 1 × 4s. Measure that distance; that dimension should be approximately 3'-1¼". Cut a 1 × 4 to the dimension measured. Spread a line of glue on the edge of the top 1 × 6 of the reveal. Place the newly cut 1 × 4 on top of the glued board and adjust it so that both ends are even with the outside edges of the long 1 × 4s. Attach the new 1 × 4 to the reveal with 6d nails or drywall screws.

4. Turn the door frame over so that it is lying face down on the 1 × 4 casing. Using the framing square, check all corners to make sure that the door frame is square. Place some white glue on the underside of each of the keystones and lay them on the back of the joints between the horizontal and vertical 1 × 4 members. Drill pilot holes and insert three ¾" flathead wood screws into the keystone on each side of the joint. Attach a 6" steel corner brace to the top outside corners of the reveal using ¾" screws also.

5. Attach the doorstop. Draw a line 1½" in from the back of the 1 × 6 reveal all the way around the perimeter of the frame. Nail or screw a 1 × 1 on that line so that the board is placed toward the front of the frame and there is a 1½" space between the edge of the doorstop and the back of the frame (Figure 3-60). Decorative moldings can be added to the casing.

Dependent Doors

Door frames may also be constructed as integral parts of a flat. Although these units cannot be moved from flat to flat, the flats with the frames intact can be saved from show to show. This is less convenient and less flexible than independent door frames, but the construction is quicker and easier.

To Construct a Dependent Door Frame for a 3'-0" × 6'-8" Door

Materials List   *Equipment List*

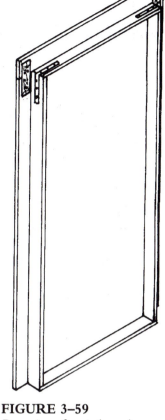

FIGURE 3–59
Rear view of an independent door frame.

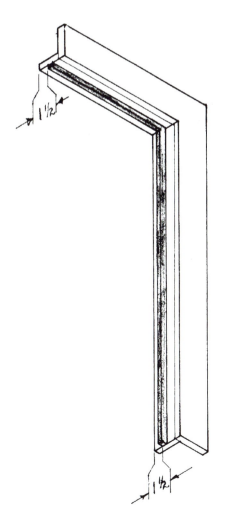

FIGURE 3–60
Attach a 1 × 1 doorstop 1½" in from the back of the frame.

1 1 × 4 × 11'-0"	Pencil
1 1 × 4 × 7'-0"	Saw
1 1 × 6 × 12'-0"	Screwdriver
1 1 × 6 × 7'-0"	Drill with ⅛" bit

50 1½" flathead wood screws
    or 1⅝" drywall screws

1. Figure 3–61. Construct the flat with a door opening of the appropriate size, allowing some clearance for the door to move within the opening. The opening for a 3'-0" × 6'-8" door should be 3'-½" wide by 6'-9" tall. This provides sufficient clearance for hardware and door movement.

2. Attach the reveal. After the flat has been constructed, covered, and painted with a prime coat, it is ready to have the door frame attached. Cut two pieces of 1 × 4 the height of the door opening, 6'-9". Attach the boards to the back of the flat on either side of the door opening with screws spaced about 18" apart.

3. Cut a third 1 × 4 to fit across the top of the opening plus the width of the two vertical 1 × 4s on the sides. This board will be approximately 3'-2" long. Using screws, attach the new 1 × 4 to the back of the flat at the top of the door opening and fasten down into the vertical 1 × 4s. These three boards constitute the reveal.

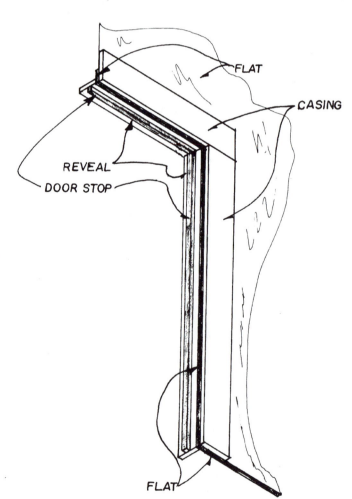

FIGURE 3–61
Anatomy of a dependent door frame.

4. Cut two more 1 × 4s the exact height of the door opening, 6'-9". Using 6d finish nails driven at an angle so they do not stick out of the back of the flat, or 1⅝" drywall screws, attach these boards to the front of the flat on either side of the door opening to form the vertical portion of the casing.

5. Measure the distance between the outside of the two 1 × 4s on the face of the flat. Cut a third 1 × 4 that dimension and attach it at the top of the door opening. These three boards make up the casing to which decorative moldings or trim can be added.

6. Draw a line all the way around the perimeter of the reveal 1½" in from the back of the frame. Attach a 1 × 1 to the inside of the reveal all the way around the opening so that the back edge of the 1 × 1 is on the line toward the face of the flat (Figure 3–60).

In either of these constructions of door frames, the reveal and casings may be replaced with wider or narrower lumber and the casings may be made from decorative moldings or some other material more appropriate to the style of the production. The square cuts at the top of the casing can be replaced with 45° mitered cuts or decorative corner moldings; this will affect the length of each board.

To Mount a Door

1. Attach the hinges. Measure 8" up from the bottom and 8" down from the top of the door on the edge where the hinges are to be located. Using flathead wood screws, attach a 1½" backflap tight pin hinge or any screen door hinge to the edge of the door. The top hinge should be placed below the 8" mark and the bottom hinge above the 8" mark, so that each hinge is 8" from the end of the door. The **butt** of the hinge, the part where the two flaps of the hinge join, must be toward the back and above the rear surface of the door.

2. Mount the door. Lay a short 1 × 3 inside the door frame. Place the door in the frame on the loose 1 × 3 and center it right and left in the opening; there should be a ¼" gap on either side and at the top of the door; the loose 1 × 3 creates a ¾" gap at the bottom of the door. Be sure that the butts of the hinges extend beyond the back of the reveal (Figure 3–62), then carefully mark the position of the hinges on the edge of the door frame. Take the door out of the opening. Place a matching unattached hinge on the edge of the frame in line with the marks that show the position of the hinges on the door. Mark the position of the holes in the hinges and drill ³⁄₃₂" diameter pilot holes in each of these for a $3/4"$ × #8 flathead wood screw. Put the door back in the frame, hold it open, and insert a screw in each hole in the hinges. If the door will be subjected to hard use, replace the screws with $3/16"$ × $1 1/2"$ flathead stove bolts.

3. Install the doorknob.   The door is now ready for a handle or knob. Standard door hardware may be used. The easiest way to put a handle on the door is to use a knob that mounts on a square shank. Drill a $1/4"$ or slightly larger hole through the door where the knob will be placed. Put the shaft through the hole, slip on and attach any decorative plates (escutcheons) that go around the knob, and then attach the doorknobs. There is usually a small screw on the side of a doorknob that must be tightened securely against the shaft. A second knob should be placed on the offstage side of the door and securely attached.

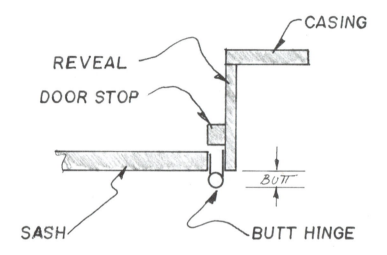

FIGURE 3–62
Placement of a butt hinge.

4. Install the latch.   The door also needs some kind of latch to keep it closed. Friction or magnetic cabinet catches are often used. One of these catches can be attached to the edge of the door near the knob or placed at the top or bottom of the door if that mounting is more convenient.

A handy way to prevent doors from moving on their own—whether closed or standing in an open position—is to screw a small ($1/4"$ thick, 2" wide) inexpensive paintbrush to the back bottom of the door so that the bristles brush the stage floor with sufficient friction that the door will not open on its own.

Although most modern doors are rectangular, it is often desirable to put doors on stage that have a curved top edge. The frame may be constructed in any desired shape by replacing the top of the casing with a piece of $3/4"$ plywood (or some other material) cut into the desired arc (see Figure 3–17). The outer edge of the casing may match the curved shape of the door or may be square to mask the opening in an existing flat. The reveal around the inside of the arc can be made from $1/8"$ standard hardboard, cardboard, or any other material that will bend. The reveal is attached to the inside edge of the casing, which shapes it and gives it support (see Figure 3–17D).

When a rounded opening is used for a door, it is sometimes difficult to make the edge of the door match the shape of the arch. It is easiest to build the arch first and then to trace that shape on the door as a guide for cutting. Hollow-core doors can be cut with any power saw. A saber saw will make the best curved cut.

Sometimes it is preferable not to cut the top of a door to match an arc (Figure 3–63). This is more economical since the door can then be preserved for other uses rather than being totally committed to this one frame. Used in this way, the door is mounted to the back of the reveal rather than within the opening of the frame. Since the door is outside of the frame it need not conform to the shape of the opening, so a standard rectangular door can be used behind any shaped door opening.

Rather than purchasing hollow-core doors from the lumberyard, doors may be constructed of 1 × 3s and covered with cardboard, hardboard, or muslin like a flat.

Paneled Doors

Moldings and trims can be added to any door and it is easy to convert a plain hollow-core door into a fancy paneled or "glass" door.

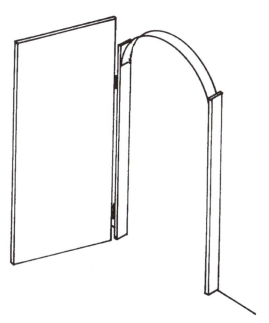

FIGURE 3–63
A rectangular door placed in an arched door frame.

To Make a Paneled Door

Materials List	*Equipment List*
Hollow-core door	Pencil
Hardboard, Plexiglas, or other material for panel backing	Saber Saw
	Table saw
	Drill with ¼" bit

2 × 4s as necessary   Hammer

9/16" staples   Staple gun

White glue

1/4" quarter-round molding
   as needed

Muslin

Dope

1. Draw the pattern of the required panel or window on the surface of the door. Drill a hole large enough for the blade of a saber saw to fit through and cut that pattern out. There will be a thin layer of wood composing each of the outer surfaces of the door and a cardboard honeycomb structure in the middle. Lightly sand the edges of the opening.

2. If it will be necessary to attach something within the opening or to the back of the opening in the door, the area around the hole must be supported. Measure the exact dimension of the *interior* space between the outer layers of wood. Using a table saw, rip enough 2 × 4 to that thickness to fill all voids around the perimeter of the hole. Lightly sand the edges of the wood (Figure 3–64).

3. Spread some white glue on the sides of the rippings, and then tap each board in place between the outer wooden layers of the door. As the board is forced into position it will compress some of the cardboard core within the door. Be sure to get the board flush with the edge of the opening. Once the lumber has been forced into position, attach the outer layers of the door to the new core with 9/16" staples or very small finishing nails.

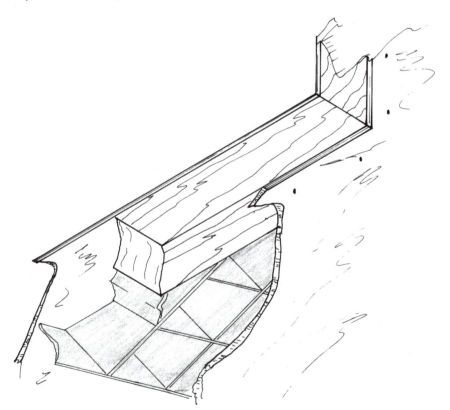

FIGURE 3–64

Filling the edges of an opening in a hollow-core door.

4. Install the panel (Figure 3–65). If only one side of the door will be seen, pieces of plywood, cardboard, hardboard, Plexiglas, or any other material can be nailed or screwed to the back of the opening. If the back of the door will be seen, panels can be placed within the hole by attaching a ¼" × ¼" strip of hardboard or ¼" quarter-round molding all the way around the perimeter just inside the edge of the opening. These moldings should be glued and nailed in place. The panel, which must be of a relatively thin material, is placed against the molding and a second set of moldings is glued and nailed on the opposite side to hold it in place. Other moldings and trim can be added to complete decoration of the door.

If the hole in the door is to be left open, the cut edge can simply be covered with muslin rather than filling the edge with wood. Tear a strip of fabric about 6" wide and coat it with dope. Also paint dope onto the surface of the door around the hole where the muslin will be applied. Lay the fabric in place and smooth it out so there are no bumps or wrinkles. Allow it to dry.

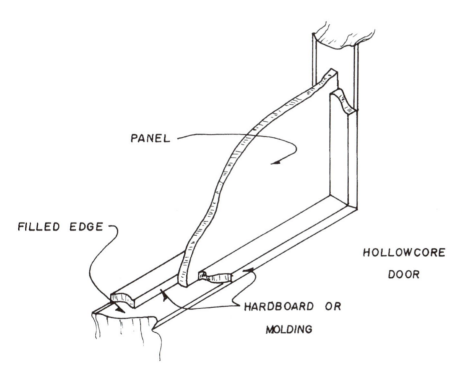

PANEL

FILLED EDGE

HOLLOWCORE
DOOR

HARDBOARD OR
MOLDING

FIGURE 3–65
Installing a panel in an opening in a hollow-core door.

Windows

Like doors, windows contribute significantly to the look of a setting and help to establish the style, period, and locale of the performance. Also like doors, windows can be time consuming and difficult to construct. The easiest windows to deal with are those that do not open and the next easiest are those that hinge rather than slide up and down.

Windows consist of a frame and a sash. The frames are constructed in a manner similar to door frames, but rather than being open on the bottom, window frames usually end with a sill 24" to 36" above the floor. Since window design varies so much, it is impossible to prescribe standard dimensions for a window frame. The best rec-ommendation is to measure existing windows in a house or apartment and use similar dimensions for stage windows.

To Construct a 2'-0" × 4'-0" Window Frame

Materials List	*Equipment List*
1 1 × 6 × 12'-6"	Framing square
1 1 × 4 × 13'-0"	Pencil
50 1½" flathead wood	Saw
screws or 1⅝"drywall	Hammer
screws	Screwdriver
48 ¾" flathead wood screws	Drill
¼ pound 6d finish nails	
White glue	
4 6" steel corner irons	
4 ¼" plywood keystones	

1. To construct the reveal (Figures 3–66 and 3–67), cut two 4'-0" long pieces of 1 × 6 and two 2'-1½" long pieces of 1 × 6. Place the boards on edge in a rectangle with the long boards between the short ones. Apply some glue to the end of each long board and assemble each corner with three screws. Check the squareness of the frame, and then

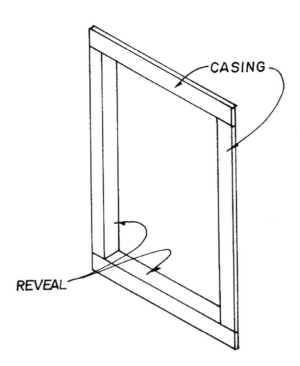

FIGURE 3–66
Front view of a typical window frame.

attach each of the four corner braces to the outside of the corners with ¾" screws.

2. Begin the casing by cutting two pieces of 1 × 4 4'-0" long. Apply white glue to the edge of the long 1 × 6s on the reveal and nail the 1 × 4s to them. Be sure that the boards are even with the top and bottom ends of these 1 × 6s and flush with their inside edge.

3. Measure the distance between the outside of the two 1 × 4s. This dimension should be approximately 2'-7". Cut two 1 × 4s to that dimension and attach them to the top and bottom of the window frame using glue and 6d finish nails.

4. Turn the frame over. Put some glue on a keystone and then attach it with ³/₄" flathead wood screws over each joint on the back of the casing.

The window frame is now ready to have a sash installed within it or attached to the back of it. It is handiest to construct independent

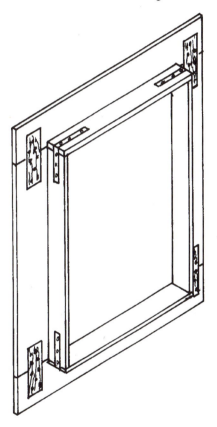

FIGURE 3–67
Rear view of a typical window frame.

window frames that have interchangeable sashes. In this way, the appearance of the window can be altered by screwing a new sash to the back of the window frame for each show. As a result, one frame can serve numerous design styles. **Mullions**, the narrow boards that divide a window into panes, can be designed in almost any pattern. They are usually made of 1 × 1s. Joints are either half-lapped (see Figure 3–10), or attached using keystones or metal mending plates. Figure 3–68 shows some possible designs for window sashes.

When a window must open on stage, it is easiest to make it swing like a door rather than slide up and down. Moving sashes may be the

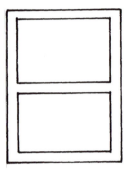  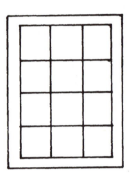 

FIGURE 3–68
Designs for window sashes.

same units as the fixed sashes described above, but they are attached to the back of the reveal with hinges rather than with screws. If it is impossible to avoid constructing a functional sliding sash window, it can be built with careful carpentry.

To Build a Functional Sliding Sash Window
2'-0" Wide × 4'-0" High

Materials List	*Equipment List*
1 1 × 1 × 16'-0"	Saw
1 1 × 2 × 8'-0"	Framing square
1 1 × 3 × 16'-0"	Hammer
2 1 × 4 × 12'-0"	Drill with $^{3}/_{32}$" and $^{1}/_{2}$" bits
1 1 × 6 × 14'-0"	
24 $^{3}/_{4}$" flathead wood screws	Screwdriver
16 $1^{1}/_{2}$" flathead wood screws or $1^{5}/_{8}$" drywall screws	Router
$^{1}/_{8}$ pound 4d common nails	
$^{1}/_{4}$ pound 6d common nails	
2 single-awning pulleys	
2 double-awning pulleys	
Rope	
2 socks	
Sand	
White glue	

1. Build the window sashes. Cut eight pieces of 1 × 3 exactly 1'-11$^{3}/_{4}$" long. Lay four pieces on the floor to form a square, with the side pieces overlapping the top and bottom boards at each corner. Using a framing square, make sure that the pieces are placed precisely at 90° to each other. This is very important. Mark each board where it overlaps or underlaps the other boards. Each board must be marked at every corner. Label the corners A, B, C, etc., so the frame can be reassembled after cutting. Following the procedures for making half-lap joints described in Figure 3–10, trim this lumber for half-lapping. Place the trimmed lumber back on the floor and once again, carefully square it into place. Put a little white glue in each joint and assemble each of the four corners with two ³/₄" flathead wood screws. Repeat for the second window frame. (If desired, a more complex mullion pattern can be designed and constructed at this time.)

2. Cut the lumber for the reveal and tracks. Cut two 1 × 6s, two 1 × 2s, and four 1 × 1s exactly 3'-10½" long. Sand each board smooth.

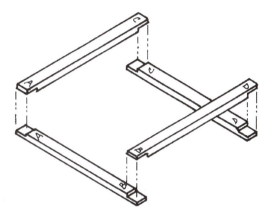

FIGURE 3–69
Assembling a half-lap window sash for a sliding window.

3. Construct the reveal/tracks. Draw a line 1" and another 2³/₄" in from the back edge of each 1 × 6. These lines must be very straight, for they will guide attachment of the 1 × 1s that will become the tracks for the sliding windows. Place a line of glue on one side of a 1 × 1. Using 4d box or finish nails, attach the 1 × 1 along the first line so there is a 1" space between the back edge of the 1 × 6 and the 1 × 1. Now, leaving another 1" space, attach a second 1 × 1 along the second pencil line. Finally, attach a 1 × 2 to the back edge of the reveal so that it faces the same side of the 1 × 6 as the 1 × 1s (Figure 3–70). Repeat this assembly procedure on the other 1 × 6.

4. Assemble the reveal. Cut two 1 × 6s exactly 2'-1½"" long. Using either three 1½" flathead wood screws or 1⁵/₈" drywall screws and white glue, attach one of these boards to the bottom of both of the

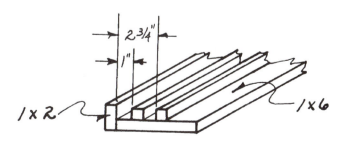

FIGURE 3–70
Assembling the tracks for a sliding window.

long 1 × 6s to form a U. Be sure to assemble the frame with the tracks facing each other and the outside corners of the boards flush to the ends of the shorter 1 × 6.

5. Place a sash in each track. Attach the remaining 1 × 6 across the top of the assembly using 1½" flathead wood screws or 1⅝" drywall screws and white glue.

6. Make and attach the casing. Cut two 1 × 4s exactly 4'-0" long and another pair of 1 × 4s 2'-7" long. Using 6d nails and white glue, attach the long 1 × 4s to the front of the long reveal boards and the short ones to the top and bottom of the reveal to complete the frame.

7. Brace the frame. Turn the frame over so that it is lying on the 1 × 4 casing. Using glue and ¾" flathead wood screws, attach a keystone over each joint on the casing. Then attach a steel outside corner brace around each corner of the reveal with screws.

8. Attach pulleys to carry operating ropes. Drill a ½" diameter hole in the 1 × 6 at the top of the window frame directly in line with the outside corners of each sash and as close to the edge of the frame as possible. There should be a total of four holes. Above one hole on one side of the frame attach a double-grooved awning pulley. In line with this first pulley, but on the opposite side of the frame, attach a single-grooved awning pulley. Attach a double-grooved awning pulley above the hole next to the single-grooved pulley and attach a single-grooved pulley next to the double-grooved one. The pulleys should be placed so that a rope can pass through the hole and over the top of the pulley.

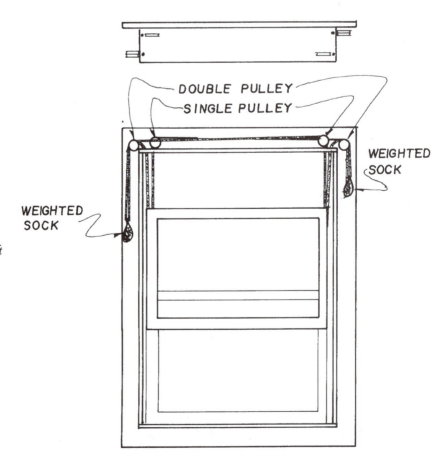

FIGURE 3–71
Rigging for a sliding sash window. The weight on the right counterbalances the front sash and the weight on the left counterbalances the rear sash.

9. Thread the operating ropes. Drop the end of a piece of ¼" cotton rope through each hole down to the top outside corner of each window sash. Attach the rope to the top corner of the sash with staples or a nail. Take the rope over the pulley above it. The rope passing through the single pulley should be brought across and passed over the double pulley, then dropped along the outside of the frame. The rope already at the double pulley should go over the wheel and down the outside of the frame also. This will result in both ropes from the front window going to one side of the frame and both ropes from the rear window going to the other side of the frame.

10. Counterbalance the sashes. With both windows at the bottom of the frame, tie each pair of ropes together a few inches below the pulleys. Put a little sand in an old sock and tie it to the end of one pair of ropes. The sock should have enough weight to counterbalance the window sash (Figure 3–71).

11. Add decorative detail to the unit. Moldings and trim may be added to the casing, and hardware can be attached to the sashes. Anything attached to the sashes must not inhibit their movement.

Glass

Whenever possible, real glass should be avoided on stage because its use causes numerous problems: it is too easy to break, too heavy to be supported by scenery, and reflects light in disastrous patterns both on stage and into the audience.

There are several alternatives to using real glass for scenery. The easiest is to use nothing at all in a window opening. This is often satisfactory; however, it is even more effective if the window is behind a drape or sheer curtain. If the window is in clear view of the audience, the audience is very close to the stage, or an actor walks behind the window as part of a scene, this shortcut tends to be obvious and breaks the sense of credibility.

The most practical solution for glass on stage is to stretch galvanized or aluminum window screening or a sheer, glossy, pale fabric such as organdy or tulle over the back of the opening. If the fabric is wrinkled or creased, it must be ironed before it is stapled in place. It must be absolutely wrinkle-free to be effective. Both the screening and the fabric will suggest the glint of glass without adding danger, weight, or glare.

The plastic material often used for drop cloths can also be used to simulate glass. Unfortunately, when it is simply stretched over an opening it looks exactly like a plastic drop cloth—complete with wrinkles and creases. This problem can be minimized by heating the plastic to shrink it tight, or by using the plastic sheeting where it can be stretched behind a complex pattern of mullions and then painted with a dilute mixture of artist's clear acrylic medium, a little light grey or light brown paint, and some water to suggest an accumulation of dirt and grime. The paint mixture should look like dirty dish water. The acrylic medium serves as a binder to adhere the paint to the plastic sheeting.

Effective materials to use for decorative glass are the flat, light weight plastic panels made to cover fluorescent lights in suspended ceilings. These inexpensive panels are available from lumberyards in sheets measuring 2'-0" wide × 4'-0" long. They come in a variety of patterns from frosted glass to colored bottle glass; even some stained-glass patterns are available.

Clear acrylic sheeting, commonly known as Plexiglas, is a rigid substitute for real glass. These plastic sheets are lightweight, moderately rigid, available in large sizes, and break resistant; they are also very expensive. To emulate the rigidity of glass, the acrylic sheet must be at least $^3/_{16}$" thick. The plastic can be very effective on stage but, like glass, will produce reflection and glare. It also scratches easily. The material can be cut and drilled with power-operated wood and metal working tools.

Gel, the thin plastic material used to color theatrical lighting instruments, can also be used as a replacement for glass. The most dilute colors should be chosen, or preferably those media known as diffusion gels, such as frost, which will produce less glare or reflection. Gel can be stapled, taped, or glued to the back of sashes. More intense colors can be assembled with electrician's tape to simulate stained glass.

Alternatives to Standard Windows

If a play takes place entirely at night, a window can be implied by painting it onto the setting, covering it with a sheer curtain, and finally dressing the window with heavy curtains hanging to ether side. The deep blue or black paint between mullions painted on the flat will be seen as an unlighted evening behind sheer curtains.

Frequently a window will be appropriate or called for in a setting but never used. An easy way to create the sense of a window is simply to hang an opaque curtain over a section of the wall. The curtain itself suggests the presence of a window—that no one looks out of it and no light enters through it will be of little consequence.

Large windows can be created by assembling several flats to form a picture window and adding 1 × 4s and 1 × 6s as the reveal and casing. Glass and curtains can be added as described above.

Mullions, the small strips that divide a window into panes, are often made from 1 × 1 lumber; however, some simple substitutes are possible. On windows that have nothing simulating the glass or on those that have been covered with sheer fabric, window screen, or gel, mullions can be implied by attaching cord, rope, or tape to the back of the frame in almost any pattern. It is best to staple the ends of substitute mullion material to the window frame. Where a material is present, rope or tape can be replaced with a line of grey or black caulk or hot-melt glue.

Trims and Moldings

Almost any building or room is decorated with moldings. The design of this architectural detail contributes to the sense of period and style of the setting as well as the play as a whole. Bearing this significance, moldings should be carefully considered when planning a setting, making selections based on research of architectural styles in paintings and photographs.

The easiest way to make moldings is the most expensive: many styles of moldings may be purchased from the lumberyard (Figure 3–72). These trim pieces can be used individually, or several moldings can be combined to create larger and more elaborate designs. Usually larger moldings for the stage are constructed on a frame so that the back of the molding is hollow, as in Figure 3–73. If the molding is to be painted (rather than stained), hardboard, cardboard, or almost any other material may be used as part of the decorative structure.

Alternatives to constructing moldings from lumber are limited only by the imagination. Styrofoam and similar plastic foams are especially useful substitutes from which to construct large moldings. Individual layers of foam can be glued together to make a thick slab that is shaped to the desired pattern with a hot wire cutter, an electric knife, or other simple tools. See Chapter 6 for a discussion of working with plastic foams, including very important safety precautions.

Moldings offer one of the broadest areas for creative use of materials in scenic construction. Almost anything may be used. Things such as carpet roller tubes cut in half or rings cut from the end of whole,

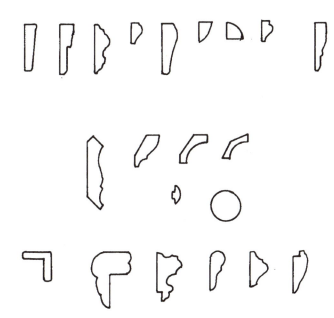

FIGURE 3–72
Some of the molding styles available from lumberyards.

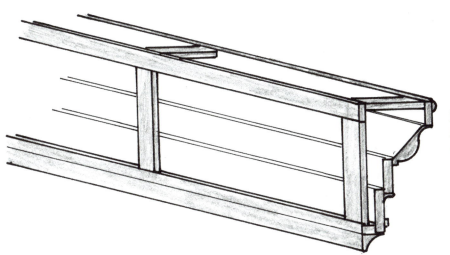

FIGURE 3–73
Hollow-backed, built-up molding.

half, or quarter tubes may be lined up. Ball fringe or string fringe may be coated with glue and attached at the top of a wall; small plastic discs, various preformed or specially made Styrofoam shapes, blocks of wood of various sizes, or teaspoons may be lined up in a row or placed on end, or any one of these or most other materials may be arranged and painted for use as moldings. The ability of the materials to give the impression of elaborate moldings is ultimately dependent on the appropriate painting and finishing techniques which are discussed in Chapter 4.

Equally challenging and exciting is the construction of railings and newel posts. Spindles and newel posts can be purchased new at the lumberyard and sometimes can be rescued from buildings being torn down. They can also be made in the shop on a lathe or created in almost as many ways as moldings from cardboard tubes, rope, illustration board, plastic foams, or anything else appropriate. For some productions they can be stylized and cut out as flat patterns.

Columns

Columns are very effective visual elements on stage and they are fairly easy to construct.

To Construct a Column 14'-0" Tall × 15" Diameter

Materials List	Equipment List
¼" plywood 2'-6" × 4'-0"	Compass
1 × 8 × 10'-0"	Saber or band saw
½ pound 1" roofing nails	Table saw
or drywall screws	Hammer
3 2 × 4 × 14'-0"	Muslin
2 pounds 4d nails	Dope

1. On a piece of ¼" plywood, draw and cut out five circles measuring 14½" in diameter.

2. Lay each circle on top of a pair of 1 × 8 boards placed side by side. Each board should be at least 15" long. Using each disc as a pattern, mark the outline of the circle on each pair of 1 × 8s and then cut out the half-circles on each board.

3. Using white glue and nails or screws, attach the 1 × 8 half-discs to their matching plywood circles. The grain on top of the plywood must be in the direction opposite the joint between the half-circles (Figure 3–74). Allow the glue to dry.

4. Cut three 2 × 4s exactly 14'-0" long. Set up a table saw to make a ¼" rip cut. Cutting through the 1½" thickness of the 2 × 4s, cut at least 31 pieces of wood ¼" × 1½" × 14'-0". Place a pencil mark at 3'-6", 7'-0", and 10'-6" on four of these strips. These marks indicate the location of the discs when the column is assembled.

5. Using white glue and 4d common nails or short drywall screws, attach each end of one of the marked strips to the side of one of the discs. Now attach a disc at each of the pencil marks (3'-6", 7'-0", and 10'-6"). Attach a second marked strip to each of the discs exactly opposite the first strip. Finally, attach the remaining two marked strips 90° around the circle from the first two strips (Figure 3–75).

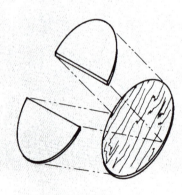

FIGURE 3–74
Discs assembled from 1 × 8 and ¼" plywood to form the core of a column.

6. Fill in the areas between the existing strips with additional rippings from the 2 × 4.

7. Paint the entire surface of the column skeleton with dope and cover it with muslin. Apply another coating of dope on the fabric after it has been stretched on the column. Allow the dope to dry.

Columns constructed in this manner can be made to appear smoother by replacing the 2 × 4 rippings with rippings from the edge of narrower lumber such as 1 × 4s. If a fluted look is desired, spacing between the wood strips can be increased so there is a strip of wood followed by an evenly spaced gap or by alternating thick (³⁄₄") and thin (¹⁄₄") rippings when assembling the column (Figure 3–76). When the

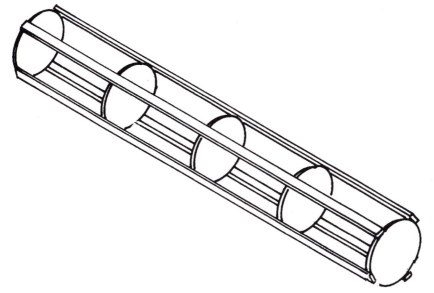

FIGURE 3–75
Rippings of ¹⁄₄" × 1¹⁄₂" wood attached to the core discs of the column.

muslin is stretched over the structure, the gaps or thin rippings will allow the fabric to sag, giving the impression of fluting. The fabric should be stapled in the depressions. Another way to create the effect is to add 1 × 1 strips evenly spaced around the outside of the basic

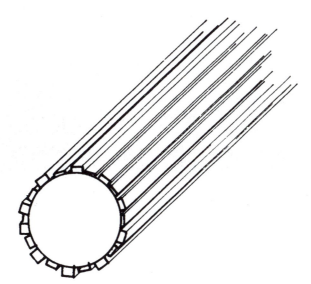

FIGURE 3–76
Add fluting to the column by alternating thick and thin rippings.

109

column after it has been covered with muslin. This would result in two layers of wood forming the structure: the base layer of ¼" thick rippings and the fluting layer of 1 × 1s.

Tapered columns can be made by reducing the size of each circle over the height of the column so that the structure becomes increasingly narrow toward the top, for instance starting with a 15" circle at the bottom, followed by a 13", an 11", and finally a 9" circle. This will require shortening some of the pieces of the ¼" rippings since there would not be room for the same number of pieces at the top as there is at the bottom of the column.

Alternative Column Techniques

An open column can be created by using the traditional column construction described above, but leaving spaces between the vertical strips and not covering the structure with muslin. This skeletal design can be very effective, especially if it is completed with an interesting base and capital.

Large-diameter solid columns can be made from cardboard or standard hardboard.

To Construct a 30" Diameter Column 12'-0" Tall

Materials List	*Equipment List*
1⅓ sheets ¾" × 4 × 8 plywood	Compass
4 1 × 3 × 12'-0"	Saber saw
3 ⅛ × 4 × 8 standard hardboard (or corrugated cardboard)	Saw
½ pound 6d nails or 1⅝" drywall screws	Hammer
2 pounds 1" plasterboard nails or 1" drywall screws	Caulking gun
Panel adhesive	
White glue	

1. On pieces of ¾" plywood, draw four squares measuring 30" on each side. Draw a diagonal from corner to corner of each square. Use the point where the diagonals cross as the center to place a compass and draw a 30" circle within each square. Cut out the circles.

2. At the end of each diagonal line on each circle cut a notch into the disc that is large enough to accept a 1 × 3. Nail or screw a 4" piece of 1 × 3 on the disc along the long edge of each notch.

3. Make the superstructure. Cut four 1 × 3s exactly 12'-0" long. Draw a line 4'-0" from each end of each board. Using white glue and 6d nails or 1⅝" drywall screws, attach one end of a 1 × 3 inside a notch on one disc; nail or screw it to the added 1 × 3 block. Attach a second disc at the first 4'-0" mark and a third disc at the second 4'-0" mark. Attach the last disc at the opposite end of the board. Attach each of the

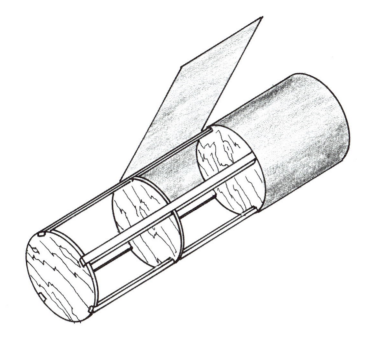

FIGURE 3–77
Constructing a large-diameter column from hardboard.

remaining boards to all of the discs, gluing and nailing or screwing to the 1 × 3 blocks.

4. Spread a line of panel adhesive around the edge of the bottom and second disc. Also spread panel adhesive on the edges of the 1 × 3s between these two discs.

5. Attach the 4'-0" wide edge of a sheet of standard hardboard at the center of one of the 1 × 3s with 1" nails or screws. Keeping the hardboard carefully aligned with the edge of the bottom disc, gently bend the material around the superstructure, putting a nail or screw in each disc at least every 6". Nail or screw to each of the vertical members also. When the hardboard completes the circle, cut off any excess material.

6. Put panel adhesive on the edge of the next disc and the 1 × 3 verticals between the second and third discs. Install a second sheet of hardboard in the same manner as the first sheet (Figure 3–77). This panel will share the second disc with the first sheet of hardboard and will share the third disc with the last sheet of hardboard. Attach the last sheet of hardboard in the same manner.

7. Cover with muslin and/or paint the assembly as desired.

Instead of using hardboard to form the skin of the columns, broadloom carpet can be attached to the perimeter of the disks with panel adhesive and roofing nails. It will be necessary to support the disks with 1 × 4s or 2 × 4s nailed or screwed between each disk to provide sufficient structure. As an alternative, the column can be suspended in a manner similar to the fabric column described below.

Both large- and small-diameter columns can be constructed from two plywood discs and fabric when it is possible to suspend the upper disc from something overhead (Figure 3–78). These columns are made by cutting two circles to the appropriate diameter and attaching the top and bottom edges of the fabric to their perimeter. A smooth column

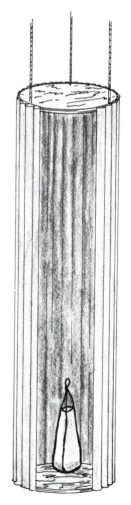

FIGURE 3–78
A column made of fabric attached to two plywood discs.

111

can be made if the fabric is stretched tightly around the discs, or the effect of a fluted column can be created by stapling the fabric to the disc in even pleats. A tapered column can be made by using a larger disc on the bottom and a smaller disc at the top. Weight of some kind, such as sandbags or concrete blocks, must be placed on the bottom disc to keep it from being lifted off the floor. The upper disc must be tied off so it does not tilt and the fabric pulls tightly and evenly against the bottom disc. Any round form, such as a bicycle wheel or a 5 gallon-bucket, can replace the plywood circles.

A simple column can be constructed from honeycomb cardboard (see page 116). Cut through the top surface and most of the depth of the structural layer of the honeycomb at evenly spaced intervals and then bend the board into a circle. Tape the edges of the honeycomb panel together to complete the circle. The cardboard can be left plain or covered with muslin or some other fabric.

The construction industry uses a material called **Sonotube** as forms for round concrete columns. These are wax-coated, rigid cardboard tubes that may be purchased from lumberyards, concrete suppliers, and even some display stores in diameters as small as 12" and as great as 48". They are available in lengths from 10'-0" to 40'-0". The tubes may be sawed, drilled, bolted, or screwed. They work especially well if wrapped with a decorative fabric or covered with muslin. Sonotube is very expensive.

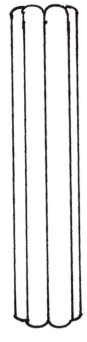

FIGURE 3–79
A column assembled from carpet roller tubes.

An interesting decorative column can be made by assembling several carpet roller tubes into a bundle (Figure 3–79). The tubes can be nailed, screwed, glued, or taped together in symmetrical or asymmetrical patterns. Columns of this design can be especially effective for Gothic settings.

Generally, columns are thought of as being round; however, it is possible to make columns with flat sides, faceted, that imply roundness but are simply boards nailed to a circular base. This works especially well in larger theatres where the audience is further from the stage. It is also very effective as a stylized design. Two or more discs 1½" narrower than the finished diameter are needed. Discs should be placed no more than 5'-0" apart, so if a column is 10'-0" tall, a top, bottom, and middle disc would be needed. 1 × 2, 1 × 3, or 1 × 4 are nailed to the discs, fitting their back edges tightly together. Each board forms a facet of the column. After assembly, the boards may simply be painted or they may be covered with muslin, thus filling the gaps between boards. In effect, this is the same concept as the traditional column, but each vertical member is so wide that it maintains its shape and does not blend into the general roundness that occurs with traditional column construction.

ALTERNATIVES TO STANDARD CONSTRUCTION MATERIALS

Each method of construction discussed so far uses traditional techniques. Although these have proven to be both economical and strong, they are not the only means by which to construct scenery. In recent years there have been numerous experiments with both old and new materials and methods. Many experiments have proven especially successful for small-staff/low-budget organizations.

Corrugated Cardboard

One of the simplest, easiest, and least expensive alternatives to standard scenic construction is the use of corrugated cardboard. It may be used for drops, instead of flats, or in place of muslin when covering flats. This versatile material can often be obtained free from furniture and appliance stores, and some large boxes may be picked up from hardware and grocery stores as well as from lumberyards and construction sites. If necessary, large sheets of cardboard can be purchased from carton manufacturers.

Corrugated cardboard is actually several layers of heavy paper assembled in a way that provides a great deal of strength (Figure 3–80). The cardboard consists of two flat, smooth, outer layers of heavy kraft paper and a center layer of paper that has been folded into tiny waves glued in evenly spaced rows. The material has its greatest strength in opposition to the direction of the folds of the center layer. These corrugations serve as little columns, which provide a great deal of strength when force is applied directly down on them, and they resist bending.

FIGURE 3–80
Construction of corrugated cardboard.

Among the advantages of cardboard are that it is free or relatively inexpensive, available in large sizes, easy to work with, and can be used with or without a frame. There are also a few disadvantages to using the material. It has a tendency to warp, will not withstand a lot of handling, and will dent and bend badly if abused. Often cardboard that is available free from stores has printing on it that is difficult to cover with paints. These problems can be minimized if care is taken during the assembly and painting processes.

When working with hand tools, the material can be cut easily. The best cut edge is obtained by using a very sharp knife held against a steel guide. The cardboard should be placed on a firm base that is smooth and covered with a soft material that may be cut into, such as the back of a piece of carpet. Straight cuts can be guided against a steel straightedge but curved lines are usually drawn on the cardboard and cut freehand. Although it is possible to cut the full depth of the cardboard in a single stroke, the most precise cuts can be achieved by making several strokes over a line, each stroke cutting deeper through the material. The first stroke might penetrate the top paper layer, the second stroke half the thickness of the corrugated layer, the third stroke will cut the rest of the corrugated layer, and the final stroke will cut the bottom layer of cardboard. Each traverse through the material should be taken slowly and carefully, following the same line; this will result in a neat, crisp edge.

If a saber saw is available, it is easy to cut straight and curved lines using a toothless saw. These blades are made expressly for this kind of work. A very sharp blade must be used and it must be replaced as soon as it becomes dull. The tool should be moved slowly through the cardboard to maintain firm control of the cut.

Cardboard can be shaped into smooth curves by bending the material in arcs that parallel the corrugation lines (Figure 3–81). Arches can be formed by gently pressing the sides of a sheet of material into position and stapling each edge to keep it in place. Although it is not mandatory to have an armature to give the arc shape, some kind of framing will ensure maintenance of a smooth, consistent curve. Frames or ribs may be cut from lumber to which the cardboard is glued and stapled. Columns can be formed by bending the cardboard into a circle around a barrel or some other mold and taping the seam where the edges join. Do not attempt to bend cardboard in opposition to the lines of corrugation: it will crimp and crease quite badly. If some of the cardboard being used is particularly resistant to bending, or if a very small radius is needed, the material can be brushed with warm water on both surfaces to soften it. After the water has soaked in slightly and while the cardboard is still moist, the sheet may be slowly and evenly bent to force it in place. The formed sheet should be fastened in position and allowed to dry so that it warps into this new shape.

It is easy to create a sharp crease or fold in a sheet of cardboard. Simply cut a line through the top layer of paper only on the open side of the fold (Figure 3–82). With the cut facing up, hold the fold line at a sharp edge, such as the edge of a table or the edge of the stage. Place a board on top of the cardboard to form a sandwich of board, cardboard, and table top. Press down on the cardboard overhanging the edge to create the crease (Figure 3–82). If the open side of the fold faces the audience, it may be desirable to cover the corner with a piece of kraft

FIGURE 3–81
Corrugated cardboard bends easily in directions parallel with the folds of the center layer.

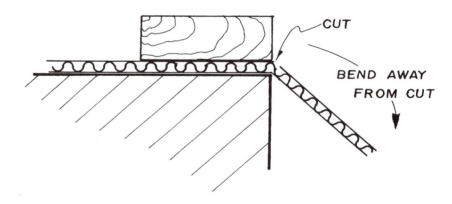

FIGURE 3–82
Making sharp folds in corrugated cardboard.

tape or a dutchman (see page 127) before painting. Whenever possible, try to plan a fold or bend so that it is parallel with the corrugations.

Corrugated cardboard may be used unframed as a simple sheet of material that is cut to shape and supported on threads, string, or wire, or it may be bent or folded to stand up by itself, like a dressing screen. It might also be used with a wooden frame constructed like a flat, complete with cornerblocks and keystones, or a frame built with folded strips of cardboard.

One method of constructing a cardboard frame is to cut a cardboard sheet into long strips about 8" wide. Following the bending instructions above, fold each strip to form an L measuring 4" wide on each leg. Cut three pieces of cardboard into 5" × 5" squares. On two edges of each square form a 1" lip by scoring and folding the cardboard. Glue the lips of all three squares of cardboard inside the L, placing one square at the top, one at the middle, and the third at the bottom (Figure 3–83). As an alternative, blocks of 1 × 4 can be used to hold the L in shape. These Ls can be used individually glued to the back of sheets of cardboard to stiffen and brace them or they may be combined to create complete frames. These shapes can provide an edge that is perpendicular to the surface of a wall and can be used to create the impression of thickness around a door or window opening. The cardboard should be glued with panel adhesive.

An even stronger brace can be made by taking long strips of cardboard with the corrugations running vertically, scoring the outside corners, and folding each strip into a rectangle or an equilateral triangle. The open edge where the vertical strips join should be taped its entire length to create a solid column (Figure 3–83B). The tube is then glued to the back of the cardboard sheets using a panel adhesive or white glue. This kind of construction provides an enormous amount of strength yet adds little weight or expense to the construction. Individual cardboard tubes may be joined together to form a frame by cutting 45° corners in a miter box; the corners are held together by gluing hardboard or plywood cornerblocks over the joints. A panel adhesive will do this job very well.

Cardboard may be stapled, nailed, or glued. In all instances, care must be taken not to dent or mar the top surface of the material, or to allow the heads of nails or staples to pull through it.

Staples are the quickest fastener used to attach the material. To ensure adequate penetration of the cardboard and its supporting material, ½" or ⁹/₁₆" long staples are needed. They should be inserted about 4" to 6" apart on surfaces that will be painted. Unpainted or previously painted cardboard usually needs staples only 12" apart. Broad headed nails ³/₄" long, such as roofing or plasterboard nails, also work well, since they penetrate deeply into the wood and provide a large surface to hold the top layer. It is very easy to dent the cardboard while hammering, so care must be taken when attaching the materials.

The best fasteners for cardboard are adhesives and glues. When dried under weight or pressure, the adhesives will make a superb bond that holds the entire glued area on the backside of the sheet without causing any denting or marring on the front surface. Although white glue is a satisfactory adhesive, it requires complete drying under pressure or weight to obtain an adequate bond. This usually necessitates a

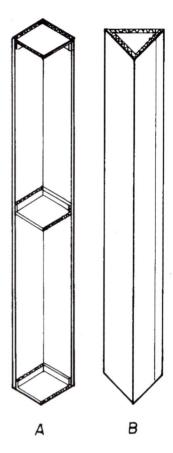

A   B

FIGURE 3–83
Structural frame members formed from folded corrugated cardboard.

12- to 24-hour drying time. Panel adhesives are the better glue for attaching cardboard. This adhesive comes in a large tube that is discharged using a caulk gun. When using panel adhesive, lay down a line of glue about ¼" wide and ¼" thick in a zigzag pattern on the frame to which the cardboard will be attached. Put the cardboard in place over the glue on the frame and put weights on top of it to hold the material firmly against the frame. Allow the glue to dry at least an hour without disturbing the materials. As an alternative, after the cardboard has been laid on top of the adhesive, staple the cardboard to the frame every 8" to 12" apart. The staples will create sufficient pressure to cause the adhesive to form a solid bond between the cardboard and the frame. Panel adhesive is especially handy when gluing cardboard (or any other material) to metals and most plastics.

Any standard scene paint or latex paint may be used on cardboard; however, care must be taken, since the material has a strong tendency to warp when moistened. The likelihood of warpage can be reduced if a prime coat is applied in the following manner. When initially painting the cardboard, *first* paint all of the edges and the *back* side of the sheet with the same paint that will be used on the front side. *While the paint is still wet,* turn the cardboard over and put the first layer of paint on the front of the sheet. With the cardboard lying flat on a solid surface (on the floor is best), allow the paint to dry *thoroughly*. Once the edges and the front and back surfaces of the cardboard have been sealed with this solid prime coat, the likelihood of warpage is significantly reduced unless later coats of paint are very heavy or very wet and badly saturate the prime coat. Dark or heavy printing on cardboard cartons should be pretreated with an opaque, dense paint such as casein primer or latex ceiling paint.

Honeycomb Cardboard

Honeycomb cardboard is a material very similar to corrugated cardboard; however, it is much thicker and has significantly greater strength (Figure 3–84). It is available under brand names such as Hexcel and Feather Panel from artist, floral, and display supply companies as well as theatrical suppliers. It is manufactured in sheets measuring 4'-0" × 8'-0"

FIGURE 3–84
The structure of honeycomb cardboard.

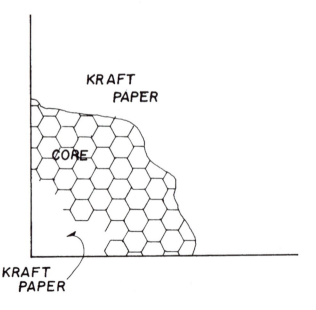

and in thicknesses from ½" to 4". Like corrugated cardboard, this material also consists of three layers: the top and bottom layers are sheets of very heavy, smooth kraft paper and the center core, which distinguishes honeycomb cardboard from other materials, is made of rows of kraft paper folded and glued into a series of hexagons. With the top layer of kraft paper removed, the middle layer of the board looks like the honeycomb of a beehive, thus giving the material its name.

Almost all techniques described for cardboard can be used with honeycomb. Due to its thickness and inherent strength, honeycomb can be effectively used without any framing. The material is easily cut with a hand or power saw that is equipped with a fine-toothed blade or a knife blade. It may be nailed and stapled in a manner similar to corrugated cardboard, and it takes adhesives, tapes, and paints well, although the thinner sheets are susceptible to warpage when made excessively wet.

When painting thin sheets of honeycomb, it is best to use the technique described above for painting corrugated cardboard: that is, paint a prime coat on the edges and on *both* sides of the sheet at one time.

The manufacturers of display materials have developed plastic seams that may be used to join sheets of honeycomb in a row to make solid walls, hinges for folding units, and edge moldings to finish the ends of panels. These accessories slip over the edge of the honeycomb panel and are held in place by friction. It may be desirable to glue these pieces in place with panel adhesive.

An alternative method to assemble solid honeycomb walls is to glue 1 × 3 boards to the back of the sheets with panel adhesive. The battens must be weighted while the adhesive is drying. This method of assembly is sufficiently strong for scenery that will not be handled a great deal. If a scenic unit is going to receive substantial handling, it would be better to attach the battens to the honeycomb with drywall screws in addition to the adhesive.

Although the kraft paper from which honeycomb is manufactured is quite sturdy, it is neither sufficiently strong nor dense to support nails, screws, or bolts adequately on its own; however, it is possible to make standard woodworking joints between honeycomb panels or to attach standard hardware to it if the edges of the panels are reinforced.

To Reinforce the Edges of a Honeycomb Panel

Materials List	*Equipment List*
Honeycomb panel	Pencil
1 2 × 4 × 8'-0"	Tape measure
White glue	Table saw with rip fence
⅜" or longer staples	Hammer
	Staple gun

1. Measure the exact thickness of the honeycomb between the inside surfaces of the outer layers of kraft paper. Set up a saw to rip a 2 × 4 to exactly that dimension. A table saw or a radial arm saw will be the easiest tool to use to make this cut; however, the lumber may be cut with a circular saw if the wood is held firmly in place on the work surface. Cut a piece of lumber for each edge of the panel.

2. Spread some white glue on the sides of the ripped boards. Using a mallet or a hammer, tap the ripped lumber into each edge of the honeycomb panel between the outer layers of kraft paper. Be careful not to damage the outer layers of the panel. As the board is tapped in place, it will force sections of honeycomb to compress at the edges within the panel.

3. Place the panel on a flat solid surface and weight the edges to maintain pressure against the boards, or staple both the top and bottom outer layers of kraft paper to the new wooden core and allow the glue to dry. This process creates a solid edge that can be nailed, stapled, screwed, or bolted.

Whether the honeycomb panels are battened with 1 × 3s glued to the back or joined together with nails, screws, or bolts, the joints between panels can be covered with brown kraft packaging tape. This wide, gummed tape will adhere well if properly applied. The gummed surface should be moistened with warm water, causing the glue to feel slightly slimy; the tape is then smoothed into place and will begin to adhere immediately. It should be allowed to dry thoroughly before moving or painting the scenery.

Honeycomb is especially useful for cutouts, such as free-standing landscapes, or to make flats in nonstandard shapes, such as trees. The arches in Figure 3–85 were formed from honeycomb.

Foam-Cored Boards

Foam-cored boards also resemble corrugated cardboard. Rather than a center layer of folded paper, the middle of these boards consists of a plastic foam similar in appearance to Styrofoam. The outer layers are either paper, coated paper, or a thin plastic skin. Standard board

FIGURE 3–85
Honeycomb cardboard was used to make the arches in this setting (The King & I). (Courtesy Theatre UNI, University of Northern Iowa.)

dimensions vary from 30" × 40" up to 4'-0" × 10'-0" and are available in thicknesses from ⅛" up to 1½". Sheets of foam-cored board are extremely lightweight but very sturdy, which makes them especially convenient for thin, hanging scenery. Perhaps the best feature of foam-cored board is the ease with which it may be cut with a sharp matte knife. Because of the density of the foam, the material finishes with a very smooth edge that makes it especially attractive for cutout pieces. The more rigid boards may be suspended or used free standing or in hinged panels as solid walls. The thinner boards may be cut out and glued to flats, walls, or other surfaces, or they may be bent to gentle curves. Most boards can be **scored**—that is, cut in parallel lines partially through the material, and bent into deep curves or round columns.

Almost any paint or ink may be used to coat the paper surfaces, but it is difficult to obtain good coverage on the edges of the interior foam layer except with acrylic paints, which may be used as a prime or finish coat. Care must be taken to avoid warping the large sheets. As with most other boards, foam-cored boards will warp if the paper surfaces are saturated excessively with liquids or if the boards are left lying on uneven surfaces or standing on end without support. In addition to being used for walls, backgrounds, and layering on flats, foam-cored boards may be used as a substitute for covering flats. The thin sheets are especially practical for lightweight, hard-surfaced coverings for flats, which may be especially desirable for plays that have a lot of door slamming or other rough activity. The primary disadvantage of foam-cored boards is that the material is fairly expensive.

Paneling

Although hardboard is not very costly compared to many other construction materials, it is often possible to find sheets of 4'-0" × 8'-0" paneling at lumberyards and discount stores that are less expensive than hardboard. Inexpensive paneling can be used on a set with the right side out to create the sense of a wood-paneled room. To be effective, the printed grain of the paneling must be sufficiently bold so that it can be distinguished from the audience, and the finish must not glare under stage lighting. The wrong side, or back, of inexpensive paneling can be used for almost any purpose for which hardboard or cardboard is used.

Any woodworking equipment and technique may be used with paneling or hardboard. It is best to use a fine-toothed (panel) saw blade for cutting, working on the backside of the material so that when cutting with a circular saw the side the audience will see faces *away* from the operator and the saw is on top. This will result in the smoothest finished edges toward the audience. Hardboard and paneling may be attached with finish nails, large-headed nails, staples, screws, bolts, or panel adhesive.

The back of paneling is often turned toward the audience when it is used to replace hardboard. This may expose a grain or flaws on that surface which may be quite noticeable. Either problem can be solved by filling serious flaws with wood putty followed by a light sanding and covering the sheet with muslin or paper. If the flaws are not too severe, coating the surface with undiluted flat latex paint will fill the grain and seal the wood in preparation for painting with scene paint.

119

Rigid Plastic Foam Boards

There are two insulation materials generically referred to as **styrofoam** that are available from lumberyards and discount stores. One of these materials is Dow Chemical Company's Styrofoam, which is blue in color, inherently flame-retardant, and comes in various textures and finishes. The Dow product is available as Styrofoam SB, a smooth-surfaced board that is manufactured in 4'-0" × 8'-0" sheets ½" to 2" thick with score lines cut in it, and as Styrofoam FR, which is coarsely textured and made in 16" and 24" wide × 8'-0" long boards ³/₄" to 4" thick. Both of these materials will produce a toxic gas when cut, sanded, or burned. *They should be worked with only in adequate ventilation.* The other kind of material commonly called styrofoam is bead board. This is a white, cellular-looking sheet that is less dense and less structurally sound than the Dow products. It is also significantly less expensive than the blue material and produces no toxic gases unless burned. Bead board is available in pieces as small as 16" wide by 8'-0" long, but is most commonly sold in 4'-0" × 8'-0" sheets from ½" to 4" thick. In spite of these differences, both products may be treated in similar ways for scenic construction.

These plastic foams may be easily cut with any standard hand or power tools, although they dull saw blades, drills, and router bits quickly. In addition, these foams may be shaped with serrated kitchen knives, electric knives, sanding machines, sandpaper, files, and almost any heating device such as a soldering gun, hot wire cutter (Figure 3–86), electric charcoal lighter, or even (with care) a propane torch.

White glue will adhere to the outer layer of plastic foam, but panel adhesives especially designed for foam plastic are the best way to attach the material. Hot-melt glues may be used but might melt the plastic due to the high temperature produced. Any glue that contains an aromatic hydrocarbon or a ketone should be avoided because it will dissolve the plastic. Check the contents on the label of the container for the presence of these solvents. In addition to gluing, foam can be nailed, bolted, or stapled in place, but it is very easy to crush the material using these fasteners.

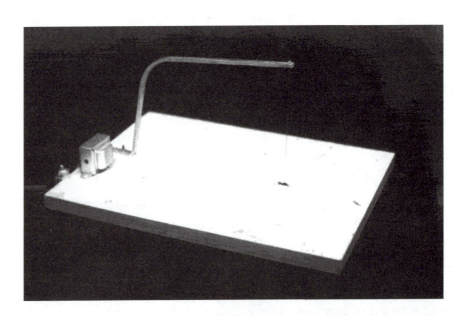

FIGURE 3–86
A simple hot wire cutter for cutting foam boards.

The surface of the foam can be protected somewhat from physical damage and made easier to paint by coating it with white glue and cheesecloth, muslin or paper, plaster of paris, thick paints, or a commerically available material especially useful for painting and prop making called Sculpt-or-Coat. Once the foam is coated with a protective layer, almost any paint can be used on it. Without protection, lacquers and paints containing aromatic hydrocarbons or any ketones must be avoided for they will dissolve the plastic.

Plastic foams can be used to cover flats with a stiff surface or as a surface that can be readily textured (see Chapter 4) to create, for instance, three-dimensional scenery such as bricks, stone, or marble. A talented artisan can carve the plastic into almost any kind of object. Wooden or metal armatures can be inserted in the foam and it can be used to make decorative table or chair legs, statutes, and even iron stoves. Most of the success achieved using plastic foams is the result of not only careful planning, carving, and design but also well-planned and well-executed painting.

Paper

Kraft (packaging) paper and butcher paper are inexpensive materials that may be used to cover flats or to make drops. These papers are available on long rolls 36" wide from school and art supply stores as well as paper and packing companies. Both materials are fairly sturdy and moisture resistant. Kraft paper is brown in color and generally less expensive than butcher paper. Butcher paper is usually white. Some butcher papers are coated with wax on one or both sides, which makes them difficult to paint. A more expensive but highly useful material is **seamless paper**, which is available from art and photo supply stores as well as from display companies. Seamless paper comes in over 100 colors, textures, and finishes in rolls 36'-0" long up to 108" (9'-0") wide.

Kraft, butcher, and seamless papers can be used to cover flats temporarily, can be stretched over the back wall of the stage to create a neutral background, or can be painted and suspended from batten or a board above the stage as a backdrop. Wherever these papers are used, they should be stretched tightly and attached at the top, bottom, and on all sides. It is best to join together edges of paper strips with kraft tape to make a continuous surface for painting. Moisture will cause the paper to warp and wrinkle, so care should be taken not to get it too wet. Usually, spraying on a prime and base coat in thin dilute layers with drying between each coat will help reduce damage. Due to the richness of most of the colors and textures, seamless paper can often be used without any additional painting or texturing.

Fabrics

In addition to unbleached muslin, almost any fabric may be used to cover flats or to make drops. Muslin is usually used because it is relatively inexpensive, available in wide widths, and can be shrunk smooth to fit the flat. Alternative fabrics such as burlap, corduroy, taffeta, felt, printed textiles, and window curtain and upholstery fabrics create interesting textures. They may be used in place of muslin or they can be stretched and stapled over an existing muslin covering as a second layer.

Loose fabric may be used as a replaceable second layer on flats. This makes it possible to double the life of a setting for a show in a very simple manner. If the ground plan for a second set can be essentially the same as the plan for the first set, perhaps with the reduction of doors or windows, it is possible to staple fabric to the top back of the flats during construction and at the scene change simply toss the stapled fabric over the top of the first set to cover it up with the second layer (Figure 3–87). The bottom edge of the fabric should be wrapped around and stapled to a 1 × 3 or some other material that will have sufficient weight to stretch the fabric tight when in place on stage. If necessary, some kind of fastener such as plastic or metal hook-and-eyes, hook-and-loop strips such as Velcro, or weights may be used to hold the bottom edge in place. Any relatively opaque fabric can be used this way. The material can be left plain or a pattern may be stenciled, painted, or sewn on it.

When covering a flat with a fabric that will not be painted, stretch the material very tightly over the frame and staple it to the outside edge or back of the flat. Care must be taken to pull the fabric tight without distorting the weave. When the fabric is stretched over the frame, it does not have to be glued; however, it must be stapled firmly with long staples. Where several layers of fabric stack on top of each other at the corners, the excess layers should be trimmed away to reduce bulk.

Crating Lumber

Crating lumber can often be obtained free where shipments are unboxed or from companies that receive a lot of goods in crates or on pallets. Although much of this lumber is very hard, quite knotty, and rough, it may be used for a variety of purposes from wonderfully rich

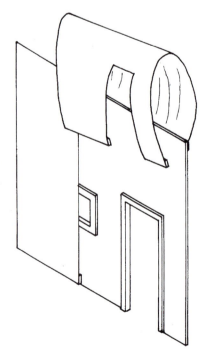

FIGURE 3–87
A loose layer of fabric is attached to the top back of the set and thrown over the top of the flats to make a new surface for a second setting with the same floor plan.

textural floors, platform facings, and even wall surfaces, to actually assembling the crate lumber as frames for flats, platforms, and stairs. Recently, a lot of better electronic equipment has been shipped in crates made of low-quality plywood and other lumber that could be used for scenery. The crates are often disposed of so it should be easy to obtain this lumber once a source has been identified.

ASSEMBLING SETTINGS

Realistic interiors usually consist of flats assembled in a variety of patterns to make walls. The methods of assembling scenery are fairly simple and may be used equally well for stationary settings as well as for changeable scenery.

Assembling Long Walls

Traditional scenic construction limits the width of standard stock flats to 6'-0", yet many settings require walls that are wider. These larger walls can be made by building larger flats or by joining several stock flats together using various techniques.

Battens

A long wall may be assembled by screwing a 1 × 3 to the top, center, and bottom on the back of the flats (Figure 3–88). These boards, called **battens,** are cut to the length of the wall, less 1½". When they are attached to the back of a group of flats, they must be kept ¾" away from the outer edges of the wall to facilitate joining walls at corners. Normally, battens are placed just above the bottom

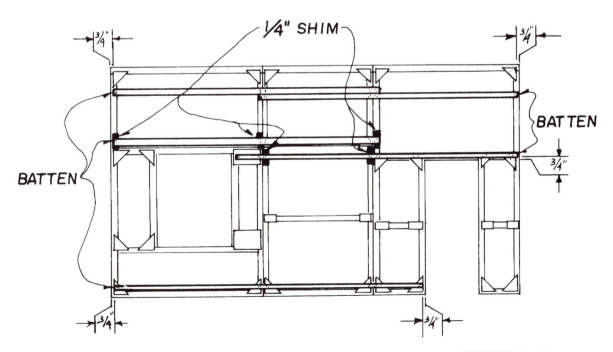

FIGURE 3–88
Battening flats together.

cornerblocks, below the cornerblocks at the top of the flats, and at the center of the wall across the toggle rails. If a batten rests on top of a cornerblock or keystone anywhere, it must rest on top of a cornerblock, keystone, or ¼" thick block of plywood or hardboard everywhere that it is attached to the flat (Figure 3–89). If the batten is not kept level in this manner, the wall will be uneven on the front, staggering in and out at the joints. Rather than looking like a smooth plane, the surface will look like it is divided into several sections. Battens are attached with two 1½" flathead wood screws or 1⅝" drywall screws at each stile they cross. When the overall length of a wall is greater than the longest boards available to assemble it, battens can be pieced together. The boards should be arranged so that the joints between pieces fall in the middle of a flat rather than on a joint between flats. A second piece of 1 × 3 at least 3'-0" long should be nailed or screwed over the top of the joint in any batten made of more than one board.

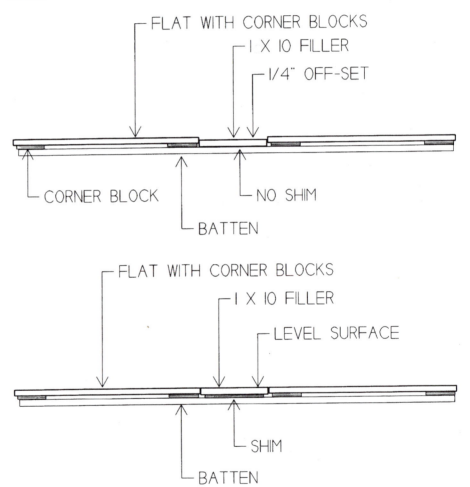

FIGURE 3–89
If a batten rests on a cornerblock or keystone anywhere, it must be placed on a ¼" shim, a cornerblock, or a keystone everywhere it is fastened, or the assembled wall of flats will be uneven.

Rigid stiffeners may replace a batten when a wall is particularly long or tends to bend easily. A **stiffener** is made from two pieces of 1 × 3 or 1 × 4 assembled in the shape of an L (Figure 3–90C). For rigid walls, the stiffener is attached to the flat in the same way as a batten. Another type of stiffener may also be used. These are single boards attached to the back of the flat with tight- or loose-pin backflap hinges so the boards stick out at a right angle to the rear surface of the flat (Figure 3–90A and B). A hinge is attached at each stile on alternate sides of the stiffener so that the first hinge is on the top of the board, the second on the bottom, and so on. Tight-pin hinges are used for settings that will not have to fold up for touring; however, if the walls are for a show that must be folded to store or pack into a truck, the boards are attached with loose-pin hinges so the stiffeners can be removed.

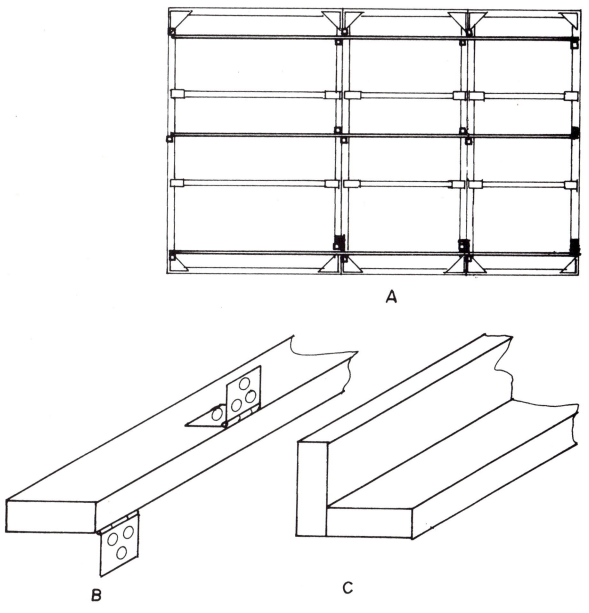

A

B

C

FIGURE 3–90
*(A) Stiffeners are attached in the same locations as battens. (B) A 1 × 3 or a 1 × 4 may become a stiffener by attaching hinges to both the top and bottom sides of the board. (C) **L-shaped** stiffeners constructed from two 1 x 4s are the most rigid.*

Hinges

It is also possible to hinge long walls so they may be folded for storage or loading on a truck. When only two flats are hinged, the joint simply requires a 1½" backflap hinge attached 12" above the bottom of the flat, another 12" below the top of the flat, and additional hinges spaced approximately 4'-0" apart between these two hinges (Figure 3–91). The hinges are put on the *front* of the flat. When more than two flats are hinged together, a tumbler is needed to allow them to lie flat when folded. A **tumbler** is a vertical board used to extend the width of a hinged joint so the overriding flats will fold together without breaking or warping (Figure 3–91). A set of hinges is attached to the edge of the flat on either side of the tumbler and both sets of hinges are also attached to the tumbler. The entire assembly is then covered with a dutchman.

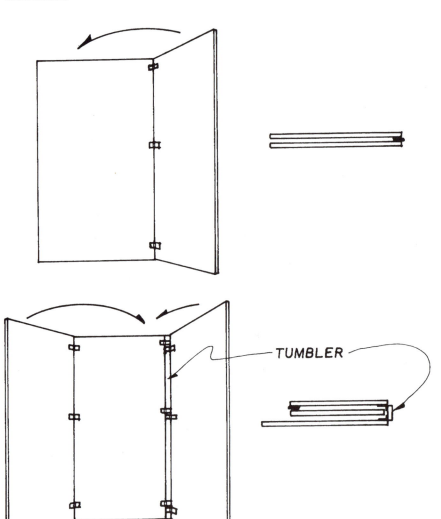

FIGURE 3–91
Hinged flats. A two-fold and a three-fold with a tumbler. These units are also called books.

Dutchman

A **dutchman** is a strip of muslin usually glued over the entire length of a joint. The dutchman is applied with **dope,** a mixture of 1 part white glue, and 3 to 5 parts water. Sometimes a filler such as whiting is added to give the mixture body. The process of applying a dutchman is fairly simple; however, it must be done well or the dutchman will peel or wrinkles and other flaws will distort the appearance of the finished scenery.

To apply a dutchman, begin by tearing a strip of fabric several inches longer than the joint to be covered. The muslin strip should be the width of the joint plus 3" on either side of the seam. If the joint between two flats is being covered, a strip of fabric about 6" wide is needed. If this joint were hinged on the face, the dutchman should extend 2" to 3" beyond the edges of the hinge so the strip would be about 9" wide. *Tear* the fabric to the necessary width. The dutchman will blend in better after painting if it has a torn rather than a cut edge. It is very important to remove all of the strings that develop as a result of tearing the fabric. After making sure the muslin strip is the right size, and having removed all loose threads, lay the fabric out flat and coat it with dope. Paint the area over which the dutchman is to be applied with dope as well. Place the saturated strip of muslin over the joint and smooth it out. Finally if desired, apply an optional coat of dope on top of the smoothed-out fabric. *Scenery with a fresh dutchman should not be moved until it has thoroughly dried.* After the dope has dried, any muslin hanging over the edge of the flat should be trimmed flush with the edge.

Joining Corners

Corners can be assembled in several different ways: they may be screwed, nailed, hinged, or lashed. After assembly, the corners may be covered with a dutchman, but this is usually only necessary in very intimate theatres where the audience is close to the stage or where the corners gap badly.

During construction, cornerblocks, keystones, battens, and stiffeners were held $3/4$" back from the edge so they would be out of the way when flats were joined together. If this has been done properly, corners should easily fit together. To assemble a corner, flats are set at the appropriate angle (it need not be a right angle) and then connected from the front or back with either 6d nails, $1\frac{1}{2}$" flathead wood screws or $1\frac{5}{8}$" drywall screws. The nails or screws are placed about 30" apart along the edge of the flat, more often if desired or necessary. Nail heads 6'-0" or more above the floor may be allowed to protrude $\frac{1}{8}$" from the wood on the offstage side of the setting. This will facilitate disassembly. However, nails within body height tend to grab costumes, so it is usually better to drive these all the way in. Since nails are intended to be put in but not taken out, screws are a better choice for this assembly. Be sure to drill a $\frac{1}{8}$" pilot hole for each screw and insert it completely. In some instances, longer screws may be required because of the angle of the walls. Drywall screws are especially convenient for assembling flats since they hold firmly, can be removed without damaging the scenery, but do not require a pilot hole.

Any corner may also be joined using a backflap hinge. After the flats are in place and ready for assembly, rather than driving nails or screws into the edge, simply attach backflap hinges on the back of the corner using $3/4" \times$ #8 flathead wood screws. A minimum of three hinges are required on each joint: one about 12" above the bottom, a second at the horizontal centerline, and the last one about 12" below the top of the flats. Walls over 12'-0" tall need four hinges evenly spaced along the joint. Once again, if the setting must be changed or the show is to tour, loose pin hinges will allow a joint to be taken apart by removing the pin, and to be reassembled at a later time when the pin is replaced.

Lashing is the most primitive assembly concept, but it is inexpensive and quite functional. With this procedure, the flats are laced together in a manner similar to a shoelace. Figure 3–92 shows one typical layout for lash hardware. Looking at the back of the flat, a $3/8"$ hole is drilled in the top-right cornerblock. A piece of $1/4"$ cotton rope (clothesline) is fed through the hole and a knot is tied between the cornerblock and muslin. A lashline cleat is attached to the stile 4'-0" below the top of the flat. Additional cleats should be placed every 4'-0" apart below that (but at least 1'-0" above or below rails, cornerblocks, or keystones) and there must be a cleat located 2'-6" above the bottom of the flat, even though that alters the pattern. On the opposite edge of the flat, a cleat is installed 2'-0" below the top of the flat and then every 4'-0" apart down the edge. There must be a cleat 2'-6" above the floor on this edge also. These cleats may be replaced with $2" \times$ #12 roundhead wood screws installed on the inside edge of the stiles at the same locations as the cleats. It is easiest to attach the lashline hardware during construction, before the flat is covered with muslin.

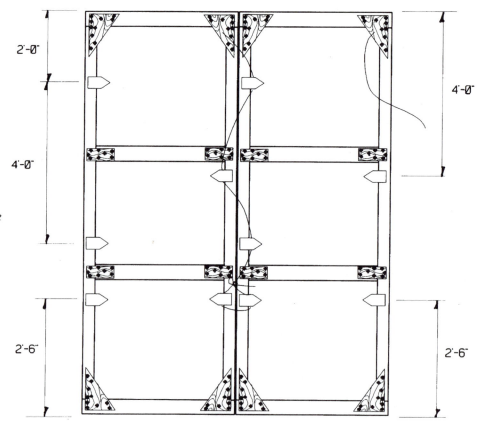

FIGURE 3–92

Placement of lashline hardware and a lashed joint.

The act of lashing flats together is a little tricky and requires some practice. The lashline is held firmly in one hand and swung in a loop to hook over each of the lashline cleats, alternating between flats in order down the edge of the joint. The line ties in a half-bow around the two cleats at the bottom cleats, 2'-6" above the floor. When completely tied, the lashed scenery is quite secure but the knot and rope allow quick assembly/disassembly for scene changes.

Alternative Joining Techniques

In a way, hinges on a joint and a dutchman do the same job: they both hold the joint together but allow the pieces to move. If a unit will not receive too rough treatment, the hinges can be eliminated and the dutchman alone used as both hinge and joint-cover. Extreme care must be taken when handling these assemblies, because a good firm pull in the wrong direction will destroy the unit and possibly the entire setting.

Another joining technique uses fabric bands instead of hinges. Burlap or some other material can be cut into strips approximately 4" wide and attached to the edges of a pair of flats with staples and glue (Figure 3–93). Each strip should start on an alternate side so the joint appears to be laced. In this way, the top strip goes from the front of the right flat to the back of the left flat, and the second strip goes from the back of the right flat to the front of the left flat, alternating all the way down the edge. The fabric must be pulled tight or the joint will be weak and sloppy.

A final joining technique uses standard C-clamps (Figure 3–94). Two flats can be joined side to side by hooking a clamp over the edges of the stiles and tightening it in place. Outside corners can be joined in the same way. However, there is no practical way to join inside corners with a C-clamp. A rope *must* be tied to the C-clamp and attached to the flat to provide a "safety" that will catch the clamp and prevent it from falling on someone should it wiggle or vibrate loose.

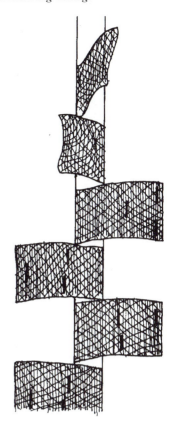

FIGURE 3–93
Strips of fabric used to make a weak hinged joint.

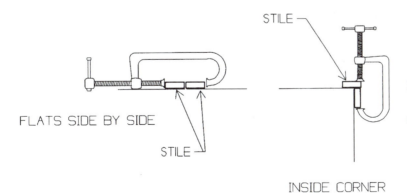

FIGURE 3–94
Using C-clamps to join the edges of flats.

129

Bracing

Flats that are hinged together and kept in some kind of folded arrangement can usually support themselves, and flats nailed or screwed
together at corners can also support themselves without any additional
bracing. However, when longer walls are assembled or a wall will be
near some severe activity, it is necessary to add braces for additional
support. There are two standard methods for bracing flats: stagebraces
and jacks.

A **stagebrace** (Figure 3–95) is a piece of specialized stage hardware especially designed to support flats. The device is made from two
pieces of hardwood that can slide past each other to telescope to length.
One end of the stagebrace has a foot iron or friction pad on it; the other
has a special hook designed to mate with a stagebrace cleat. A **stagebrace cleat** (Figure 3–96) is attached to the stile on the back of a flat
with ¾" flathead wood screws. It is placed facing the center of the flat
and located within the top one-third of the height of the flat.

FIGURE 3–95
A stagebrace supporting a flat.

FIGURE 3–96
*A stagebrace properly installed
in a stagebrace cleat.*

To install the stagebrace, the hook is turned toward the flat and
slipped into the hole in the stagebrace cleat. The brace is then rotated
180° so that the hook that is not engaged in the stagebrace cleat is
pushing against the back of the stile (Figure 3–96). A **stage screw**

(Figure 3–97) is turned into the stage floor through a hole in the foot iron. On those stages where it is not possible or permitted to insert stage screws into the floor, a less secure but adequate solution is to use stagebraces with foot pads (Figure 3–98). These pads are large, flat, wooden plates covered with rubber on the underside. The rubber resists slippage and, when loaded with weights, adequately braces most scenery.

FIGURE 3–97
A stage screw.

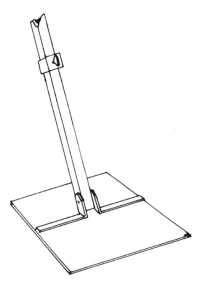

FIGURE 3–98
A stagebrace foot pad. Weights are loaded on the pad to keep it from slipping.

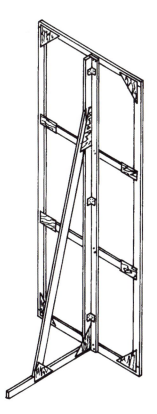

Whereas stagebraces are purchased hardware, jacks are homemade devices. A **jack** (Figure 3–99) is a triangular brace constructed from 1 × 3 and cornerblocks that is attached to the back of a flat with screws or hinges. The base of the jack is loaded with sandbags or some other weight. It may be as tall and as substantial as necessary.

To Construct a jack for 12'-0" Tall Scenery

Materials List	*Equipment List*
3 1 × 3 × 12'-0"	Saw
3 cornerblocks	Hammer
White glue	Framing square
1¼" plaster board nails or 1⅝" drywall screws	Pencil

1. Cut a 1 × 3 to 3'-6" long and label it *bottom rail.*

2. Place the square end of the remaining 12'-0" 1 × 3 against the side of the bottom rail. Hook a tape measure over the side of the bottom rail and measure the height of the flat to be supported, less ³/₄", on the long board. Cut this board on that mark and label it *stile.* The new board will be approximately 11'-8⅝" long.

3. Lay out the bottom rail and the stile to form a right angle by placing each board against one edge of a framing square. Draw a line ³/₄" above the bottom edge of the bottom rail. Spread some white glue

FIGURE 3–99
A jack.

131

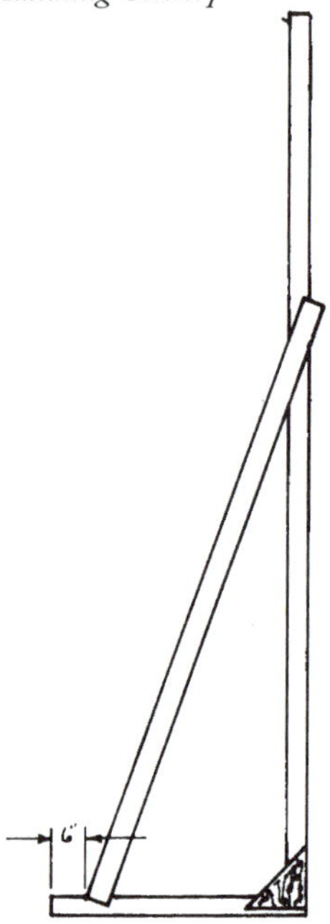

FIGURE 3–100
Laying out the diagonal brace on a jack.

on the underside of a cornerblock and place it on the pencil line flush with the edge of the stile. Make sure that the top grain of the cornerblock is running vertically. Using the pattern shown in Figure 3–14A (see page 53), attach the cornerblock to the bottom rail and stile.

4. Draw a line 6" in from the unattached end of the bottom rail. Put the remaining 1 × 3 on top of the two assembled pieces so that it forms a diagonal beginning at the 6" mark on the bottom board and extending as high as possible on the long board (Figure 3–100). Mark the angle at which the diagonal crosses the other two pieces and cut each end of the diagonal 1 × 3 on those lines.

5. Put the cut diagonal board back in place and trim a cornerblock to fit each new assembly point. The grain on the top cornerblock should run horizontally and the block should be even with the outside edge of the jack. The cornerblock on the bottom should extend no lower than the line ³/₄" above the bottom edge and the grain should run vertically. Using glue, nails, or screws attach the trimmed cornerblocks.

6. Cut the last 1 × 3 the same length as the overall height of the jack. Place the jack on edge against the 1 × 3. Using three 1¹/₂" backflap hinges, attach the jack to the board.

7. Place the jack against the back of the flat. Screw the hinged board to the top and bottom rail and each of the toggle rails on the flat with 1¹/₂" flathead wood screws.

After the jack is attached, it will support the flat if weights are placed on the bottom rail or a foot iron is attached to the jack and then connected to the floor with a stage screw.

Where it is possible to nail to the floor, stagebraces and jacks can be replaced in a very simple manner. A scrap block of wood is nailed or screwed to the back of a flat near its top edge. Any sturdy board long enough to reach the floor at an angle is nailed to the side of the block on the flat and then attached to the side of another block of wood, which is nailed or screwed to the floor. This creates a long, sturdy brace for scenery that will not have to be shifted.

CHANGING SCENERY

Multiset shows require careful planning early in the production process to get the scenery on and off the stage. There are four traditional ways to change scenery: running, flying, tracking, and rolling.

Running

Running simply means that scenery or props are picked up and carried away. No special techniques are needed to move most things in this way. However, there is a traditional way to handle flats that makes scene shifting safe and efficient. The technique requires some practice. The person moving the flat stands sideways next to the edge of the flat, facing the direction the scenery will move. The hand closest to the scenery is placed over the edge of the flat at about chin height and the

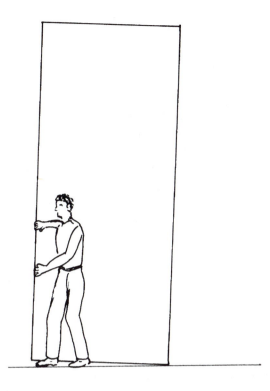

FIGURE 3–101
Running a flat.

hand farthest from the flat is placed on the edge at about hip height (Figure 3–101). Lift the leading edge of the flat about 2" or 3" off of the floor—the back end *must* drag on the floor—and walk rapidly, dragging the flat alongside. The toe of the near foot and elbow of the near arm can be used for leverage to guide the flat and to maintain balance.

1. Always keep the flat vertical.
2. Only lift the leading edge of the flat high enough to allow it to move.
3. Whenever possible, lead with the edge of the flat. Avoid moving the wide surface of the flat against the wind.

Moving flats begins with standing them up. There are two ways to do this. The first technique can be performed by two or three people. The bottom edge of the flat is either shoved against a wall or some other stationary object, or someone "foots" it by placing a toe against the bottom edge. The purpose of the wall or toe is to keep the bottom of the flat from lifting up or sliding away while the top is being raised. With the bottom edge of the flat braced or held in place by a toe, two or more people raise the top of the flat high enough to allow them to get under the flat and move hand-over-hand along the stiles, raising up the top edge (Figure 3–102). Hands should always be on wood, not on unsupported fabric. Everyone lifting must be at about the same point in the height of the flat at all times. Once the flat reaches an angle of about 45°, it is very susceptible to breaking as it bends during the raising process. It is best to work relatively quickly at that point to reduce the likelihood of damage.

The other technique for raising flats may be performed by one or two people. The flat is put on edge. A person at the bottom end of the flat places a toe at the bottom corner and pulls the upper edge toward him or her (Figure 3–102). This will cause the flat to stand up, pivoting on the bottom corner where the toe has been footing the flat. If a second person is available, he or she walks along the lower edge to help raise the flat.

A flat or a large wall may be laid down by walking it down in the same manner as walking it up, or a flat or wall that does not have any door or window openings in it or fragile or heavy trim on it can be **floated** down. This is done by clearing an area for the flat to fall, footing the bottom edge with a toe, and just letting go of the unit. As the flat moves, the air will cushion the fall and the scenery will gently settle to the floor. Once the flat starts to fall, do not try to stop it. Always make sure that no one is in the path of the falling scenery and that the floor where the flat will land is clear.

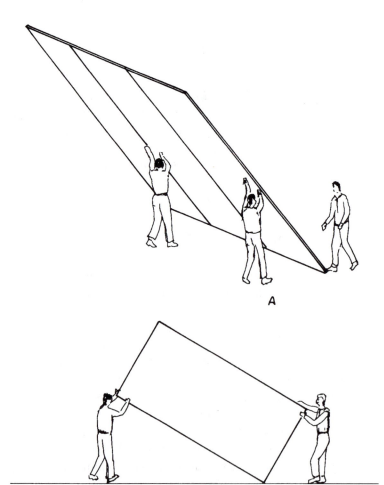

FIGURE 3–102

Standing up a wall or walking up a flat.

A

B

Flying

Flying means to suspend scenery overhead and raise or lower it in the acting area. Many theatres are equipped with specialized equipment for this specific purpose. The parts of that rigging and the basic operation of those systems are discussed in Chapter 1. The safety rules for operating a counterweight system are repeated here.

Rules for Operating Counterweight Systems

1. Always keep excess weight at the floor. When it is possible to load scenery and weight at the same time, load the scenery first; then add the weights to the arbor. When unloading, always remove the excess weight first, then unload the scenery.

2. For rigging, use only ropes, cables, and hardware that are in good condition. Inspect them regularly for wear. Have equipment and systems professionally inspected at least every other year.

3. Always plan a safety factor. Professional theatre riggers use a minimum safety factor of 8; that is, they make things eight times stronger than minimum breaking strength.

4. Only move scenery on battens when someone is able to watch the scenery move, preferably the operator of the batten. If this is not possible, someone with a loud voice and a keen eye for potential problems should watch the scenery while the batten is being moved.

Drops, drapes, and other soft scenery are attached to battens with tielines that are usually placed every 12" across the top of a drop or drape. The tielines should be tied in bows, just like a shoelace bow. This allows the tieline to be quickly tied and easily untied.

Hard scenery, such as flats, may be attached to a batten in several different ways. When the lines will not be seen by the audience, ½" hemp rope is often used. A **bowline knot** (Figure 3–103C) is tied to **hanger irons** (Figure 3–104A and B) at the bottom of the flats and the rope passes through a **Top hanger iron** at the top of the flat. The rope is then tied to the batten using a **clove hitch** knot (Figure 3–103B) with a **half-hitch** (Figure 3–103A) tied as a safety after the clove hitch. Grade 8 or Grade 80 chain, which is rated for overhead lifting, may be substituted for the hemp rope. It is attached at each end with a properly rated **shackle** of appropriate size for the load (Figure 3–105). A shackle is double-ended connector used especially with chains. S-hooks, bolts, and most other hardware should *not* be used when attaching or installing chain.

If the means of suspension will be seen by the audience or if an especially heavy load will be placed overhead, **galvanized aircraft**

FIGURE 3–103
The most used knots: (A) half-hitch, (B) clove hitch, (C) bowline.

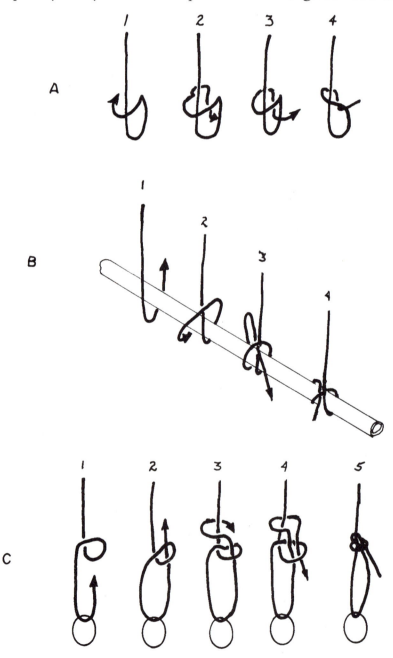

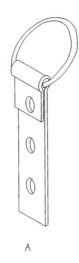
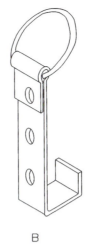

FIGURE 3–104
(A) Top hanger iron, (B) Bottom hanger iron. When installing, use at least one bolt in a hanger iron.

A   B

A

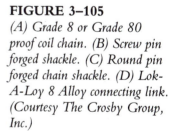

FIGURE 3–105
(A) Grade 8 or Grade 80 proof coil chain. (B) Screw pin forged shackle. (C) Round pin forged chain shackle. (D) Lok-A-Loy 8 Alloy connecting link. (Courtesy The Crosby Group, Inc.)

B   C

D

cable, flexible rope made from galvanized and braided wire strands (Figure 3–106), may be used. Aircraft cable and all other wire rope is rated by *ultimate* breaking strength. It is normal practice in theatre production to use aircraft cable with an ultimate breaking strength five to eight times greater than the anticipated load. Thus, a piece of scenery weighing 150 pounds would be supported on a cable with an ultimate breaking strength between 750 and 1,100 pounds to assure an adequate factor of safety. Aircraft cable is attached using forged cable clamps or compression fittings. Cable clamps (Figure 3–107A, B, and C) are two-part devices. One section is a u-bolt with threaded legs; the other section is forged steel to create a saddle that the wire rope fits in. The two pieces are bolted together. The correct number of the proper-sized clamps must be installed with the proper spacing and in the proper direction. The nuts *must* be on the section of cable that is supporting the weight of the load (Figure 3–107D).

Compression fittings (Figure 3–108) are attached using a special tool that develops sufficient force to make a satisfactory connection. The proper-sized fitting and compression tool must be used. Compres-

FIGURE 3–106

The construction of wire rope.

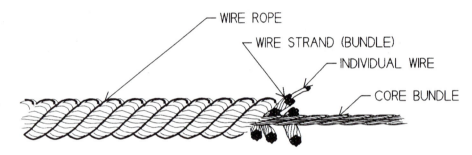

FIGURE 3–107

Wire rope hardware. (A) Forged fist grip clip, (B) forged wire rope clip; (C) standard wire rope thimble (Courtesy The Crosby Group, Inc.) (D) Properly installed wire rope clips: the U-bolt is around the "short" line and the forged fitting is around the line carrying the load. Clips must be properly spaced and the nuts properly tightened (not over or under tightened) to develop safe, maximum working strength.

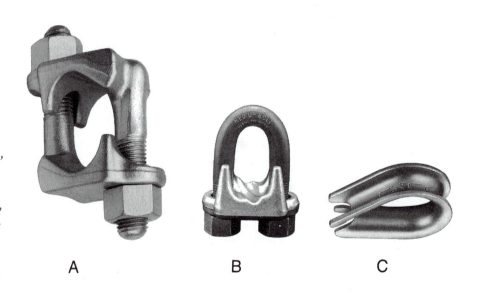

A   B   C

D

sions on the fitting must be made in the proper location and with sufficient force. A "Go-gauge" is a small tester that can be used to check the depth of compression of the fitting. If the gauge fits over the compressed area, the fitting has been properly installed.

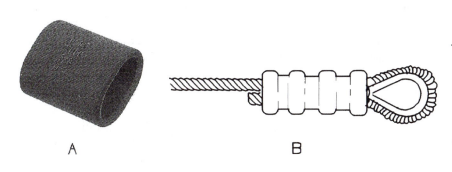

A   B

FIGURE 3–108
(A) A swage (or compression) fitting (Courtesy The Crosby Group, Inc.). (B) These oval sleeves are compressed onto wire rope with tools specifically designed for this purpose. Compressions must be of the proper depth and spacing to develop maximum safe working strength.

Alternative Flying Techniques

Many performance spaces do not have any means to raise or lower scenery. Although this can greatly reduce the flexibility of the stage, there are alternatives that may be used.

Block-and-Tackle Flying

If it is possible to reach the structure supporting the ceiling over the stage, and that structure is of sufficient strength to bear the load, it is also possible to fly scenery, even to make it move during a performance. Using two or more block and tackle, a primitive hemp set can be devised (Figure 3–109). A very sturdy batten the entire width of the

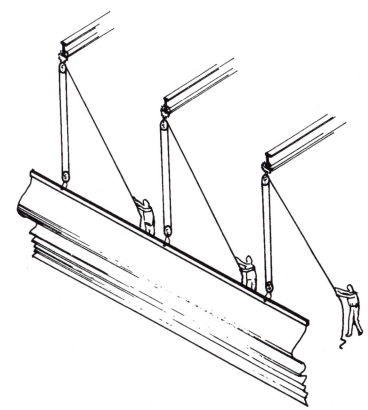

FIGURE 3–109
Block and tackle rigging for a drop.

139

drop to be flown is needed as well as three to four locations from which to suspend block and tackle. One end of each block and tackle is attached overhead to a solid part of the ceiling or roof and the other is hooked to the batten carrying the drop. Be sure there are functioning fail-safe safety devices at each point of attachment. The drop can be quickly raised into place from the floor in this manner. If it is necessary to change drops during a performance, the batten can be lowered, the old drop untied, and a new drop tied in its place, or the entire drop and batten can be removed from the rigging and replaced with another drop already tied to a batten. If the stage is arranged so that a downstage drop or curtain can hide an upstage drop during the performance, it would be possible to change drops several times, even though there is no theatrical rigging in the performance area.

There are four problems with this system. (1) Block and tackle tend to be quite squeaky. The blocks must be of good quality and well lubricated to minimize the amount of noise they make while in use, which is especially important when changing drops during a performance. (2) Block and tackle can be rigged for quite heavy loads and can give significant mechanical advantage for raising and lowering heavy objects; however, care must be taken not to overload the structure of the building. (3) Because it is possible to lift very heavy loads, it is important to have a sufficiently strong and large enough crew to be able to handle the load. (4) There must be a solid and sufficiently sturdy place to tie off the ropes when the batten is suspended in the air.

When there is not enough room overhead to fly a drop all the way out of sightlines, it may be tripped. **Tripping** is a way of folding a drop so that it takes up less vertical space overhead. If a drop has tielines on both the top and bottom edge, it can easily be tripped by tying the bottom of the drop to the next batten upstage or downstage (Figure 3–110A and B). Both lines are flown out, folding the drop so that it only requires 50 percent of its usual height for storage. If the drop is painted on both sides, the tielines that held the top edge of the drop could be untied and the drop suspended upside down and backwards to reveal a new scene painted on the back of the drop (3–110C). The painting must be planned very carefully to avoid bleeding through the fabric. Care must be taken to deal with the change in weight when drops are tripped or moved from batten to batten. It would be very easy to lose control of an overweighted pipe.

FIGURE 3–110
Tripping. (A) Tie the bottom of the drop to the next up- or downstage batten. (B) The drop folded on two battens may be stored in the loft in this manner. (C) The drop is released from the downstage batten and hangs upside down and backwards, revealing a new set.

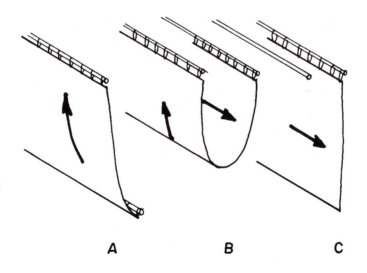

A   B   C

Another way to handle drops when rigging space or equipment is limited is to rig a roll drop. Roll drops are often used when reproducing the sense of the nineteenth-century theatre. The technique is still useful for the contemporary theatre.

To Rig a Roll Drop 15'-0" High × 20'-0" Wide

Materials List

1   2 × 4 batten 24'-0" long
2   1 × 4 × 12'-0"
1   1 × 4 × 2'-0"
4   2 × 2 × 12'-0"
2   2 × 2 × 2'-0"
Carpet roller tube
White glue
8d box nails
½" staples
Glue
1 single-groove awning
   pulley
1 double-groove awning
   pulley
125'-150' of cotton rope

Equipment List

Saw
Hammer
Matte knife
Stapler

1. Firmly attach the top of the drop to a batten. It may be tied, stapled and glued, or nailed in place.

2. The roller for the bottom of the drop should be at least 4'-0" longer than the width of the drop. Since this drop is 20'-0" wide, the roller will be 24'-0" long. Make the roller. This may be done several different ways. However, it is imperative that the roller carry its own weight plus the weight of the drop without sagging, even though it is only supported at the ends. Rigid 4" plastic drainpipe is excellent for this if the roller is constructed with reinforced joints between the sections of pipe. The best way to reinforce this joint is to insert a core of another piece of plastic pipe that firmly fits the inside of the roller. The reinforcing pipe should be 3'-0" to 5'-0" long and glued in place.

A less costly alternative to plastic drainpipe is to build a roller from carpet roller tube. The cardboard tube must be assembled with a core to prevent it from bending. The core can be made from a piece of 1 × 4 ripped to the width of the inside diameter of the tube. This primary board is then assembled with two additional pieces of wood to form a cross that is equal in all dimensions (Figure 3–111). If a splice is needed to make the support lumber long enough, as it is for this example, the joints between boards should be staggered. To assemble the core for the carpet roller tube, rip the 2 × 2s so that when they are attached to the sides of the 1 × 4 they will fill the inside diameter of the carpet roller tube. Put a line of glue on the edge of the 2 × 2, center it on the side of the 1 × 4, and fasten it in place with 8d nails or drywall screws. Repeat the assembly on the opposite side of the 1 × 4. Force the core into the carpet roller tube. It may be necessary to tap the core

FIGURE 3–111
End view of reinforced carpet roller tube to be used for a drop roller.

with a rubber mallet to get the parts to fit together. Drive a few roofing or plasterboard nails through the tube into the core to ensure that the wooden core will not slip.

3. Attach the bottom edge of the drop to the roller. The drop should be glued and stapled to the roller. If plastic pipe is used, a thin narrow strip of wood can be placed over the bottom edge of the drop and glued and screwed to the plastic roller; if a carpet roller tube is used, the drop can be glued and stapled to the roller.

4. Hang a single pulley above the stage right end of the roller and a double pulley above the stage left end of the roller (of course, the pulleys can be reversed).

5. Cotton clothesline ¼" in diameter will be used to operate this drop. Rig the drop while the roller is down. Fasten one end of the rope to the roller just below the stage-right pulley. Since the drop is 15'-0" high, wrap 15'-0" or more cotton rope around that end of the roller. Do not cut the rope. Run the line up from the roller through the groove of the single pulley, over one groove of the double pulley, and down to the stage floor (Figure 3–112). Cut the rope even with the stage floor at the offstage end.

FIGURE 3–112
Rigging a roll drop.

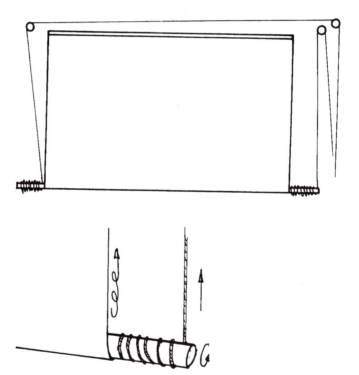

6. Rig the opposite end of the roll drop by attaching a second piece of cotton rope to the roller directly below the stage-left pulley. Wrap 15'-0" or more rope around the roller in the same direction as the first rope. Pass the rope over the remaining groove in the double pulley and pass it to the floor. Cut the rope even with the floor.

To operate, simply pull down on the free ends of the ropes. They should unwind from the roller, causing it to turn and wind the drop up around it. When the drop is fully raised, the ropes must be tied off, for they are carrying the weight of the entire drop and the roller. When the drop is to be unrolled, release the ropes and stand back. The drop will automatically unroll, rewinding the cotton ropes around the roller. Roll drops wider than 25'-0" are difficult to make work well.

Tracking

If a spare traveller drape track is available, drops can be hung on the track and pulled across the stage. It is best if the track is arranged to allow the drop to be a solid unbroken piece of fabric so that it can close entirely from one side. If a commercial track is not available, a homemade track is possible, or rigging that uses common hardware store materials can be devised.

A homemade traveller track can take several forms. The kind of track and carriers used for sliding doors will work for almost all moderate-weight scenery. This hardware can be purchased from a lumberyard and attached to a 1 × 3 for support. Try to find as enclosed a track as possible to reduce the likelihood of the carriers coming out of the grooves. Somewhat heavier scenery will stay in the track better than very lightweight scenery. The board carrying the track can be suspended with wire or rope from the ceiling. If it is desirable to rig a one-way drop, a stagehand can walk behind the leading edge of the drop and pull it across the stage, or a rope can be tied to the first carrier at one end to pull the leading edge of the drop across the stage. To pull the drop offstage, a second rope must be attached to the same carrier to pull it back to the same side of the stage from which it came.

A homemade track can be constructed from 1 × 3s to fit carriers purchased from theatrical suppliers or from a lumberyard. These homemade systems are seldom as quiet or as smooth to operate as a commercially made track, but they can be arranged to do the job.

Another way to change drops during a performance actually requires the use of flats in place of the drops. This system uses **shutters**, sliding panels of flats, mounted in **grooves**, tracks on the floor and overhead. The "drop" is made by assembling stock flats to make two large walls, each half the width of the required drop. A number of techniques can be used to make the "shutters" move.

Furniture glides ³/₄" in diameter can be placed approximately 2'-0" apart along the bottom edge of the flats. Additional glides should be placed on the front and back surfaces of the flats along the top edge (Figure 3–113).

Two tracks are needed for each shutter location, one at the bottom and the other at the top of the drop. The track at the bottom may be attached to the stage floor, placed on top of a platform, or arranged to fall between a pair of platforms as a recessed groove. A simple track can be made by nailing or screwing two 1 × 1s to the floor 1⅛" apart. The boards must be straight, smooth, and well sanded. Portable tracks can be assembled by attaching two 1 × 1s to the top of a 1 × 3. The 1 × 1s should be spaced 1⅛" apart. Since a normal 1 × 3 is usually 2⅝" wide, two ³/₄" × ³/₄" track guides and a 1⅛" space are exactly the width of the board. It is very important that the boards are straight and well sanded.

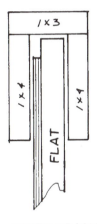

UPPER TRACK

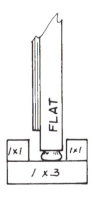

FIGURE 3–113
A track system for flats sliding in tracks.

The upper track should be deeper than the bottom track. This track is constructed from a 1 × 3 on top and a 1 × 4 on each side to form a deep U-shaped channel. Once again, the boards must be straight and well sanded. Although it can be suspended on a batten, the upper track must be fastened firmly in place. It cannot tip, swing, or move while the track is in use or it will cause the shutters to jam. The upper track should be braced to the side walls of the stage or stiffened with large jacks extending to the stage floor (Figure 3–114).

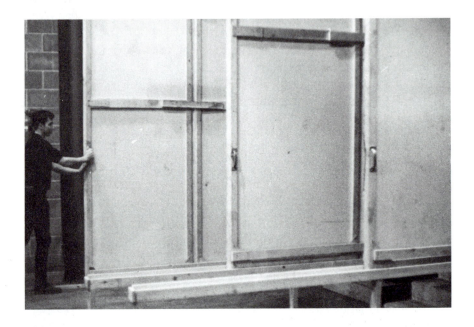

FIGURE 3–114
"Shutters-in-grooves"—flats in tracks. A modern adaptation of an ancient system of scene shifting.

It is helpful to rub paraffin inside the tracks or to spray them with a *dry* silicone lubricant.

When scenes are changed a shutter is slid onstage from each wing or pulled offstage to each wing. With some practice, stagehands can get the two sections to reach center or the offstage ends at the same time.

If it is possible to install two or more tracks, perhaps one far downstage, one at midstage and a third far upstage, a multiset show could easily be mounted by changing shutters in each set of grooves when the units are pulled offstage. This requires quite a bit of wing space to continue to pull flats offstage into storage areas, but it can be a quick and efficient method of scene shifting.

Rolling

Putting scenery on wheels is one of the most efficient ways to move it around. Pieces of settings or entire scenes can be rolled to facilitate scene shifts and to enhance the spectacle of a performance.

Wagons are platforms that move on casters. They may be specially built or converted from standard platforms by adding wheels.

The most practical caster for stage use is a plate-mounted 2½" to 3" hard rubber swivel caster with oilite or ball bearings rated for 250 to 300 pound loads. Its overall height should be 4" to 5". Casters of greater capacity and size may be used but are seldom necessary. For a standard

3×6 or 4×8 wagon, six casters are needed. To ensure clearance between the frame and the floor, facilitate movement, and ease additional construction on the wagon, it is best to shim each caster so that the top of the wagon is exactly 6" above the floor.

To Convert a Standard Platform into a Wagon

Materials List

1 standard 4×8 platform

6   3" swivel casters

24   $1/4$" $\times$ $2\frac{1}{2}$" flathead stove bolts with nuts and lock washers

Shims as needed

$1/8$ pound 4d common nails

Equipment List

Drill with $1/4$" bit

Screwdriver

Wrench

Saw

1. Determine the shim height.   Rest four casters on their plates on a table, and then balance any small board on the wheels. Measure the height from the table top to the underside of the board. This dimension should be approximately $4\frac{1}{2}$". The top of the wagon must be 6" high. Since a standard platform is being used, the thickness of the platform lid is $3/4$". This caster plus the thickness of the lid equals $5\frac{1}{4}$", so it will be necessary to shim these casters an additional $3/4$". Cut six blocks of 1×6 approximately 6" long (any $3/4$" thick lumber could be used). These will be the shims. Other combinations of lumber and hardboard can be used to make shims of appropriate height.

2. Locate the casters.   Put a standard 4×8 platform upside-down on a set of sawhorses. Place a caster as close as possible to each corner. *Rotate the caster to be sure that it does not come in contact with the frame at any point.* There should be a minimum clearance of $1/4$" between the caster and the frame, but there should be no more than 1" clearance or the caster will not adequately support the corner. In addition, locate casters at the center of the platform near the sides. Slip a shim under each caster and nail it to the bottom of the platform lid with two or three 4d common nails.

3. Attach the casters.   Drill a $1/4$" hole through the shim, platform lid, and padding where there are holes in the caster mounting plates. Slip a $1/4$" $\times$ $2\frac{1}{4}$" flathead stove bolt in each hole from the top of the platform through the padding, lid, shim, and caster. Slide a lock washer over the bolt and attach the nut, tightening firmly. Make sure that the bolts do not impede the movement of the caster. If necessary, cut off any extra length on the bolts with a hacksaw or bolt cutter. Repeat for each caster.

4. Turn the wagon over and cover each group of bolt heads with a dutchman.

Large wagons may be assembled by bolting or battening two, three, or more 4×8 units together through the sides or edges of the frame. To assemble the units with bolts, use three $3/8$" $\times$ 4" carriage bolts to join two long sides together or two bolts to join ends together. If a large wagon is assembled in this way, casters only need to be installed on one side at the joint. While it is preferable to attach casters with stove bolts, if the weight being carried on the wagon is not too heavy and the floor is smooth, $\frac{1}{4}$" × $1\frac{1}{2}$" lag screws may be used instead. To batten units together, a solid 1 × 4, 1 × 6, or 2 × 4 is nailed, screwed, or bolted to the side of the assembly to hold the units together (Figure 3–115).

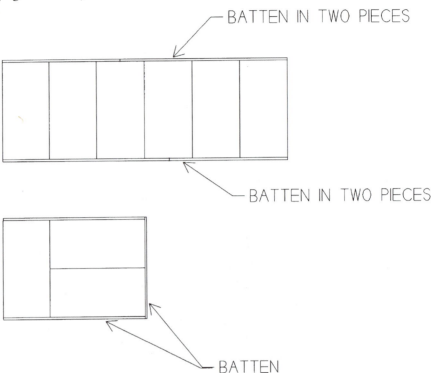

FIGURE 3–115
Wagons can be assembled by nailing, screwing, or bolting battens to their perimeter.

A simple replacement for a small wagon can easily be made by attaching furniture glides 2'-0" on center to the bottom of a sheet of $\frac{3}{4}$" plywood. The plywood is strong enough to carry a reasonable load without a frame and the furniture glides permit fairly easy movement. A rope can be attached to the sheet of plywood to use as a pull handle.

Wagons may move freely about the stage or they may be mounted on pivots or guided on tracks. A **slip stage** is a wagon guided in a track. After the basic wagon is assembled, a track and a knife guide are needed to make this system work. The guide can be made from a 2 × 2 and the track from two pieces of 1 × 1.

To Make a Slip Stage 8'-0" × 16'-0"

Materials List	*Equipment List*
Assembled wagon	Saber saw
1 2 × 4 × 16'-0"	Drill with $\frac{1}{4}$" bit and $\frac{3}{4}$" bit
1 1 × 6 × 16'-0"	Hammer
5 $\frac{1}{4}$" × 2" lag screws or drywall screws	Socket wrench with $\frac{7}{16}$" socket
$\frac{1}{4}$ pound 6d nails	Table saw
Dry silicone spray lubricant	
Sandpaper	

1. Before the assembled wagon is turned over to rest on its wheels, make and attach the knife guide. Using a table saw, rip a 16'-0" long 2 × 4 to exactly 1½" × 1½" square. Cut another piece of 2 × 4 2'-0" long and rip it to the same dimensions; label it *spacer* and set it aside. At each end of the 16'-0" board, cut an arc to form a quarter circle. Sand the board completely smooth.

2. At each end of the wagon, measure 3'-11¼" from one long side toward the opposite long side. Snap a chalkline on those marks. Place the side of the knife guide on the chalkline so that the center of the board is exactly 4'-0" from each long side of the wagon. The rounded ends should be turned away from the wagon. At each end and at each point where the knife guide crosses a pair of 2 × 4s on the underside of the wagon, drill a 1"-diameter hole *half* the depth of the knife guide. In the center of each hole, drill a ⅛" hole the rest of the way through the 2 × 2 and into the platform frame. Insert a ¼" × 2" lag screw in each hole and tighten it into the frame using the socket wrench. Sand off any rough edges (Figure 3–116).

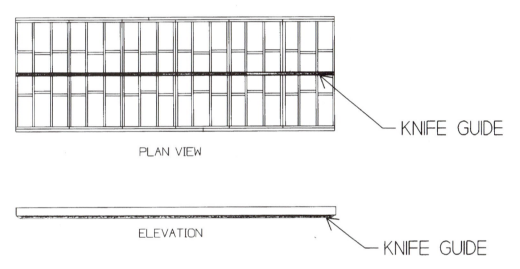

PLAN VIEW

ELEVATION

FIGURE 3–116
Placement of a knife guide on the underside of platforms assembled as a slip stage.

3. The amount of track needed depends on the distance the slip stage must travel. This example assumes that the unit moves its own length, 16'-0", thus requiring a total of 32'-0" of track. Using a table saw, rip a 1 × 6 into four pieces of lumber ¾" × 1" × 16'-0" long. Sand the boards smooth.

4. Mark the position on the floor that coincides with the downstage edge of the knife guide. Using 1½" flathead wood screws or 1⅝" drywall screws placed approximately 2'-0" apart, attach two of the ¾" × 1" track boards end to end on this line with the 1" dimensions up.

5. Attach a piece of ⅛" hardboard to one side of the board that was marked *spacer* which was cut in step 1. The spacer will now measure 1½" × 1⅝". Starting at one end of the track, place the 1½" side of the spacer on the floor with the hardboard against the upstage side of the ¾" × 1" track that has already been installed. Put another piece of ¾" × 1" track against the other side of the spacer so the two track boards are separated by a distance of 1⅝". Insert a screw. Moving the spacer to each location a screw is to be inserted, attach the track to the floor. The spacer will keep the track boards properly aligned and spaced apart (Figure 3–117).

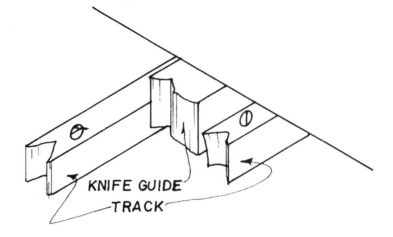

FIGURE 3–117
Knife guide and track for a slip stage.

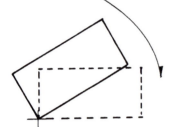

A

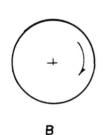

B

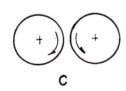

C

FIGURE 3–118
Typical wagon rotation patterns.

6. Sand smooth the joint in the track. Sweep out the space between the tracks and spray it with the dry silicone lubricant.

7. Slide the wagon with the knife guide into the track.

Pushsticks made of 2 × 4s can be attached to the end of the slip stage with large hinges, or stagehands can simply push on the edge of the wagon to move the slip stage in and out of the acting area.

Pivoting Wagons

Wagons can be assembled to rotate on a fixed point, which may be at the center of the unit, along a side, or at a corner of the wagon. Pivots are usually made of steel (Figure 3–118).

A very simple pivot can be made by screwing a short piece of $1\frac{1}{2}$" pipe into a floor flange and bolting the flange to the stage floor with lag screws (Figure 3–119). The edge or corner of a wagon is put against the pipe, and one end of a piece of pipe strap is attached to the face of the wagon with two $\frac{1}{4}$" lag screws; flat washers should be used between the lag screws and pipe strap. The strap is brought tightly around the pipe and the other end is also attached to the wagon with lag screws and washers. Two pipe straps are needed, one above the other. The pivot should be sprayed well with dry silicone lubricant. If all connections are well made, this will be a stiff but adequate pivot to use at the side or corner of a small wagon.

A significantly better pivot requires a $\frac{3}{4}$" pillow-block bearing and a piece of $\frac{3}{4}$" × 6" cold-rolled shaft welded solidly to the center of a $\frac{1}{4}$" × 6" × 6" mild steel plate. The plate with the shaft is attached to the floor with lag screws. The pillow-block bearing is slid over the shaft and bolted to the side of the wagon at the pivot point. The wagon will easily rotate around the shaft guided by the bearing. This system works very well. If the equipment and skill are available, this is the best choice (Figure 3–120).

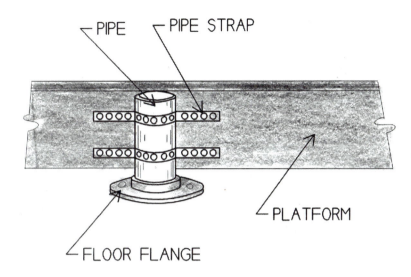

FIGURE 3–119
A wagon pivot constructed from a floor flange, pipe, and pipe strap.

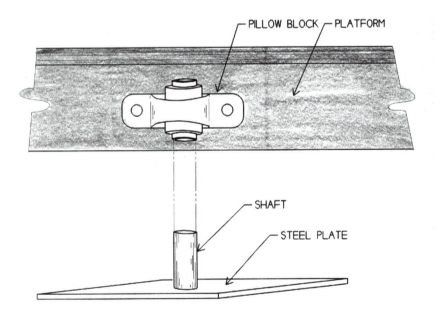

FIGURE 3–120
A wagon pivot assembled from a pillow-block bearing and a steel shaft and plate.

A revolving stage or "revolve" may be almost any shape; usually, they are circles with a central pivot. The most effective pivot is constructed by welding a steel shaft of sufficient diameter to withstand any bending forces and sufficient length to mate with a bearing mounted to the floor on a steel plate. The plate is then bolted to the underside of the wagon at the pivot point. A second plate is constructed with a **cushion bearing** (Figure 3–121) bolted to it. This plate is bolted to the stage floor at the pivot point of the wagon. The wagon, with the shaft plate already attached, is moved over the plate attached to the floor and then maneuvered until the shaft is dropped into the hole in the cushion bearing. If the wagon is large, this could require quite a bit of work. The bearing should be properly lubricated before the wagon is connected to it.

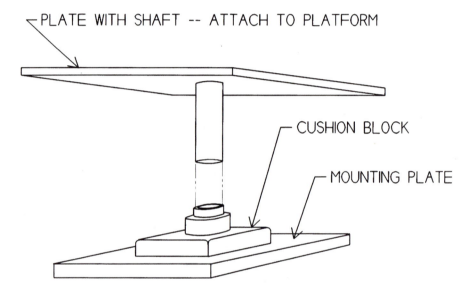

FIGURE 3–121
A wagon pivot assembled from a cushion bearing and a steel shaft and plate.

Whenever wagons or other rolling scenery are used on stage, great care should be taken to remove every bit of dirt and debris. The slightest interruption—a nail, screw, or a wood chip—can prevent a caster from turning or can totally stop a scene change.

CONCLUSION

Numerous traditional methods of scenic construction have been presented, in addition to a variety of alternative techniques and materials that can be either time or money saving. Although many of these practices will yield well-built scenery, it is not always possible or practical to work within these guidelines because of budget, staff, or time limitations or unexpected events. Unforeseeable problems often result in creative solutions. In addition, new materials or techniques may be discovered that are preferable to established practice. No solution should be discarded simply because it has not been used before or does not exist in a book. If an idea seems practical and safe, it should be tested; if it works, it should be used. The methods and techniques described in this chapter should provide the foundation for basic construction as well as creative thinking to solve problems.

Building scenery is only one element of making a setting. After the scenery has been constructed, it must also be painted and the setting completed with properties. These are equally challenging tasks that may be approached with as much creativity as scenic construction.

CHAPTER 4

Painting and Texturing

INTRODUCTION

Scenery and properties for a production are not complete until they have been finished with appropriate textures and paints. Painting and texturing are two of the most important processes in the creation of a setting. After all, the audience sees the paint, not the raw muslin or wood used to construct a flat or the plastic cups and foam balls used to make a prop. The paint should create an appropriate effect that is credible, attractive, and durable. It should tell the audience what something is or is supposed to be and the condition that it is in.

The final appearance of the paint is seriously affected by the quality and character of the foundation on which it is applied. For that reason, great care must be taken to prepare surfaces for painting. The preparation may simply be a well-done size coat on a drop or a joyously applied three-dimensional texture on a wall. Whatever the base, the final product depends on the combination of the foundation and its coatings.

Determining the colors and techniques to use for any of the effects described below is exciting but can be a challenge. The basis for making any choice is very simple: observe the world. Whether painting walls, trees, windows, or wood grains, the careful artist will take some time to study how these things appear in real life. Careful analysis of the colors that contribute to the complex beauty of wood or brick will help anyone painting scenery determine which colors to use, the order in which to apply them, and the processes that may be most effective. The techniques described here should be considered as guides from which to begin; observation of the world will give understanding and richness to the results. If observation of the world is combined with research to develop and produce a design, an exciting and appropriate setting can be the result.

As with scenic construction, there are traditional painting tools, materials, and techniques that have become standardized, and there are also many alternatives that are inexpensive, convenient, and practical. In this chapter, materials and processes to obtain specific effects are described in detail and guidance regarding the selection and mixing of colors is provided. Chapter 5 should be read in conjunction with this chapter because it offers further guidance about color.

PAINTING MATERIALS AND EQUIPMENT

Scenery may be painted with almost anything. Household paints and industrial coatings are as applicable as the specialized paints that have been formulated to meet the particular needs of scenic artists and designers. In addition to paints, other materials are also used on scenery, such as dyes, bronzing powders, glitters, even ground glass and sawdust. The selection of painting materials depends on the needs of the show, preferences of the painter, budget, and availability of paints and colors. Although there is no restriction that only scene paints be used on scenery, many experienced painters use and prefer them because of their special qualities, described below, that make mixing, application, and creation of effects easier.

Standard Scene Paints

All paints consist of three components: pigment, vehicle, and binder. **Pigment** is the material that gives paint its color. It may be a clay material or dye-impregnated neutral matter. **Vehicle** is the material in which the pigment is suspended or diluted. For most scene painting applications, the vehicle is water. **Binder** is the material that adheres the pigment to the surface on which it is applied; in effect, it is glue. All scene paints use similar pigments, and water is the usual vehicle. They differ most radically in the kind of binder that is used—which seriously affects all of the other characteristics of the paints.

There are several requirements for scene paint:

1. Readily available
2. Relatively inexpensive
3. Easily mix to new colors with predictable results
4. Easily mix to painting consistency
5. Dry rapidly
6. Dry to a flat nongloss finish
7. Withstand handling and the abuse of scene shifting

Better scene paints are characterized by the following additional characteristics:

1. Readily available in a broad range of colors so that a complete palette may be mixed
2. Consistent in color formulations
3. Usable as a thick paste, in a normal painting consistency, or as a dilute glaze
4. Maintain its color when diluted
5. Withstand overpainting with other colors and media
6. Easily flow from the brush in a smooth, controlled manner at any degree of dilution
7. May be applied with any equipment or process, including brush, roller, and sprayer

There are three standard scene paints that have all of these characteristics: scenic dry color, casein, and a family of acrylic paints. Although each of these media has specific attributes that distinguish it, they share several features. All three paints are water based, which means they are diluted and cleaned up with water; they are also somewhat water soluble after they have dried so that in many cases

155

they may be washed off things on completion of painting; but some might also dissolve and run if the dried paint is saturated with water. Each of the paints is available in a fairly broad range of similar intense colors that may be mixed within their own family to create a complete palette. They may be applied as a thick paste, a standard density coating, or as a very dilute wash or glaze; the paints may be built up in successive layers to create apparent or actual three-dimensional textures. After application, they may be treated with commercial coatings such as varnish to create additional effects and for physical protection.

Scenic dry color is purchased as a dry powder that must be mixed with water and glue to make a usable compound. Historically, ground gelatin glue (animal glue) was used as the binder; however, in the modern theatre, diluted white glue is used instead. Scenic dry color is difficult to ship, store, and use.

Casein has been one of the most popular scene paints. It is sold as a thick paste already mixed with vehicle and binder in 1- and 5-gallon buckets. There are approximately 30 colors available, and they may be intermixed to create a complete palette. This paint is easy to mix since the only concerns are attaining the appropriate color and spreading consistency. There are several advantages to casein scene paint.

1. It is available in strong colors that dilute well into tints.
2. At normal painting consistency, the opacity of the paint usually allows one-coat coverage.
3. The finish is flat and does not reflect light.
4. It is moderately durable.
5. The paint is reasonably resistant to water, which permits several layers of paint to be built up without lifting preceding coatings.

The paint also has a few disadvantages:

1. As water is added to casein, the color pales, becoming increasingly a tint, so that as the paint is brought to brushing consistency, the strength of color is weakened.
2. Moist casein paint will fade in the bucket if left exposed to air for several days.
3. Because it is a wet medium, it is difficult to predict what a mixed color will be until a sample of the paint is dried.
4. The paint works very well on porous surfaces such as muslin and wood, but the binder must be strengthened with clear acrylic for application to metal or plastics.
5. Once a bucket is opened, it must be resealed well or the paint will dry out and become useless.

Mixing casein paint is an easy process. With the final color in mind, a sample batch of paint is mixed, measuring the paste with tablespoons to determine the proportions of each color. The recipe should be written down. The sample is then brought to normal painting consistency by adding 1 part water to 2 parts paint. It is tested on the actual surface to be painted or on a similar material. The color of the paint can be determined only after the sample has dried completely because it will dry lighter than the color in the bucket. If the color requires modification, a new batch should be mixed and tested. When the color is correct, the recipe is translated into measuring cups in the same proportions as the sample. The mixed pigments are then brought to painting consistency, usually 2 parts casein to 1 part water, and stirred vigorously until smooth.

Figure C–1 represents the complete palette of colors available in casein paints from one manufacturer.

Acrylic paints include acrylic latex and vinyl acrylics, which are characterized by a chemically formulated binder. They are sold in very concentrated pastes that must be diluted for use. Since they are also a paste, acrylics share some characteristics with casein paints. They are shipped in cans completely mixed with their binder. When put to use, the paints need only be mixed to the appropriate color and brought to proper painting consistency.

1. A broad range of strong, vibrant colors is available.
2. They dry to a flat, nonreflective finish.
3. The paint can be mixed to be opaque or can be diluted for very thin washes and glazes.
4. It maintains its strength of color when diluted or exposed to air.
5. It is the most moisture resistant of the scene paints and will resist spills and overpainting without bleeding or lifting off the surface.
6. The paint does not rot, putrefy, or mildew.

The mixing process for acrylics is the same as for casein paints. A sample batch of carefully measured colors is mixed and tested, the recipe modified, and the final mixture prepared. The paint is then brought to the proper dilution and stirred until smooth. The amount of water required depends on the specific paint and the painting process used. The paint from one manufacturer requires a minimum dilution of 1 part paint to 1 part water; paints from other manufacturers require different dilutions.

One supplier manufactures an inexpensive acrylic paint that is ready for use from the can. The paint is available in a broad range of colors and bears the positive characteristics of the professional lines of acrylic scene paints. These paints have been especially developed for the nonprofessional theatre technician.

An alternative paint that may be used for the stage is household **flat interior latex** and household **acrylic latex**. These paints are available from local hardware, discount, and paint stores in hundreds of colors.

1. The paints are readily available.
2. They may be purchased premixed in a broad range of colors.
3. Pale colors are moderately inexpensive.
4. The paints provide a good opaque coating.
5. They are fairly water resistant.

There are, however, numerous disadvantages to the use of these paints.

1. They do not dry completely flat, thus they tend to cause stage lighting to reflect in a glaring manner.
2. Colors are generally weak and do not permit significant dilution.
3. The consistency is very thick, but the paints cannot be diluted and still maintain opacity. This means that the coating of paint applied to the scenery will be heavy and will make it necessary to recover flats more frequently.
4. Detail painting is hampered because undiluted latex paint does not flow easily from the brush.

Although these paints are not the best choice for scene painting, they are conveniently available and moderately inexpensive. They can be purchased in a broad range of premixed colors, making them a satisfactory alternative to paints especially formulated for the stage, but scene paints are definitely preferred. Some scenic latex paints available from theatrical suppliers match the color palettes of casein and acrylic paints; however, they have most of the characteristics of household paints and are more expensive.

Painting Equipment

The basic equipment necessary for scene painting is very limited. A modestly equipped shop should have several old 1 gallon paint cans and some clean No. 10 cans, in addition to 10 quart pails and 5 gallon buckets. The shop should also have an assortment of good **lay-in brushes**, about 4" wide for putting on base coats; **trim brushes**, usually 2" to 3" wide for working in smaller areas; and **lining brushes** for detail painting, as well as some small inexpensive brushes to apply dope (Figure 4–1).

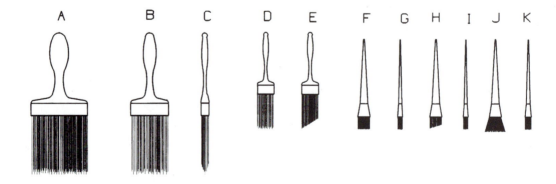

FIGURE 4–1
(A) 4" and (B) 2" lay-in brushes are used for prime and base coats and some detail painting. (C) Side view of a typical lay-in brush; note the tapered and flagged bristles. (D) Straight and (E) tapered trim brushes. (F) Straight liner (G) side view. (H) Angular liner (I) side view. (J) Foliage brush or Fitch (K) side view.

Brushes

Lay-in and trim brushes should be of decent quality. Better brushes are made with polyester bristles in a block that is at least ½" thick and 4" long. The bristles are somewhat springy when pressed into an arc and their ends are tapered and flagged (split to hold paint) and feel soft to the touch. They are used to apply paint over large areas and for some detail painting. Dope brushes should be the least expensive small nylon brush that can be found. Lay-in, trim, and dope brushes can be purchased at local hardware, paint, and discount stores, as well as from theatrical suppliers. **Lining brushes** are made from natural bristles; synthetic bristles are unacceptable because they do not hold sufficient quantities of paint nor do they respond well on the painting surface. The bristles should be fairly long and full and must stay in a neat block pattern. The **ferrule**, the metal band that attaches the bristles to the handle, must be firm and tight. Handles should be fairly long and comfortable to hold. Several different sizes of liners are usually needed, ranging from ¼" wide up to 2" wide. Although good lining brushes are expensive, if they are properly cared for, they will not only make painting easier but will also last a long time. They usually must be purchased from a theatrical supply company. **Fitches** or **foliage brushes** are, in effect, wide, thick liners. They are used for painting foliage and for wide lines and other detail painting where control is needed in broad strokes. They are usually very expensive because of their large size.

If properly cared for, paintbrushes can last a long time. There are only a few important rules for brush care.

1. Never leave a brush standing on its bristles in the bucket. If the paint is deep, the handle will absorb pigment and will always have some of that color running into any new color being used—even after washing. Also, a brush stood on end in a pail for some time will warp into a permanent curve, making it difficult to control. Finally, the handle will swell from the liquid and break the ferrule so the bristles will eventually fall off the brush.

2. Always clean the brush when done painting. Rinse in the proper solvent or scrub the bristles on a bar of hand soap or in mild detergent to break up the paint. Rinse the brush thoroughly in warm—not hot—water until the water runs clean. Repeat scrubbing if necessary.

3. After washing, shake out the excess water, shape the bristles into a block, and hang the brush up, bristles down, to allow it to dry. Alternatively, wrap the moist bristles in paper towels to keep the bristle block tight and well formed. Store the wrapped brush flat where air can circulate around it.

4. Never bang the ferrule against the edge of the sink or bucket. Banging the ferrule will damage the brush and cause it to fall apart.

Other Tools

In addition to paintbrushes, the equipment shown in Figure 4–2 is needed for scene painting. Most of these items can be purchased from theatrical suppliers or local paint, hardware, or discount stores. However, the lining stick or straightedge and muslin stomp are shop made because they are not commercially available.

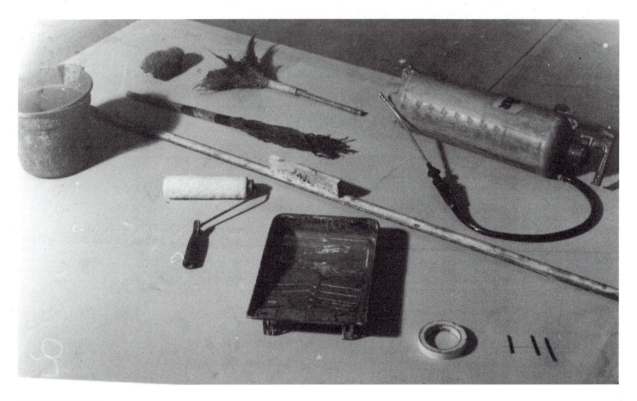

FIGURE 4–2
Painting equipment. From top left: natural sea-wool sponge; real ostrich feather duster; garden (Hudson) sprayer; muslin stomp; straight edge or lining stick; buckets, cans, and pails; paint roller and roller tray; masking tape; charcoal.

A **straightedge** is used to guide painting straight lines. It is made from a piece of 1" or wider cove molding about 6'-0" long. The molding may be purchased from a lumberyard. Cut a piece of 1 × 2 approximately 12" long. Cut a notch on one edge of the 1 × 2 to form the inside of a handle and then sand it smooth. Place the center of the handle over the center of the decorative side of the molding. Drive nails or screws from the flat side through the molding to attach the handle at the center of the decorative side of the molding (Figure 4–3). The flat side of the molding will go against the surface of the scenery being painted. Lightly sand the straightedge and then coat it with gloss exterior varnish or an exterior paint. This will reduce the likelihood of its warping.

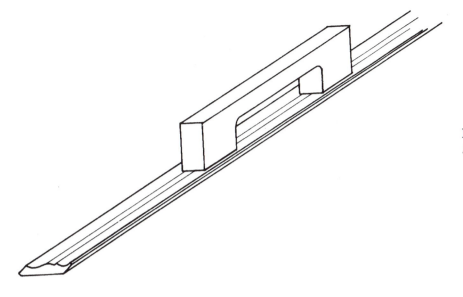

FIGURE 4–3
Straightedge or lining stick.

To make the muslin stomp (Figure 4–4), cut a piece of 2 × 2 approximately 3'-0" long and sand it smooth. Cut a strip of muslin approximately 2'-0" wide and 6'-0" long. Draw a line 6" from one edge of the muslin. On the opposite edge, tear the muslin to the line in 2" wide strips so that the muslin strip looks like a shaggy fringe. Wrap the solid part of the fabric around the end of the 2 × 2 and nail or staple it to the stick.

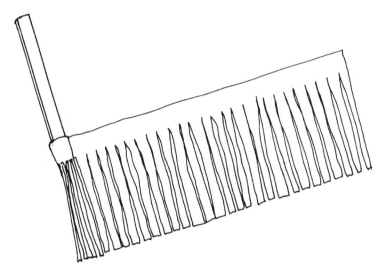

FIGURE 4–4
Muslin stomp.

GENERAL PAINTING TECHNIQUES

Scenery can be treated with up to four different painting processes: the size coat and prime coat prepare the surface, and the base coat and detail painting are finishing processes. Each process serves a specific function, although to save time some functions may be combined.

Surface Preparation

Size Coat

The **size coat** shrinks muslin to a tight, smooth painting surface. It is usually applied to flats as part of the construction process and on drops as the first step of painting. **Size** is a dilute mixture of white glue and water. Sometimes **whiting**, a neutral paint filler or a bit of dry pigment, is added to the mixture to give it body and opacity. It is necessary to put a size coat on individual flats after they have been covered with new muslin or on a new drop in preparation for painting. The size coat may be applied with a brush or roller, or by spraying the material on the surface.

Prime Coat

The **prime coat** is the first layer of paint applied to the surface after the scenery is assembled and the dutchmen have been applied and trimmed. It fills pores in the fabric, hides the dutchmen, and covers any previous coating to make a consistent surface in preparation for base coating. The prime coat is usually a thin- to medium-density mixture of scene paint. A pastel color in the range of the base coat that will follow, performs this function well. If necessary, the prime coat may be the same as the size coat; however, this is less effective at filling the pores of new muslin and hiding the dutchmen than if separate treatments are done. Occasionally, the prime coat might serve as a base coat. The prime coat may be applied with a brush, paint roller, or sprayer.

Finishing Processes

Base Coat

The **base coat** is the underlying color applied to the scenery. It is the first finishing treatment on the setting and is the foundation of what the audience will see. The base coat may be applied with a brush, paint roller, or sprayer. Often, more than one color will be used to base coat different parts of a set. For instance, the major portion of the walls might be a medium blue topped by a light yellow border and brown moldings at the edges. It is best to mark the lines between the areas of color in preparation for base coating and then to paint only the desired colors in the appropriate sections of the flat. This is called **laying in**. Marks should be placed at the edges of the scenery and chalklines snapped across the walls to identify the borders between colors.

The line of demarcation between colors can be dealt with fairly easily. The lightest of the colors is painted first. The paint should be carried to or just over the chalkline. The darker color can be applied after the first color has dried. At the point where the colors change, a crisp line of the darker color is painted with the aid of a straightedge and lining brush. This requires a little practice. The side of the straightedge is placed on the line, and a 1" wide lining brush is loaded with paint and then lightly pulled along guided by the straightedge (see page 172, Figure 4–15). If the straightedge is held firmly and the brush is gently pulled along it, a smooth, straight, crisp line appears. The darker color is painted up to and blended into the guided line. It may be tempting to use masking tape to create a straight line on a wall, but when the tape is removed, it tends to pull off the previous layer of paint.

Detail paint and painted or three-dimensional textures give dimensionality to the base coat and create specific effects. Textures of some sort help to give scenery a sense of credibility and hide distortions of imperfect surfaces.

Each coat of paint is extremely important because it provides the foundation for all subsequent painting. In many instances, one of these coatings can serve multiple functions; for instance, the size coat and prime coat can be a single treatment if necessary. Often, a prime coat is eliminated and the base color is painted directly over the size coat.

Scenery can be painted while it is standing up or lying down. Standing scenery must be protected from runs and dribbles. When scenery is painted lying down, puddles must be avoided and care must be taken not to leave footprints or cause other damage to the surface.

Lay-in Techniques

Crosshatch

The direction in which the base coat is applied affects the way successive paint treatments behave and the manner in which the setting reflects light, so any decisions in this regard must be made with care. It is usually desirable to apply the base coat in a way that does not create an identifiable pattern. For this reason, size, prime, and base paints are usually applied with a **crosshatch** brush stroke (Fig. 4–5A). To do this, the paintbrush is moved in a random, overlapping X-pattern. When the base coat is applied with a sprayer or paint roller, it is equally important to avoid creating a pattern. Once again, some randomness to the direction of application is desirable. In some specific instances, such as when paint is being applied in a narrow area or if a wood grain (or some other directional pattern) is to be painted, it may be desirable to paint the base coat in a specific direction.

A.

B.

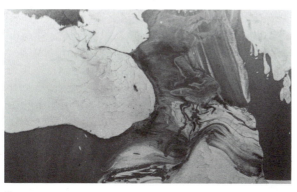

C.

FIGURE 4–5
Base painting techniques: (A) crosshatching. (B) wet blend, (C) puddle.

163

Wet Blend

A **wet blend** (Figure 4–5B) is another method of applying a base coat. This painting technique provides a variegated base of color in preparation for later detail painting. With this technique, at least two different colors of paint are applied to the scenery at the same time. A separate brush must be used for each color. First, one color is brushed on the scenery in a relatively small area. While this color is still wet, a second color is painted next to the first. Some of the second color is brushed into the first color until there is an area of transition where the two paints blend together. If the paint is brushed too much, the colors will mix, making a muddy area rather than a blended area. It may be necessary to wash a brush during the painting process if too much of the alternate color collects on it. This technique provides a rich base for many effects, especially woods such as oak or old, dirty, crumbling plaster, rocks, or marble.

Puddling

Puddling (Figure 4–5C) is another wet blending technique that can be used to apply a base coat. Rather than brushing two or more areas of color on the scenery, a base coat is laid in and while it is still wet one or more other color paints are poured onto it. A thicker paint is usually used for the base paint and a dilute mixture is used for the poured color. The wet paints run and blend together on their own. In some areas the poured paint may simply stay in a puddle and in others it may merge with the base paint. When this technique is used on flats, some control can be obtained by lifting and tilting the scenery to cause the puddles to run together or flow in a particular direction. This allows the paints to maintain their integrity in puddles. Puddling provides a good foundation for painting effects such as rough, textured walls, terrazzo floors, stone walls, or any highly variegated surface.

DETAIL AND TEXTURE PAINTING

After the base coat has dried, painted texture and detail are applied to the scenery.

Techniques

Each of the following techniques may be used alone with one or several colors or may be combined with other techniques to create specific effects. Each requires practice to develop sufficient control to obtain predictable results. Any technique that has not been attempted previously or has not been used for some time should be practiced on something other than the actual setting. All color combinations should also be tested in areas that will not affect the final setting. When applying the base coat to the setting, it is helpful to paint a spare flat or piece of cardboard on which to test colors and to use as a test surface to try out texture and detail techniques before attempting them on the actual setting.

Spattering

Spattering is one of the most common texturing techniques used in the theatre. Virtually everything in the world has some kind of texture to it. Spattering creates the effect of a neutral texture (Figure 4–6). It may be applied in a fine, even pattern or as a very coarse texture. There are three ways to apply this texture. Each method has its own advantages and problems.

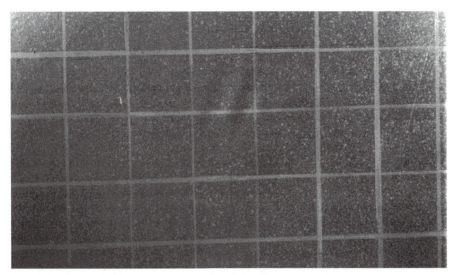

FIGURE 4–6
A spattered wall.

1. The hand slap (Figure 4–7). Protect the floor, drapes, and other set pieces in the vicinity of the scenery to be textured. Experiment with the technique in a test area. Dip a lay-in brush into the paint, and then wipe it off so it is not too wet. With the brush held

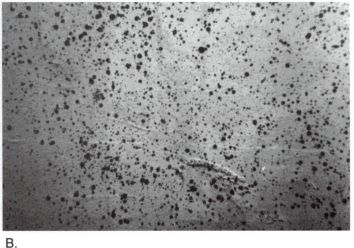

FIGURE 4–7
Spattering: (A) the hand slap, (B) the effect of this technique.

A.

B.

165

firmly in one hand, slap the ferrule against the fatty part of the palm of the other hand or against a block of wood held in the other hand. As the brush strikes, it lets off a spray of little dots of paint that spatter onto the surface of the scenery. With each stroke, rotate the brush to a different direction and move around the scenery so that no pattern develops. Continue to strike the brush against the wooden block until it no longer produces an adequate spray of paint, and then re-dip it. Take a practice shot on a test area away from the actual scenery being painted to judge the amount of paint on the brush; then continue to spatter the scenery.

2. The toss (Figure 4–8). After preparing the scenery and work area, dip a lay-in brush in the paint. Standing at the edge of the scenery, hold the brush so the bristles are straight up. Flip the bristles toward the flat in a quick jerk. Once again, a pattern of little dots will spatter the surface of the flat. (*Caution:* It is very easy to continually lay down a specific pattern of dots with this technique. The neutral texture that is desired can quickly become a badly patterned surface. Be sure to move around the scenery and continually change both position and angle from which the paint is being tossed.)

3. The sprayer (Figure 4–9). Garden sprayers, such as Hudson sprayers, are frequently used to spatter scenery. Paint must be mixed to a very smooth and fairly dilute consistency, strained at least twice through nylon stockings, and then funneled into the garden sprayer. The sprayer is pumped up and the nozzle adjusted for the desired texture. The spray shoud be tested in an area off the scenery before beginning to spatter. After making all adjustments, the spatter is applied by holding the wand about 3'-0 to 5'-0" from the scenery and moving

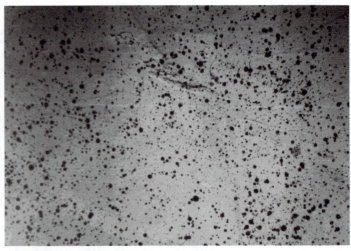

FIGURE 4–8
Spattering: (A) the toss, (B) the effect of this technique.

A.

B.

A.

B.

FIGURE 4–9
Spattering: (A) garden sprayer, (B) the effect of this technique.

it in complete overlapping circles so no specific pattern develops. If the paint is the proper dilution, the sprayer properly adjusted, and the operator moves smoothly, a very consistent, richly textured surface can be painted. The sprayer must be washed thoroughly after use.

Although there are no "rules," as a general guideline, at least two colors of spatter are normally painted over a base coat. Safe and effective choices are a tint and a shade of the base color. The tint is made by adding a significant amount of white to the base color. The shade is mixed by adding to the base color some vandyke brown, black, or the primary dark or intense color from which the base color was originally mixed. Almost any other colors might be used as a spatter as well. An exciting wall color can be built up with a base coat in one hue and spatters in several other colors; for instance, a rich lavender can be painted by base coating a wall in blue and spraying red and white spatters over it. This might require as many as five or six different spatter coats to obtain the precise color desired.

Spatter also may be used to correct color problems. (See Chapter 5 for a discussion of color.) For instance, if a wall is too dark, it might be spattered with white or a very light tint of the base color to lighten it; a wall that is too intensely blue might be spattered with a very fine mist of its complementary color, orange, to reduce the intensity yet maintain the sense of the original color. This is a very delicate process and should only be attempted after reasonable experimentation with the spattering technique and the color. Spatter can also be used to create numerous effects, from the shaded edges of walls in an old room with collected grime in the corners to the impression of a patina of dust on walls, windows, and furniture. Although any of the three tech-

167

niques can be used, spraying produces the most consistent results for most effects achieved by spattering.

Dribbling

Dribbling (Figure 4–10) is a painting technique that is used when moderate or large dots of paint are desired, such as the base coat for a terrazzo floor or marble. Although the effect bears similarities to that of spattering, the technique is significantly different: when scenery is spattered, paint is tossed at the surface; when the painting technique is dribbling, paint is simply allowed to drop off a brush onto the scenery. The paintbrush is dipped into the paint and held parallel with the floor straight out from the body. Rather than shaking the brush, which would cause the paint to spatter, the brush is slowly twisted about 60° up and down to encourage the paint to drop off it. The brush must move continually and the painter must constantly relocate to avoid developing a pattern. Color choice for dribbling depends primarily on the effect sought.

Sponging

Sponging (Figure 4–11) differs entirely from spattering and dribbling. With this technique, a pattern of the ridges of a natural sea-wool sponge is pressed on the scenery. A sponge is dipped into a bucket of paint and then partially squeezed dry. Holding the sponge firmly, it is gently pressed against the surface of the scenery so that the ridges on the sponge imprint their pattern on the setting. The sponge is lifted off the scenery, rotated a few degrees, and once again pressed against it. The sponge must be rotated between each impression to avoid a repetitious pattern. Random, overlapping imprints should be made to create a continuous texture. (*Caution*: It is very easy to rush this painting and

A.

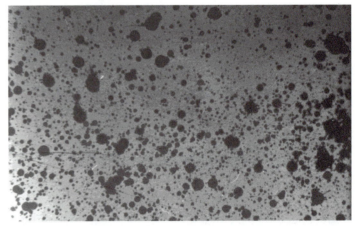

B.

FIGURE 4–10
(A) Dribbling, (B) the effect of this technique.

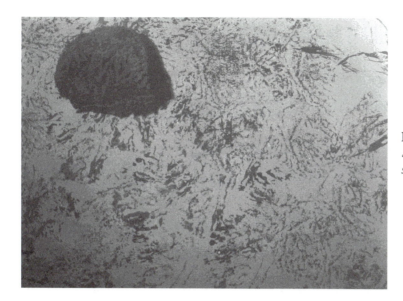

FIGURE 4–11
Sponging with a natural seawool sponge.

rotate the sponge while it is touching the scenery, which will create unsightly swirls that are very difficult to hide.) Be careful not to allow a sopping wet sponge to be used, for it will make blobs rather than an imprint of the ridges on the sponge. Artificial sponges can be used but they are not nearly as effective as natural sponges. The texture may be applied with the scenery standing up or lying down and in a single color or with several colors. The technique may be used effectively to create a neutral texture over large areas or may be easily confined to small spaces where the application of a spatter would be too messy. Sponging is an effective technique to create the specific textures of coarse plaster, stucco walls, brick, and stone. Natural sponges can be purchased at professional paint stores.

Scumbling

Scumbling can be applied in a random arrangement to create a coarse, neutral texture or in a specific direction to establish the base for another effect. The technique may be performed two different ways, yielding significantly different results.

1. Rag roll (Figure 4–12A). Take any fairly large rag and twist it into a roll about 1'-0" long and 2" to 3" in diameter. Dip the roll into paint and squeeze it partially dry. Roll it over the scenery while pressing

FIGURE 4–12
Scumbling: (A) rag roll, (B) taped paint roller.

A.

B.

down only hard enough to print an impression of the ridges on the rag roll. The roll may be moved in a straight line intentionally to create a pattern or may be maneuvered in a random pattern to create a neutral texture. The final effect of the technique depends on color choice, direction of movement, and coarseness of the rag roll.

2. Paint roller (Figure 4–12B). Wrap masking tape tightly around a paint roller in a random criss-cross pattern that covers some of the nap and leaves other sections exposed. Wrapping in a spiral from left to right and then in a spiral in the opposite direction works well, but any other pattern will do. Dip the roller into paint and make a test stroke on an area off the scenery to be sure that only the exposed portions of the nap on the roller are making an imprint. If the paint on the tape is printing, either it was not wrapped tightly enough or there is too much paint on the roller. Make whatever corrections are necessary. Moving the roller in a straight line creates a directional texture that is a wonderful base for wallpaper. Strokes must be placed adjacent and parallel with each other but not overlapping. If the roller is moved in a random pattern, it creates a distinctive texture that can be used alone or as the base for another painted effect.

Feather Dusting

Feather dusting (Figure 4–13A) creates a rich elaborate texture that can serve as wallpaper or it can be utilized as a textured base for a wallpaper stencil. Once again, the effectiveness of the technique depends on the means of application as well as on the selection of color. A real ostrich-feather duster is used. The feathers are dipped into the paint, wrung partially dry, and tested on an area off the scenery to determine the amount of paint on the feathers. Holding the duster by the handle, the feathers are swirled so they spread out like a fan; while in the extended position, they are dropped onto the surface of the scenery, leaving an impression of the swirling feathers. The duster is lifted, rotated in the opposite direction, and dropped onto the scenery again, repeating the process in random, overlapping patterns. The duster must be lifted and rotated between each impression; the feathers should not move on the surface. If a feather duster is not available; a muslin stomp may be used in exactly the same way.

FIGURE 4–13
(A) Feather dusting, (B) flogging with muslin stomp.

A.

B.

Flogging

Flogging (Figure 4–13B) uses a muslin stomp in a slightly different technique than the feather duster. The stomp is dipped into paint, wrung out, and then shaken to loosen the individual strands of material. The stomp is then slapped against the surface of the scenery, applying a long, slightly swirled, and slightly feather-like pattern in a triangular shape. After each hit, the stomp should be lifted straight off the scenery. Random, overlapping patterns at various angles should be achieved.

Dry Brush

Dry Brush (Figure 4–14) is a technique often used to paint wood grains although it can be utilized for numerous other effects as well. Any brush, preferably an older one that has badly separated bristles, is dipped in paint and then wiped almost dry. The brush is dragged lightly over the scenery, leaving behind a pattern of thin lines of paint. With some practice, a brush more heavily loaded with paint can be used to paint longer lines. When more than one stroke is necessary to complete a line of dry brushing, the location where strokes overlap must be treated delicately to avoid obvious impressions of the beginning and ending of strokes. As a brush runs out of paint, the arm carrying the brush should be swept up in an arc that tapers the brush stroke off the surface rather than ending it in a blunt line. The freshly dipped brush should be swept into the end of the previous stroke of paint also in an arc so the two lines of paint overlap lightly, avoiding a blunt mark where the old stroke ends and the new one begins.

FIGURE 4–14
Dry brushing.

Lining

Lining is the process of painting lines onto scenery. These may be highlights and shadows on moldings, brick, or clapboard siding or lines to create some other effect. Whatever the purpose, the technique is the same. When a straight line is needed, a lining stick or straightedge is used. The straightedge is held against the scenery and a lining brush is grasped far back on the handle with the opposite hand. The brush is pulled along the straightedge in a smooth, consistent, continuous stroke (Figure 4–15). The brush should be held so neither the bristles nor paint will get under the straightedge and cause a smudge. Line width depends on the brush used and the pressure applied to it: a narrow brush makes a narrow line, but if the bristles are pressed firmly against the surface, the line will be wider. A dilute paint is easiest to use for lining because it will permit long lines to be painted with the fewest breaks (Figure 4–16).

FIGURE 4–15
Lining with a straightedge.

FIGURE 4–16
An entire set painted with lines (The Miser). *(Courtesy Theatre UNI, University of Northern Iowa.)*

Stencils

Stencils are often used to produce wallpaper patterns and templates for repeated forms such as brick. The best material for making the patterns is **stencil board**. This is a heavy paper with a special coating that makes the material moisture resistant. If necessary, stencils may be cut in illustration board, cardboard, or even hardboard. All of these materials must be mounted in a frame and treated with a moisture-resistant coating (Figure 4–17). A design is transferred to the stencil paper and cut out with a matte knife. The stencil paper is then glued and stapled to a frame constructed from 1 × 3s. After the glue dries, the frame and stencil are painted with several coats of exterior varnish to further protect it from moisture that may accumulate during the stenciling process.

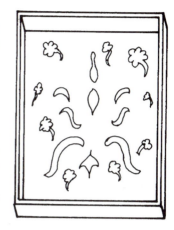

FIGURE 4–17
A stencil mounted in a frame.

To apply a stencil, the pattern is held against the scenery and then lightly sprayed with the desired color paint. A garden sprayer or even aerosol spray paints may be used (*be sure to read the cautions on the paint label*). If necessary, the pattern can be transferred to the surface of the scenery by dabbing the end of a stiff brush or a sponge through each of the openings in the stencil. The stencil board should be wiped clean between each impression so it does not collect paint that will then run onto the surface of the scenery. It is handy to make several copies of the stencil and alternate them during the painting process. This also provides protection in the event a stencil becomes damaged during painting.

The stencil must be designed and laid out with some care. Open areas must not be too small and areas between openings must be wide enough to support the stencil. In addition, the pattern should contain **keys** in the corners that allow the first stencil that is applied to align automatically with the next stencil by overlapping the painted keys with the key openings in the stencil. Some elaborate designs may require two, three, or more stencils in different colors to complete the image desired. This painting is also facilitated by keys that allow alignment of successive layers of stencils.

Stencils need not be limited to long-term multiple applications. If it is necessary to paint a very detailed and specific pattern on the scenery only once or twice, a pattern could be laid out on kraft or butcher paper, cut out, and sprayed. As an alternative, the pattern could be perforated with holes on the lines and aerosol paint sprayed over it or chalk dust rubbed over the pattern to transfer it to the scenery to use as a guide for painting.

Stamping

Stamping is a fairly easy process. A piece of evenly napped carpet or foam rubber is cut into the pattern to be stamped: the carpet or foam rubber is then attached to a block of wood. The stamp is dipped into paint and pressed on the surface of the scenery. This process may be used to transfer specific images or simply a texture. Using a piece of fairly coarse carpet might be an effective way to stamp a brick pattern.

A commercial paint roller is available from paint stores and theatrical suppliers that uses interchangeable patterned rollers that imprint a design such as birds or flowers. The rollers may be used with any paint to create a wallpaper pattern. A homemade version of this device might be manufactured by cutting designs out of carpet and gluing them to a fiber or metal tube that fits a paint roller.

Glaze

A **glaze** is a very dilute coating of paint brushed over a previously painted surface with the intention of modifying the underlayer, not covering it up. Glazes are often used to paint shadows or to create a patina of some kind, or they can be coated over an entire surface to modify the color of the base coat. Several layers of glaze can be built up to create very rich surfaces.

Painted Effects

The preceding techniques are easy to learn and can be quickly mastered with a little practice. Each can be used independently as a neutral texture or as a texture representing a specific material. Techniques also may be combined with each other and a base coat to build a particular painted effect. Careful planning from the beginning of construction produces the best results. This allows the development of a good foundation on which to paint, application of an appropriate base coat, and execution of well-planned textures. The proper choice of techniques and colors is the key to success. Some color suggestions are made in the following examples, but exact selections should be tested for the desired effect. All paints described in the following examples refer to the color chart in Figure C–1.

Wood Grain #1 (Mahogany or Walnut) (Figure 4–18)

1. Add white pigment to burnt umber paint to make a medium-brown color. Use that color to base coat the wood area. Large areas should be painted with a crosshatched stroke, whereas smaller areas can be painted in the long direction of what will become the boards. Also paint a test area located off the actual scenery on which to check color and density of the graining paints.

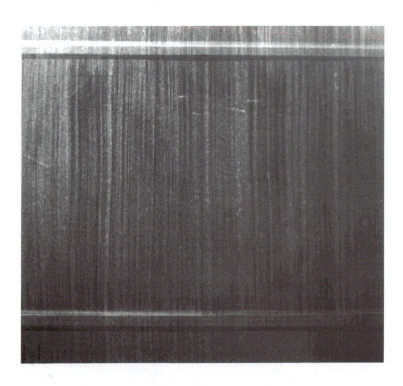

FIGURE 4–18
Painted mahogany wood grain.

2. Pour about 1" of the base color into another bucket. Add more white pigment, creating a color close to that of coffee-with-cream. The color in the pail will have a red tone to it rather than the yellowish color of coffee-with-cream. Pour 1" of base color into a third bucket of paint. Add enough vandyke brown to make the paint look like the color of moist coffee grounds. Select a brush for graining. An old brush that splits badly when used for base coating is excellent for dry brushing.

3. Try out the color mixture and technique on the prepared test area. Grain with the lightest paint first. This color will be easier to cover with the dark paint used to create the grain should the first graining color be applied too heavily. Dip the brush into the paint, wipe it almost dry, and paint a stroke on the test area. The pattern of the bristles should appear. The brush stroke should be at least the entire distance that can be reached without taking a step. If the paint does not flow on or will not extend at least one arm's length, or if it is too intense, dilute it with water, adding no more than a half cup at a time. Keep adding water until the paint flows easily yet allows sufficient coverage. If the paint flows on as a solid mass rather than producing the pattern of individual bristles, the brush is too wet; remove paint from the brush. Usually, only very light pressure is needed to produce an acceptable dry brush stroke. After producing an acceptable stroke, allow the paint to dry. If it is very white, add a little of the burnt umber to it; if it is too dark, add a little white and then adjust the amount of water in the paint to compensate for the added paint. Repeat this test with the dark color and make whatever adjustments are needed.

4. Determine the direction of each painted board on the set. Mark joints between boards with a pencil line. Look at a piece of real wood that has been stained and varnished. Mahogany is often used on doors in modern homes, and walnut may be found in a lot of contemporary furniture. It is better to look at actual grains rather than at pictures of grains, but if the right kind of actual wood cannot be found, a picture is the next best choice. Using the light color, dry brush all of the base-coated wood grain in the appropriate direction and style as determined by observation of the actual wood.

5. Dry brush with the dark grain.

6. If desired, a gloss medium—such as gloss varnish, lacquer, or even diluted white glue—can be applied over the completed graining to give a more realistic appearance to the effect. (*Caution:* Some gloss finishes will dramatically change the color of the paint. *Caution:* Most water-base paints will not cover or adhere to varnished or lacquered surfaces.)

175

Wood Grain #2 (Oak) (Figure 4–19)

1. Study the appearance of a piece of finished oak. Note all of the complexities of the grain as well as the colors of the wood.

2. Prepare a bucket of burnt sienna and another of raw sienna for base coating and a bucket of burnt umber and one of vandyke brown for graining.

3. Using both the raw sienna and the burnt sienna, paint a wetblend base coat in the long direction of each board. Do not crosshatch. While the paint is still damp, dribble a few small droplets of vandyke brown into the base coat. Drag a clean, dry brush through the dribbles of the vandyke to elongate the spots into dark streaks. Allow the paint to dry.

FIGURE 4–19
Painted oak grain.

4. With a pencil and straightedge or with a chalkline, mark the edges and ends of each board. These lines indicate where the painted grain patterns are to change.

5. Add just a little bit of raw sienna to some burnt umber. Use this color to paint the knots, cut grain, and coarse grains that typify oak. Select a good 1" or smaller lining brush. Hold it far back on the handle and work freehand to paint the grain. Roll, rotate, and turn the brush to obtain the variety needed (Figure 4–20). Be careful not to become repetitious while painting the pattern and do not let a grain pattern extend beyond the pencil lines or the boards will appear to merge together.

6. Using a dilute mixture of vandyke brown and a very narrow brush, paint narrow broken lines within about half of the coarse grains. The vandyke brown should fall mostly within the darker color and follow the same pattern of the previously painted coarse grain.

7. In another bucket, add a little white paint to some raw sienna. Using a narrow lining brush, add occasional highlights to the edges of the dark coarse grain. The highlights should occur infrequently.

FIGURE 4–20
Roll the brush to paint a checkered grain.

176

8. Dilute the highlight color. Using little paint, lightly dry brush the entire grained area and then dry brush more heavily with vandyke brown. The dry-brushed grain should be mostly straight but may waver and bend around knots.

Wood Grain #3 (Weathered Wood) (Figure 4–21)

1. Study a photograph or a painting of old, greyed wood.

2. Mix a base coat of approximately 5 parts white paint and 2 parts black. Adjust the mixture to obtain a light medium grey. Using a crosshatch stroke, base coat the area to be painted.

3. Use a 1" lining brush and black paint to detail knots, cracks, and splits in the wood. Use all edges of the brush to get a lot of variety to the lines. Cracks will develop in old wood around knots and splits at the ends of boards and all through the wood. A checkered effect (Figure 4–20) can be achieved by pulling the brush sideways and rolling it from side to edge, then back to the side again. Be as free, but logical, with the painting of this grain as possible.

4. Determine where the source of light will be for this scene. Use a very narrow lining brush to paint very thin, infrequent white lines on edges where the light will strike, such as the top edge of a rail or the bottom edge of a crack or the joint between two boards. The highlight must be painted as very narrow lines and kept quite minimal. Highlight is often accompanied by a shadow so the white lines are almost always paired with black lines.

5. Dilute a little bit of white paint to the density of skim milk and paint a light, finely textured grain over the coarse grains; repeat with the black paint.

FIGURE 4–21
Weathered wood.

Brick #1

1. Add a little bit of raw umber to some white paint. The mixture should be a slightly greyed off-white to use as a mortar color between the joints. Base coat the entire brick area with this paint.

2. Using either the hand slap or the toss method, spatter the base coat with both white and vandyke brown.

3. Either prepare a stencil in a brick pattern or lay ½" or ¾" masking tape on the scenery in the joint pattern of bricks. (Figure 4–22). (There is some danger that the tape will lift the base coat.)

FIGURE 4–22
Brick painted over masking tape that is pulled up to reveal the joints.

4. Mix a red or red-orange brick color with burnt sienna, a little orange, and some white paint. Test and adjust the color. Paint the brick stencil pattern onto the spattered base and allow it to dry.

5. Pull up the tape and then spatter the brick with a very fine coating of the mortar color and a coarse spatter of vandyke brown.

6. Prepare a very dilute mixture of white to use as a glaze. The paint should look like dilute skim milk. Determine from which side of the stage light will be coming for the scene in which the brick appears. Using a brush about two-thirds the width of the brick, paint less than half of each brick in a random pattern on each corner facing the source of light.

7. An optional highlight and shadow may be added to give the brick extra dimensionality. Using white, paint each brick with a very narrow line (⅛" wide) along half the top edge and the side facing the light. Then, using vandyke brown, paint the edge of the brick away from the light and most of the bottom edge to create a shadow line. Allow the top and bottom lines to taper off near the center of each brick (Figure 4–23).

Brick #2

1. Base coat the entire area with a brick color mixed from burnt sienna, orange, and white. Test and adjust the color before making a general application.

FIGURE 4–23
Painted brick wall with glazes for highlight.

2. At each side of the bricked area, mark the location of each horizontal joint, normally about 4" apart. At the top and bottom edges, mark one-half the width of each brick, every 5". With red chalk on the string, snap a chalkline on each set of marks. There should be a chalkline grid on the scenery about 4" × 5".

3. Mix a mortar color by adding a small amount of raw umber to white paint. This shall be used to paint the joint lines between the bricks. Use a ½" or ¾" wide lining brush and a straightedge. Remember: only every *other vertical* line is to be painted to obtain the image of staggered bricks on a wall.

4. Sponge the entire wall with burnt umber (Figure 4–24).

5. Determine which side of the stage will have the source of light for this scene. Dilute the mortar color and sponge a small amount of it on the side of the brick facing the light and on the upper edge of each brick.

FIGURE 4–24
Brick joints lined and texture applied with a sponge.

179

6. An optional highlight and shadow may be added to give the brick extra dimensionality. Using white, paint each brick with a very narrow line (⅛" wide) along approximately half the top edge and the side facing the light. Then, using vandyke brown, paint the edge of the brick away from the light and most of the bottom edge. Allow the top and bottom lines to taper off near the center of each brick.

Stone Wall

1. Mix a light grey color composed of 6 parts white and 1 part black. Evenly divide the mixture into two separate buckets. Add ¼ part of navy blue paint to one bucket and an equal amount of burnt sienna to the other bucket. The paints should be medium grey warm and medium grey cold. Base coat the area to become stones with these paints using a random wet-blend technique (Figure 4–25).

FIGURE 4–25
A block wall painted with a sponge to create highlight and shadow (Charley's Aunt). (Courtesy Theatre UNI, University of Northern Iowa.)

2. Mix a mortar color composed of 10 parts white and 1 part raw umber. Study an actual or painted stone wall. Using a 1½" lining brush, paint the joints between what will become the stones. Rotate the brush and roll it on to its side to paint various-width lines between each of the stones. Try to give lots of variety to the shape and size of the stones.

3. Pour some of the warm base color into two separate buckets and pour some of the cool base color into two separate buckets as well. Add some white to one bucket of each color to make a highlight and some black to the other bucket of each color to make a shade.

4. Using the highlight colors interchangeably but each with its own sponge, sponge the center of each stone and the side toward the source of light. Then, using the darkened paints, sponge all the edges facing away from the source of light to create shadow. This painting technique is especially effective if vines or some kind of foliage is painted over it.

Foliage (Generic Tree) (Figure 4–26)

1. Paint the area behind the foliage with whatever is to be seen through the trees.

2. To paint the bark, prepare a medium grey-brown mixture by mixing 4 parts white with 3 parts vandyke brown and 3 parts burnt umber. Test and adjust the color. Base coat the trunk and all the branches of the tree.

3. Mix a highlight color by adding white to the base paint and a shadow color by adding black to it. Paint the highlight and then the shadow on the bark by pulling a 1" lining brush down the length of the tree while continually rolling the brush from the flat side to the edge and back again. Be sure to work free-hand more or less following the contour of the trunk and limbs. Do not use a straightedge. There should be several long vertical rows of heavily textured bark. Paint the branches in this manner, making the bark on the smaller limbs less severe.

4. Prepare some dark green, chrome oxide green, emerald green, and finally a very light green made from 1 part emerald green and 8 parts white. These paints will be used for the foliage.

5. Foliage is painted by slapping the flat side of a fitch against the scenery and leaving an imprint of the bristles. The brush should be constantly rotated to a new orientation so that the leaves are applied in various directions. These brushes are fairly thick, with the bristles arranged in somewhat of a fan shape. Sometimes trim, lay-in, or lining brushes can be used to paint foliage as well.

Start with the leaves around the branches. These leaves are the oldest, darkest, most mature, and least exposed to light. Use the darkest color green and a brush about 3" wide. Dip the brush in the paint and

FIGURE 4–26
Detail of a forest drop.

181

slap the scenery with it. Concentrate the painting in the area of the upper trunk and close to the branches. Be sure to allow the background and branches to show through the clusters of leaves.

6. Select the next lightest color and apply another group of leaves. These grow further out from the branches and the center of the tree to form most of the ball of foliage in heavy clusters. Use a 2" foliage brush.

7. The new leaves will be the next lightest color and are all around the outer portion of the ball of leaves. They occur individually and in small clusters. These leaves are smaller than the medium leaves; use a 1" to 1½" foliage or lining brush.

8. The lightest color is the highlight, which is seen on leaves facing the source of light. Determine the direction of the source of light and paint several clusters of leaves on that side of the ball of foliage. Also, paint some additional leaf clusters on other sides of the tree where light might strike leaves directly.

9. If needed, fill in the bottom side of the ball of foliage opposite the extreme highlight with some additional large dark leaves.

Ivy, bushes, brush, and other foliage can be painted in similar impressionistic styles by modifying the layout and leaf size (Figure 4–25). This is clearly not a realistic style of painting. Although it works well on the proscenium stage when seen in shadows or from a distance, it is not especially effective when brightly lit or close to the audience, unless it is consistent with the theatricality of the rest of the design.

Plaster

Plastered walls are among the easiest textured effects to achieve. The walls may be in good condition and perhaps even freshly painted, or they may be old and cracked with peeling paint, or somewhere between these extremes. The wall is simply base coated with cross-hatched strokes and then spattered using any one of the techniques described above. A new, smooth, or freshly painted wall is implied best by an even spatter applied with a garden sprayer. A smooth consistent texture in low-contrast colors works well. A light yellow wall, for instance, can be base coated with a mixture of white and yellow ocher; a dark spatter is mixed by adding additional yellow ocher in the base color. If a stronger color is desired, straight yellow ocher or raw sienna could be used for the spatter. The dark spatter should be followed by a spattering of the base color mixed with white or with straight white paint.

If this light yellow wall were in an old, dirty room, the same base coat and spatter colors could be used with dark, murky shadows, stains on the wall, and dirty corners suggested by applying a thicker layer of the dark spatter and shading it heavily into the corners. Older plaster usually has a coarser appearance. This is best accomplished by using the hand slap or toss spatter techniques and higher-contrast spatter colors, such as a darker brown or even a complementary color, in this case violet.

Tricks such as showing the location where a photo used to hang on the wall can be accomplished by covering a rectangular area with a piece of cardboard or paper while the spatter is being applied and then removing the covering to expose a lighter-colored wall area.

The cracks in plaster can be painted with a stiff feather dipped into the dark spattering color. The edge is used to paint fine cracks, and areas of fractured paint can be achieved by turning the feather to pull it sideways, obtaining a mass of thin lines (Figure 4–27). A little highlight painted alongside the dark cracks strengthens the effect.

FIGURE 4–27
Cracks in plaster painted with a feather.

Stucco

Stucco is a kind of plaster used on the exterior of buildings, especially the half-timbered houses of Gothic England. It is easily painted with a few simple techniques (Figure 4–28).

1. Base coat the scenery with a mixture of approximately 1 part yellow ocher and 8 parts white.

2. Pour about 1" of white paint in a bucket and add enough of the base paint to make a new color that is just off-white. Also prepare a dilute mixture of yellow ocher. Using the widest brush available, dry

FIGURE 4–28
Stucco painted by dry brushing in an arc.

brush over the base coat with the darker paint in randomly placed, overlapping, semicircular strokes. Repeat with the off-white paint.

3. Using either the hand slap or the toss, spatter the painted area with the off-white paint, the yellow ocher paint, and a mixture of 1 part raw umber and 3 parts yellow ocher.

Marble

Marble often appears in temples and government buildings. Although there are several hundred kinds of marble, audiences generally assume the presence of veining as an indication of the material. Study a photo or actual sample of marble in preparation for painting (Figure 4–29).

FIGURE 4–29

Marble painted on a wet-blended base then dribbling over the top, followed by veining painted with a feather.

1. Prepare a fairly thick mixture of white paint and pour it into two buckets. In one bucket, slowly add small amounts of raw sienna until the paint looks like coffee-with-cream. In the second bucket, add burnt sienna until the paint is about as dark as the first color. Both paints should be mixed to the consistency of heavy cream. Prepare some additional white paint with a normal painting consistency.

2. Using these thick mixtures of raw and burnt sienna, paint a wet blend on the scenery. Some of the paint should blend, and some should just border the other color without blending. Paint an area no larger than 4'-0" × 4'-0".

3. While the base coat is still wet, dribble the white paint over it. The dribbles should hit the wet paint and blend, bleed, and run; some will simply remain as large dots. The scenery can be lifted a little and tilted to encourage movement of the dribbles. The white paint will behave differently on various parts of the surface depending on the wetness of the base coat. Blending into the edge of previously painted sections, repeat the process of wet blending and dribbling in 4'-0" × 4'-0" areas until the entire surface has been base coated. Allow the paint to dry.

4. Mix the veining colors. Veins in marble are usually of two or three different colors that may be related or that may have quite a bit of contrast. Mix a light sky blue and a very deep blue, and reclaim the bucket of white paint that was used for dribbling. Use a feather to paint the veins. The darkest lines should be painted first. Hold the feather by its very end. Dip it into the paint and then paint the veining, moving the feather on its edge in crisp lines and then sideways to paint sudden masses of fine veins. Keep the lines varied but somewhat parallel. After veining the entire surface with the dark color, add some veins with the light blue and finally a few more with the white. The white should be considered a highlight and used in a very limited way.

5. Add a little bit of black to the darkest veining color. Using any of the spattering techniques, apply a very fine spatter to the surface of the marble and repeat the spatter with white paint.

6. Add only enough water to some white glue to make it possible to brush onto the scenery. Coat the entire marbled surface with the glue to give it a slight gloss. The more dilute the glue, the less gloss will be achieved.

Wallpaper

Wallpaper is one of the most effective means to give character to an interior setting. There are endless ways to create the effect, including the use of real wallpaper.

Real Wallpaper

It is not uncommon to find inexpensive wallpaper at stores having clearance sales or at Goodwill stores. When available at a reasonable cost, real wallpaper can be a practical way to finish a setting if a sufficient quantity of glare-free paper in an appropriate color and pattern can be purchased. The wallpaper can be attached with staples or glued with wallpaper paste or wheat paste. Care must be taken to align the patterns properly and to smooth the seams.

Real wallpaper can be a practical solution to finish a setting. However, it is often difficult to find an appropriate paper to use that is within the budget and color range. In addition, matching patterns from strip to strip is a time consuming and annoying task. There are both simple and complex painting techniques that can be used to create attractive wallpaper for much less expense, and several are less time consuming than applying real wallpaper.

Wallpaper #1

1. Add enough purple paint to a bucket of white to make a pleasant pastel lavender color. Using a crosshatch stroke, base coat the setting.

2. Mix some purple paint with a little bit of black to make a very dark purple color. Put about 1" of white paint in a second bucket and add enough of the pastel lavender base color to make a lavender off-white color. Spatter the set with these two colors.

3. At the top and bottom edges of the area that is to be wallpaper, place marks over the entire set in the following spacing: 3", 8", 3", 8".

Snap a chalkline on each pair of marks. These lines should run top to bottom on the walls.

4. Using a lining brush, paint a ³⁄₄" wide line in the dark purple spatter color on each of the chalklines.

5. Using a ¹⁄₄" lining brush, paint a very narrow line with the off-white color on either side of the dark lines. When the lining is completed, there should be three painted lines at each chalkline: a ¹⁄₄" off-white line, a ³⁄₄" dark purple line, and another ¹⁄₄" off-white line.

This pattern could be varied by modifying the colors used, the width of the lines, the number of lines, or the spacing between lines.

Wallpaper #2

1. Mix a pastel green color by adding emerald green to white paint. If the mixture is too intense, add just a drop of red paint to the bucket. (*Caution:* If too much red is added the mixture will turn brown!) Base coat the set with this color.

2. Prepare a bucket of yellow ocher, another of cerulean blue, and a third bucket with chrome oxide green paint. Feather dust the entire set with each of these colors. Each paint should be allowed to show through the next color but the feather dusting patterns should overlap to create a rich texture. Any other colors could be selected for this technique (Figure 4–30).

FIGURE 4–30
*Feather-dusted and dribbled wallpaper. (*The Odd Couple*). (Courtesy Theatre UNI, University of Northern Iowa.)*

Wallpaper #3

1. Mix a pastel pink color by adding magenta, red, or dark red to white paint. Base coat the setting with this color using crosshatched brush strokes.

2. Spatter the entire set with magenta.

3. Obtain a roll of any nonabsorbent paper such as butcher, kraft, or even computer printout paper. Using a band saw, cut a 5" wide roll of paper off the side of the big roll. At the top and bottom edges of the wallpaper area, place marks 17" apart the entire width of the set. Roll out a piece of the 5" wide paper and place it next to each set of marks. Using either masking tape or staples, attach the 5" wide strip of paper to the flat. This will result in exposed 12" wide strips and covered 5" wide strips.

4. Mix two colors for feather dusting, perhaps a purple and a deep red. Feather dust the entire setting, allowing the paint to lap onto the paper strips. Remove the paper strips to expose a pattern of a textured stripe and an untextured plain stripe.

5. The feather-dusted stripes can be left plain or a more complete effect can be achieved by painting a ¼" wide line with one of the spatter colors on either side of the feather dusted areas. Once again, any variety of colors may be used, the width of the stripes may be varied, a muslin stomp may be substituted for the feather duster, or more or less lining may be applied (Figure 4–31).

FIGURE 4–31
Feather-dusted stripped wallpaper. (Charley's Aunt). (Courtesy Theatre UNI, University of Northern Iowa.)

Exactly the same technique of preparing a surface with a base coat, spatter, mask, and then texturing over it can be used with other painting techniques such as scumbling, dry brushing in hatched patterns, or even additional spatters in other colors. The idea is to create stripes by coating one portion of the wall with more treatments than the other portion. The variety of techniques that can be used or combined to accomplish this is endless.

Wallpaper #4

1. Mix a very pastel orange color by adding orange to white paint. Base coat the setting with this color. (*Caution*: Orange is a very difficult color to use on stage—keep it very pale.)

2. Prepare a paint roller for scumbling by tightly wrapping it with masking tape as described on page 170; slip it onto the roller frame and attach a long handle to it.

3. Standing at the bottom of the scenery, dip the roller into some golden yellow paint and test it on some cardboard to be sure the pattern will appear. Place the roller along the edge of the scenery and very carefully move it up the wall in a straight line. A vertical pattern of parallel impressions should appear. Paint another line of texture next to and parallel with the first line. Continue working across the set in this manner. If the paints have been properly chosen and mixed, when completed this effect should suggest watered silk or moiré wallpaper.

Wallpaper #5

The most common technique to paint wallpaper on stage is stenciling (Figure 4–32). Any pattern may be designed and it can be painted over any texture or combined with one of the stripes described above.

FIGURE 4–32
A stenciled pattern.

Wallpaper #6

A stencil can be replaced with a stamp to create a wallpaper effect. Once again, any texture or any stripe may provide a base for the effect.

THREE-DIMENSIONAL TEXTURES

All of the textures described so far are painted to create the illusion of a three-dimensional surface. At times it is possible or even necessary to use actual textures to achieve the appropriate effect. The combination of an applied three-dimensional texture and paint can be easier, quicker, and more effective than trying to create an illusion of texture with paint alone.

Plastic Foams

A setting may be constructed from any structure to form a base onto which plastic foams are applied and treated to become three-dimensional textures.

For most scenic applications, either of two products generically called *styrofoam* may be used. One of these materials is a coarse textured blue board manufactured by Dow Chemical Company under the brand name Styrofoam. It is available from lumberyards in 16" and 24" wide sheets 1" to 4" thick and 8'-0" long. The other material is called *bead board* and appears to be composed of the white foam pellets similar to those used to make disposable coffee cups. It is available ¹/₂" to 4" thick in 4'-0" × 8'-0" sheets. Either product may be used for the textures described below. However, safety precautions must be noted and carefully observed. *(CAUTION:* **Styrofoam [the blue material] yields cyanide gas when cut, burned, or sanded. Work with this material only in adequate ventilation! A toxic level will cause headache, nausea, and drowsiness. In the event of illness, immediately remove the victim to fresh air. If symptoms continue or are severe, seek medical treatment immediately!)** Both bead board and styrofoam give off odious fumes when burned. Work only in a well-ventilated atmosphere to prevent excessive build-up. Finally, both plastic foams produce annoying dust when the materials are cut or sanded. Use a particle mask when performing these tasks and clean the work area well after use.

Brick #1

1. Draw the brick pattern onto a piece of foam. Pull the edge of a heated electric charcoal lighter along each line, burning the point into the plastic foam. Be careful not to burn all the way through the plastic (Figure 4–33).

2. Turn the charcoal lighter flat, and within the outline of each brick burn off a slight recess so that each brick surface is irregular and uneven.

FIGURE 4–33
Styrofoam brick formed and textured with an electric charcoal lighter.

189

3. Add a little bit of raw umber to some white paint to make slightly warm, very light grey base mortar color. Base coat the foam brick with this paint.

4. Using either the hand slap or the toss, spatter the dried base coat with both vandyke brown and white.

5. Mix a red or red-orange brick color from burnt sienna, orange, and white. Using a paint roller, base coat the brick over the mortar paint.

6. Prepare a very dilute mixture of burnt umber to use as a glaze. Determine which side of the stage light will be coming from for the scene in which this set appears. Using a brush about two-thirds the width of each brick, paint about half of each brick in a random pattern on the corner opposite the source of light (Figure 4–34).

FIGURE 4–34
Three-dimensional styrofoam brick on a set for Street Scene; *Shan Ayers, scenic artist. (Courtesy Theatre UNI, University of Northern Iowa).*

Brick #2

1. Draw a brick pattern onto the plastic foam. Prepare a mixture of 2 parts lacquer thinner and 1 part water. (*CAUTION:* **Work in a well-ventilated space and wear hand and eye protection.**) Use a narrow lining brush and a straightedge to paint the joints between the brick with the lacquer thinner mixture. Free-hand lines may be painted but will be very rough; they should be reserved for stones and rock.

2. Spatter and dribble the lacquer thinner mixture over the entire surface of the brick (Figure 4–35).

3. Prepare a mixture of burnt sienna and white to produce a light-red brick color. Base coat the brick with that color. Allow the paint to puddle in the textured areas and do not be concerned about small areas that do not accept paint. This variety will contribute to the appearance of the brick.

4. Mix a little bit of raw sienna into some white paint to make a mortar color. Paint the joints with this mixture.

Of course, other color brick could be made and the brick can be enlarged or reduced in size. In fact, by adjusting the space between the lines and altering the paint colors, concrete block or old stone walls could easily be created.

FIGURE 4–35
Styrofoam brick formed and textured with lacquer thinner.

Old Granite/Marble Walls

1. Use only 1" or thicker blue Styrofoam for this process. (*CAUTION:* **Work out of doors or in extremely good ventilation. Provide a fire extinguisher and bucket of water to deal with emergencies.**)

2. Prepare a mixture of light beige latex paint. Do not dilute the paint. Set up a butane or propane torch with a very wide nozzle. The nozzle provided for paint scraping is best.

3. Working in areas about 2'-0" × 2'-0", spatter the foam with the paint. While the paint is still wet, burn the surface of the plastic with the torch. The foam that does not have paint on it will melt quickly, developing a coarse glossy texture with some portions turning black. The paint will resist the heat, may turn colors, and will dry from the heat (Figure 4–36).

Larger areas may be painted and burned at the same time after the technique is mastered. Care must be taken not to burn all the way through the Styrofoam. The blue Styrofoam boards are manufactured

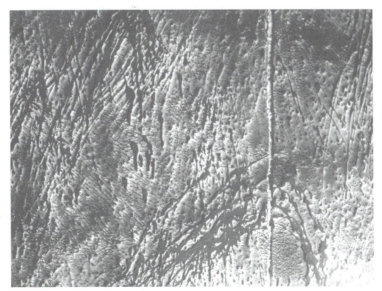

FIGURE 4–36
Three-dimenisionial granite or marble made from burned styrofoam.

191

with a chemical that makes them self-extinguishing when the source of heat is removed. If an area starts to burn on its own, remove the flame and splash some water on it.

A welder's acetylene torch may also be used in this process if controlled very carefully and no oxygen is put into the mixture. Once again, a broad tip should be used on the nozzle. Acetylene produces a black soot that will deposit on the foam and mix with the paint; this adds an exciting dimension to the texture.

Rock and Stone Walls #1

1. Roughly cut individual rocks or stones from 2" or thicker plastic foam. Use a hacksaw blade or a band saw to make the cuts.

2. Burn the surface of each rock with the flame from a butane or propane torch. The flame should smooth the edges and lightly seal the surface of the plastic (Figure 4–37).

FIGURE 4–37
A rock cut out of styrofoam and then burned with a torch.

3. Paint a base coat of light blue-grey or beige latex paint onto the stones. Complete coverage is not necessary and puddling is acceptable.

4. Using dilute glazes of red-grey or blue-grey, paint shadows in some of the depressions and sponge over other portions of each rock.

5. Using a mortar color, base coat the surface on which the rocks are to be attached and then spatter it with white and grey or black.

6. Glue each rock to the wall using a special foam cement or panel adhesive.

Rock and Stone Walls #2

1. Attach 2" or thicker sheets of plastic foam to the scenery with panel adhesive. It might be necessary to push 6d nails through the foam into the supporting surface while the adhesive is drying.

2. Draw the pattern of a rock wall on the foam. Prepare a mixture of 2 parts lacquer thinner and 1 part water. (*CAUTION*: **Work in a well-ventilated space and wear hand and eye protection.**) Paint the joints between each rock with the lacquer thinner mixture. Allow to dry thoroughly.

3. Burn the surface of each rock with the flame from a butane or propane torch. The flame should smooth the edges and lightly seal the surface of the plastic.

4. Paint as described under Stone and Rock Walls #1.

Joint Compound

Joint compound is the material used to cover the seams between pieces of drywall in buildings. It is heavy, inexpensive, and easy to use, and it cleans up with water. The material is available in paste form from lumberyards in small quantities and in 5-gallon pails. There are no serious health hazards with this material, but as with all compounds, some users might have a skin reaction to extensive exposure.

Stucco Walls #1

1. Apply a very thin coating of joint compound to the surface of a flat.

2. Take a single sheet of newspaper and loosely ball it up. Press it into the joint compound on the flat and spread another very thin layer of joint compound over the newspaper. Depending on the desired texture, the newspaper can be pressed quite flat onto the surface or may be left very three-dimensional, creating an extremely deep texture. Do not move the scenery for at least an hour after the joint compound has been applied (Figure 4–38).

3. After the joint compound has dried, base coat the scenery in the desired color. If the texture is extremely coarse, it will be easier to apply the base coat with a sprayer, although brushing is possible, just tedious. Spatter with one or two colors of paint (Figure 4–39).

FIGURE 4–38
Stucco made from joint compound and newspaper.

FIGURE 4–39
A three-dimensional wall made from joint compound and newspaper (A Flea in Her Ear). (Courtesy Theatre UNI, University of Northern Iowa).

193

Stucco Walls #2

1. Spread a very thin layer of joint compound evenly over the surface of the scenery. Work in areas no larger than 5'-0" × 5'-0".

2. While the joint compound is wet, drag a wire brush through the material in broad, sweeping, random arcs, leaving the impression of the bristles. Do not move the scenery for a least an hour after this texture has been applied.

3. Brush, spray, or roll on a base coat of paint. If the texture reads clearly and there are no flat smooth areas, a spatter will not be needed. The texture can be intensified by lightly dry brushing or rolling paint in a random pattern to highlight the ridges of the joint compound (Figure 4–40).

FIGURE 4-40
Three-dimensional texture in joint compound formed with a wire brush dragged in an arc.

Stucco Walls #3

1. Working in an area no larger than 5'-0" × 5'-", spread a coating of joint compound onto the surface of the scenery.

2. While the joint compound is still wet, run fingers through it in broad, sweeping, random, overlapping arcs. Since this coating is thicker than the previous treatments, it must dry for a longer time before moving the scenery.

3. Brush, spray, or roll on a base coat of paint. If the texture reads clearly and there are no flat smooth areas, a spatter will not be needed (Figure 4–41).

Brick

1. Using ³/₄" masking tape, lay out the pattern of brick joints on the scenery. Spread a ¹/₈" thick layer of joint compound over the taped area.

2. While the compound is still wet, texture the surface all over by pressing a hand into the material and lifting straight up; then lightly

FIGURE 4–41
Three-dimensional texture in joint compound formed by means of fingers dragged through in overlapping pattens.

brush over the top of the spiked peaks that this forms to smooth them out but leave a distinctive texture on each brick.

3. After the joint compound has dried for at least 30 minutes, but no longer than 1 hour, pull up the tape, leaving the three-dimensional brick pattern. Allow the joint compound to dry thoroughly without moving the scenery (Figure 4–42).

4. Spray, roll, or brush the surface with a base coat the color of the mortar. Allow that paint to dry, and then spatter it with white and black or raw sienna.

FIGURE 4–42
Making a three-dimensional brick wall with joint compound over lines of tape.

195

Painting and Texturing

5. Using a paint roller, roll the brick color over the textured surface. Do not use a roller that is too wet or paint will run into the joints between the brick. Allow the paint to dry. The three-dimensional texture should be quite visible; however, if necessary, a spatter in highlight or shadow color might be added (Figure 4–43).

FIGURE 4–43
A three-dimenisional brick wall (The Wager). *(Courtesy Theatre UNI, University of Northern Iowa)*

Rough Plaster

1. Spread a thin, variegated layer of joint compound over the surface of the scenery. While the compound is still wet, sprinkle sawdust over it and gently press the sawdust into the compound. Allow it to dry.

2. Using a paint roller, base coat the textured scenery as desired. Spattering or any other painted texture should not be necessary.

Paper and White Glue

A variety of textures and effects can be created by gluing different kinds of papers to the surface of scenery. The papers provide a three-dimensional texture that is easily highlighted with basic painting techniques, especially dry brushing.

Peeling Paint (Figure 4–44)

1. Coat an area of the scenery about 1'-0" wide by 4'-0" long with undiluted white glue.

2. Lay a piece of toilet paper loosely on top of the glued area. It must *not* lay flat and smooth: *do* allow air bubbles, ripples, and all kinds of flaws to occur. Lay another piece of toilet paper next to the first, and continue laying toilet paper on the glued area until it is entirely covered with bubbled, twisted, wadded strips of material (Figure 4–44A).

196

FIGURE 4–44
Peeling paint texture. (A) Lay toilet paper over moist white glue. (B) Brush white glue over the top of the toilet paper and allow to dry. (C) After base coating, dry brush over the textured area, picking up the three-dimensional texture with the highlight color.

3. Brush over the top of the toilet paper with additional white glue. This will flatten the paper, press the air out of the bubbles, and pull and tear the paper in the direction the brush moves (Figure 4–44B). Repeat over the entire area and allow the materials to dry.

4. Brush, roll, or spray a base coat on the textured area. Allow it to dry.

5. Lightly dry brush over the texture with at least two colors. The dry brush should apply a highlight and shadow on the texture without painting a heavy wood grain (Figure 4–44C).

Clapboard Siding (Figure 4–45)

1. Paint an area of the setting with undiluted white glue.

2. Unfold several brown paper hand towels, the kind that are put in paper towel dispensers in public restrooms.

3. While the glue is still wet, lay out a row of towels along the bottom edge of the scenery. Each towel should lie flat in an even row and abut the one next to it.

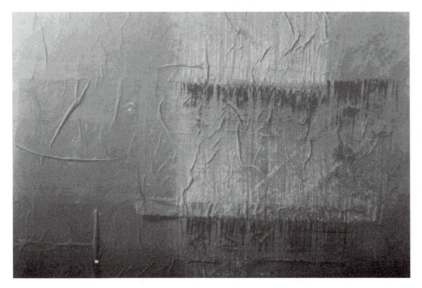

FIGURE 4–45
Shingles or siding. (A) Lay paper towels in a row over moist white glue and paint white glue over the towels. (B) After the towels have dried, base coat and dry brush over the towels.

4. Dilute some white glue into a mixture of 1 part water to 2 parts glue. Coat the top of the first row of towels with that mixture.

5. Lay out the next row of towels so the bottom edge overlaps the top edge of the first row of towels and press the towels into the wet glue. The joints between the towels of the second row should line up with the centerline of each towel in the first row. Repeat the pattern until all of the scenery has been covered with towels and coated with glue. Allow it to dry.

6. Paint a base coat on the towels and allow it to dry.

7. Mix a highlight color by adding the base paint to some white; mix a shadow color by adding some vandyke brown to the base paint. Using a dry-brush technique, and painting from bottom to top, paint the bottom edge of each row of towels with the highlight color. The highlight should be strong at the bottom edge and taper off as it extends 3" to 4" toward the top of each towel.

8. Using a dry brush technique and painting from top to bottom, paint the top edge of each row of towels with the shadow color. The shadow should be strong at the top edge and taper off as it extends 4" to 5" down toward the bottom of each towel. The two colors may leave an untextured void at the center or may overlap and blend into each other (Figure 4–45).

The same technique may be used to paint shingles. Heavily textured paper towels may be substituted for the smoother brown towels to achieve a different effect. Any other paper might be used in the same manner to attain the effect of siding, shingles, tile, or other overlapping materials.

COMMERCIAL FINISHES

There are several commercial finishes that can be used on scenery and props. All are available from paint, hardware, and discount stores. Most of these materials are compounded with solvents that require awareness of safety concerns, including flammability, toxic vapor buildup, particle accumulation, and potential skin or eye damage. (*CAUTION:* **The safety precautions on the label of all of these materials must be read carefully and fully understood: the hazards are extensive!**)

Each of these materials requires its own special solvent for dilution and clean-up, None of the materials are water based. Using water or the improper solvent will ruin brushes, destroy equipment, and gum up plumbing. A separate set of brushes should be kept for use with these finishes. If that is not practical, after brushes and equipment have been thoroughly cleaned with the proper solvent, each item should be washed with soap and warm water to remove the solvent cleaner and prepare the equipment for use with water-based scene paints again. *CAUTION:* **It is illegal to dispose of most paints and almost all solvents in sink or floor drains, toilets, or any other means leading to the sewer system. It is also illegal to dump these materials where they will soak into the ground. All paints and solvents must be disposed of in containers approved for haz-**

ardous waste and processed according to hazardous waste guidelines.

Aerosol Paint

Aerosol paints, available as (oil-based) enamels or lacquers, are among the handiest of the commercial finishes. These paints come in a broad array of colors from basic black, white, and earth tones to fluorescent colors and metallics. They are convenient, easy to use, and not too expensive. Some of the paints are manufactured with special characteristics such as quick-drying coatings and heat or corrosion resistant finishes. They may be sprayed over most materials; however, some of these paints react with other finishes and certain plastics and will cause damage. (*CAUTION*: **Always read the warnings on the label of aerosol paint.**)

CAUTION: **Aerosol paints should only be used in a well-ventilated atmosphere. However, they cannot be used in a drafty space or the paint will be blown away from the surface, coat unevenly, and dry in ripples and waves. It is usually better to apply two or three thin coats of aerosol paint than to attempt to get complete coverage with a single coating.**

When using aerosol paints:

1. Read the instructions and safety precautions on the label.

2. Always work in a well-ventilated atmosphere.

3. Shake the can well.

4. If a great deal of spray painting is to be done, **wear a particle mask.**

5. Hold the can about 12" away from the surface to be painted and spray only a light coating onto the surface.

6. Allow the paint to dry as recommended on the can, and repeat the coating two or three times as necessary.

7. When done painting, clean the nozzle by holding the can upside down and spraying into the air until all paint ceases to come out of the can (when clean, the can will continue to spray propellent but no material will come out). This will prevent clogging the nozzle and preserve the life of the can of paint.

8. Clean up any overspray with the appropriate solvent.

Wood Stains

Commercial wood stains are used to give transparent color to wood finishes. The stains come in a variety of colors that have different effects on different kinds of woods. Each color should be tested on the actual wood to be stained before an all-over application is made. Wood stains are manufactured as a water-based and as an oil-based material; each requires a different solvent for dilution and clean-up; check the label for clarification. (*CAUTION*: **Rubber gloves should be worn when applying any stain.**)

1. Read the instructions and safety precautions on the label.

2. *Stir*—do not shake—the stain thoroughly and frequently to prevent settling of the pigment.

Always prepare a sample stained area as follows: Use a clean brush in good condition to apply an even coating of stain onto the wood, moving the brush only in the long direction of the grain. Allow the stain to rest undisturbed on the surface of the wood. Every 10 minutes use a soft, lint-free cloth to wipe the stain off a section of wood to determine the depth of color achieved. Keep careful track of the time elapsed. After the desired color apparently has been achieved, allow the wiped-off areas to dry overnight and again check the color. The stained wood will change slightly in appearance after a 24-hour drying time. Select the color desired and use that timing to guide the work.

Color the wood by brushing stain on in the direction of the grain, allowing it to stand the time determined in the sampling process; then using a lint-free cloth, wipe off the excess stain in the same direction it was applied. Allow the stain to dry overnight and coat it with a protective finish.

Varnish

Varnish is the most commonly used protective and gloss finish for woods. It is coated over well-sanded raw or stained materials and can even be used over scene paints. It dries to a hard, mar-resistant finish that may have a low sheen (satin finish) or may be shiny (gloss finish). There are several different kinds of varnishes available, including interior, exterior, marine, and polyurethane, any of which may be used for the stage. Usually the least expensive varnish is the most practical. Most varnishes dilute and clean up with turpentine, mineral spirits, or paint thinner.

1. Read the instructions and safety precautions on the label.

2. Wipe the surface clean of all dirt and dust.

3. *Stir*—do not shake—the varnish.

Use a good brush to apply varnish in long, overlapping strokes in the long direction of the wood. After a board or section has been coated, hold the brush very lightly and draw it the entire length of the board in a smooth, straight line. Do not stop and restart strokes. Repeat the long, continuous strokes over the entire board. Allow the varnish to dry in a dust-free and draft-free area.

Lacquer

Lacquer is a plastic-like material that serves a similar function to varnish. It is very fast drying. *It is also more flammable than varnish and may damage paints over which it is coated.* There are several different kinds of lacquer that may be used, the most practical of which is interior or exterior gloss lacquer. (*CAUTION:* **Lacquer and lacquer thinner**

are highly flammable. Lacquer produces an intense vapor that will cause headaches and nausea; it should be used in a well-ventilated environment.) Clean-up is only with lacquer thinner.

1. Read the instructions and safety precautions on the label.

   2. Wipe the surface clean of all dirt and dust.

   3. *Stir*—do not shake—the lacquer.

Use a good brush or paint roller and apply lacquer in long, overlapping strokes in the long direction of the wood. After a board or section has been coated, draw the brush or roller the entire length of the board in a smooth, straight line. Do not stop and restart strokes. Repeat the long, continuous strokes over the entire board or area. Allow the lacquer to dry in a dust-free and draft-free area.

Shellac

Shellac is used as a wood sealant in preparation for other painting procedures such as surfaces that would resist direct coating with scene paints or that might absorb excessive amounts of paint. Shellac contains a colored filler that may be either orange or white; there are also filled shellacs for special purposes. Neither shellac nor surfaces coated with shellac are water resistant. Shellac is cleaned up with denatured alcohol.

CONCLUSION

The appearance of a setting depends on the combination of the ground plan, construction of scenic elements, and the finishing processes applied to them. Texturing and painting greatly affect the character of the setting. They are primary to the look of a show and should never be considered as afterthoughts in the process of planning a production. Traditional materials and methods of scene painting may be used or more innovative techniques can be applied to enrich or simplify the painting task. The choices available are numerous, but the importance of those choices cannot be underestimated. Care must be taken to prepare items and surfaces properly for painting and then determine the best painting techniques. *Best* may mean the fastest, or the least expensive, or the easiest, or the most dramatic. The choice becomes a matter of the need of the production and no choice is absolutely right or wrong. Once the processes and materials of texturing and painting have been determined, the appropriate colors must be selected and mixed to achieve the desired effect. Color mixing, whether it is the pouring together of pigments or the selection of upholstery to go with drapes, is a very demanding artistic process. It must be approached with care and understanding of the purpose and effect of each choice. The effects, techniques, and materials described in this chapter will gain value and meaning by a clear understanding of color and color mixing described in Chapter 5.

CHAPTER 5

Color

INTRODUCTION

Color has significant influence on our lives. Although we may not be conscious of it, color contributes to our moods and attitudes and affects our choice of clothing, automobiles, and even the food we eat. Some colors evoke such strong sensations they instantly communicate attitudes or ideas: bright red suggests danger, white evokes a sense of purity or sterility, green implies nature, and black suggests death. These responses to color contribute to choices made by artists and designers. In the performing arts, color may be the most vital element of design. Not only do colors bear significant meanings, they contribute to the interest and attention of audiences. Properly employed, color can be used to control focus and to create psychological and emotional effects. It can create a sense of form, style, and mood and suggest the period or locale of a performance. With all of these attributes, color is one of the most important elements on the stage.

THE COMPONENTS OF COLOR

Color is also one of the most challenging elements with which to work. Unlike other design elements such as line, mass, or texture, color is multifaceted. It consists of three interrelated components: hue, value, and chroma. The hue of a color is its name, distinguishing it from all other colors; the value is the whiteness or blackness of a color; and chroma is the brightness or intensity of a color. Each of these components may be treated individually or in relation to the others.

Hue

Hue is the term used to differentiate one color from another. In technical terms, individual colors are made from light. When a beam of light is passed through a prism, it produces stripes of color like a rainbow (Figure 5–1). Each colored stripe is composed of a different wavelength of light. A colored material reflects one or more of these wavelengths. Each hue is distinguished by the wavelengths of light it reflects. On this basis hues can be arranged in a logical pattern on a color wheel.

A basic **color wheel** (Figure C–2) is composed of three primary colors, three secondary colors, and six intermediate colors, equally spaced around the perimeter of a circle. The **primary colors**—red, yellow, and blue—are essential to the formation of the color wheel. Primary colors may be mixed with each other in varying proportions to form other hues, but mixing two or more hues together will not create primary colors. This color system depends on the previous existence of

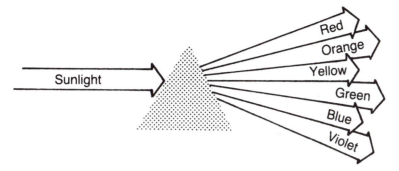

FIGURE 5–1
*When sunlight is passed
through a glass prism, the
beam of light is divided into
individual wavelengths. Each
wavelength is seen as a
different color of light.*

the primary colors. **Secondary colors** are created by mixing equal proportions of two adjacent primary hues. The secondary colors are orange (red plus yellow), green (yellow plus blue), and violet (blue plus red). They occur halfway between the primary colors on the perimeter of the color wheel. **Intermediate colors** are mixed from equal amounts of neighboring primary and secondary colors. The intermediate colors are red-orange, yellow-orange, yellow-green, blue-green, blue-violet, and red-violet. They occur halfway between each primary and secondary hue on the color wheel. An almost infinite variety of additional colors can be mixed by combining two or more hues, located in any position on the color wheel.

The position of a hue on the color wheel gives its characteristics and its relationship to other colors. **Analogous colors** are located next to each other on the color wheel (Figure 5–2). Thus, orange and red-orange are analogous; both colors contain a quantity of a common hue, in this case orange. Orange and yellow-orange are also analogous colors, with orange common to both hues. Continuing around the circle, yellow-orange and yellow are analogous colors, but yellow is the common hue rather than orange. Analogous pairs of colors can be listed all the way around the color wheel.

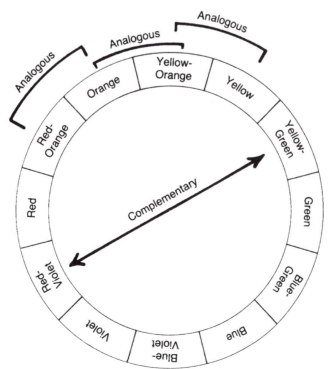

FIGURE 5–2
*The color wheel. Colors located
next to each other are analogous
hues; colors located opposite each
other are complementary hues.*

Also, two colors that are directly opposite each other on the color wheel—for example, orange and blue—have a specific relationship. Any hue directly opposite another color on the color wheel is its **complementary color**. In this way, blue and orange are complementary colors. A secondary color always occurs opposite a primary color, so that red/green and yellow/violet are pairs of complementary colors. Intermediate colors occur opposite other intermediate colors, so the complement of blue-violet is yellow-orange, the complement of yellow-green is red-violet, and red-orange is the complement of blue-green. These color pairings become important in the mixing of colors and selection of palettes.

Value

Hue describes only one characteristic of a color. In addition, a color may be bright or dull, light or dark. **Value** describes the lightness or darkness of a color. Lightness and darkness are qualities of illumination. In drawing and painting, these qualities are represented as white, grey, and black.

The **value scale** (Figure 5–3) represents the range of greys that can be mixed from black and white. Neither black nor white has any hue; they are described as **neutral** or **achromatic** (without hue) colors. When mixed together, they form a range of greys that are also neutral. An almost endless number of subtle gradations of grey can be mixed from black and white. Most artists limit the value scale to nine colors, with black at the bottom (Value 1), white at the top (Value 9), and medium grey in the middle (Value 5). Medium grey represents a totally neutral visual condition. It contains no hue and seems to consist of an equal quantity of white and black. Medium grey occurs at the center of the color wheel equidistant from all hues (Figure 5–4). Values 1 through 4 are shades and fall below the wheel; Values 6 through 9 are tints and rise above the plane of the color wheel to establish a perpendicular axis around which the hues are located.

Hues also have characteristics of lightness and darkness. Every hue has its own natural value relative to white, grey, and black. This may be seen when a chip of yellow pigment is placed next to a chip of blue and compared to black and white (Figure C–3). In this relationship, yellow appears much lighter than blue; it is more similar to white than to black. On the other hand, blue appears to be more similar to black. These are differences in the natural value of these hues. Figure C–4 shows the hues of the basic color wheel arranged in order of relative natural value.

Hues and neutrals may be treated independently to render light and shade, or they may be combined to form new colors. A hue may be mixed with white or black to form a nine-step value scale of a color (Figure C–5). Black is at the bottom of the scale (Value 1), the base hue is at the middle (Value 5), and white is at the top of the scale (Value 9). All gradations below the base hue (Values 1 through 4) are shades of the base color; all gradations above the base hue (Values 6 through 9) are tints. These nine even gradations indicate the range of values to which a color may be mixed. Many subtle gradations between each tint and shade are possible.

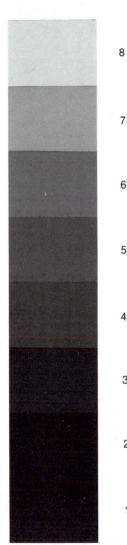

FIGURE 5–3

The value scale. This scale represents the range of grey colors that can be mixed by combining black and white. Value 1 is black, Value 5 is medium grey, and Value 9 is white.

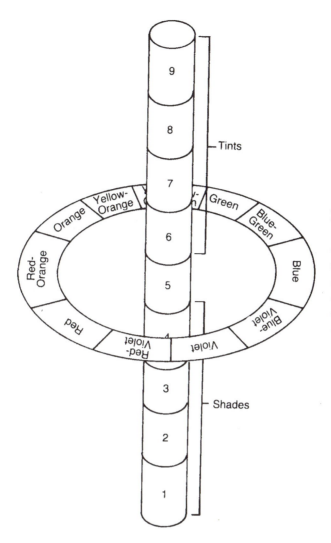

FIGURE 5–4

The value scale is a column located at the center of the color wheel. Value 5 is located on the same plane as the hues of the color wheel. Each value is equidistant from all hues on the color wheel.

Additional variety can be obtained by mixing a hue with *both* black and white *at the same time*. The seven gradations of greys that occur between black and white on the neutral value scale can be mixed in varying proportions with a hue to form **tones**. Unlike tints, which consist of a base hue plus white, or shades, which contain a base hue plus black, tones are mixed with the base hue plus white plus black. The ratio among the components of this mixture may vary widely. It may contain, for instance, one part orange, two parts black, and six parts white; or two parts orange, five parts black, and one part white; or any other proportion of hue and neutrals. These mixtures tend to subdue colors, resulting in soft, muted tones (Figure C–6).

Chroma

Hue names a color; value describes its lightness or darkness. The third component of color is **chroma**. This term refers to brightness or intensity of a color. Chroma is distinct from value. A color may be light (that is, a tint) but at the same time not be bright or intense. An example may help an observer identify chroma. Both a fire engine and a radish are red, but they are certainly not the same color. The color of the fire engine appears bright—it almost seems to glow. The radish, however, appears dull. Neither object is lighter or darker than the other; the difference in color is *brightness*. Although both objects are red, the radish has a weaker chroma. The red skin of the radish is dulled by the presence of a small quantity of green pigment, the complement of red. A color is at its strongest chroma in pure form—as it appears on the perimeter of the color wheel. The chroma of a color is weakened by the presence of its complementary hue. In this way, pure red can be made duller by adding a small amount of green pigment. Eventually, a sufficient quantity of green may be added to absorb the red color entirely; the color then becomes neutral. Any pair of complementary colors may be mixed in this manner to reduce the chroma-strength of one member of the pair, and ultimately in this way the color will be neutralized. Each hue on the color wheel requires a different quantity of additions of its complementary color to reach a neutral level. Stated another way, every hue has its own natural maximum chroma that is not equal to the maximum chroma of other hues. The 12 hues on the color wheel are listed according to strength of chroma in Table 5–1.

TABLE 5–1

Relative number of chroma steps for hues.

Color	Number of Chroma Steps
Yellow	9
Yellow-orange	8
Orange	8
Red-orange	9
Red	10
Red-violet	6
Voilet	6
Blue-violet	9
Blue	6
Blue-green	7
Green	7
Yellow-green	8

Summary of Color Terms

Color   the combination of hue, value, and chroma perceived as a result of reflected light.

Hue   the name of a color distinguishing it from all other colors, based on the wavelengths of light it reflects.

Chromatic   a color having hue.

Achromatic   a color lacking hue, including black, white, and greys mixed from black and white.

Color wheel   hues arranged around the perimeter of a circle according to the wavelengths of light each reflects.

Primary colors   hues that cannot be mixed from other colors but can be used to mix other colors. The primaries are red, blue, and yellow.

5550 PRIMING WHITE

5551 WHITE

5566 LEMON YELLOW

5567 GOLDEN YELLOW

5563 ORANGE

5562 BRIGHT RED

5560 RED

5561 DARK RED

5569 MAGENTA

5568 PURPLE

5570 TURQUOISE BLUE

5572 CERULEAN BLUE

5559 ULTRAMARINE BLUE

5573 NAVY BLUE

5552 BLACK

5571 DARK GREEN

5565 CHROME OXIDE GREEN

5564 EMERALD GREEN

5553 YELLOW OCHRE

5555 RAW SIENNA

5557 RAW UMBER

5556 BURNT SIENNA

5554 BURNT UMBER

5558 VAN DYKE BROWN

FIGURE C–1
Iddings Deep Color casein paints.

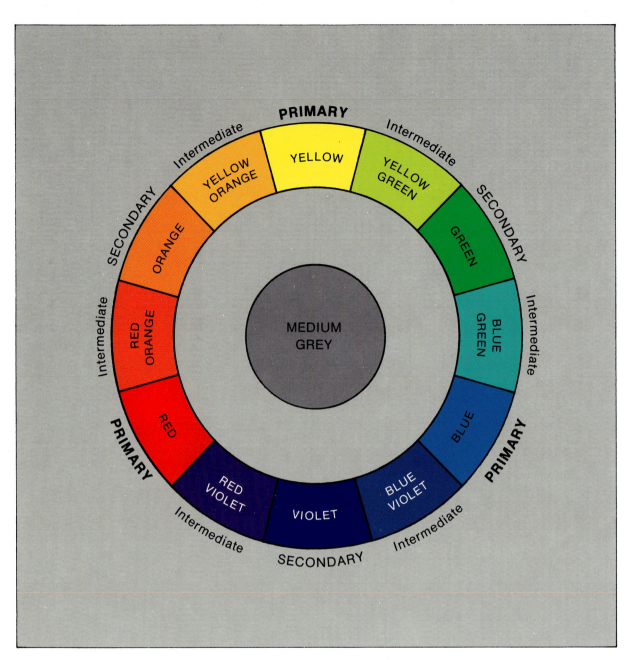

FIGURE C–2
The color wheel.

FIGURE C-3

Every hue has its own characteristic of lightness and darkness. Yellow and blue compared to black and white.

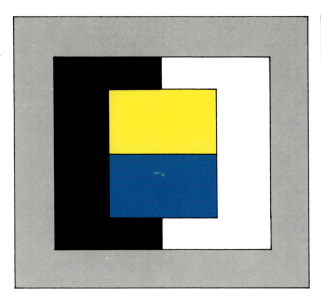

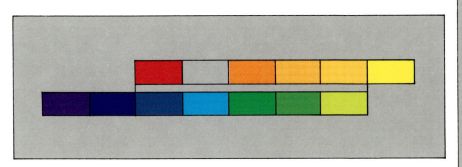

FIGURE C-4

Every hue has its own natural value. The hues of the color wheel are arranged here in order based on their natural value.

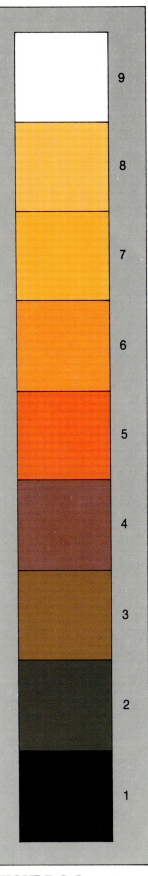

FIGURE C-5

A hue may be mixed with white and black to form a nine-step value scale in color.

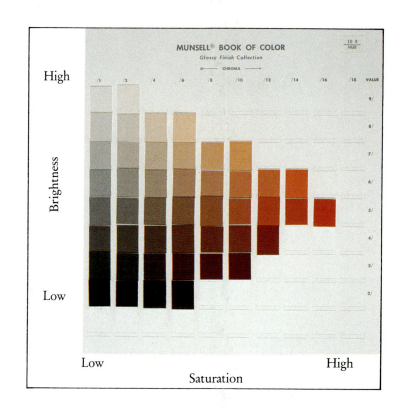

FIGURE C–6
Tones of orange.

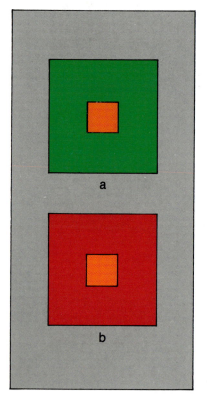

FIGURE C–7
Color perception—color temperature.

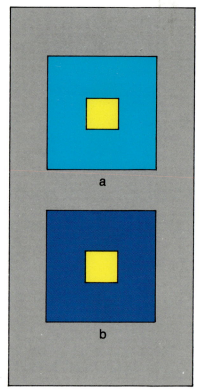

FIGURE C–8
Color perception—color perspective.

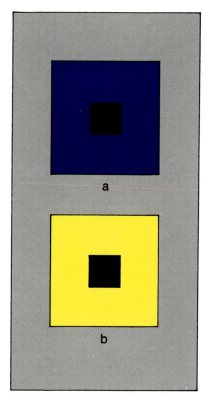

FIGURE C–9
Color perception—color perspective.

Secondary colors hues mixed from visually equal amounts of neighboring primary colors and located halfway between each primary on the color wheel. These hues are orange, violet, and green.

Intermediate colors hues mixed by combining neighboring primary and secondary colors. On a basic color wheel, these hues are red-violet, red-orange, yellow-orange, yellow-green, blue-green, and blue-violet.

Analogous colors hues located next to each other on the color wheel, such as red, red-orange, and orange.

Complementary colors hues located opposite each other on the color wheel, such as red/green or blue/orange.

Neutral colors colors without hue. These include black, white, and all greys mixed from black and white.

Value the relative lightness or darkness of a color in relation to black and white. Values are described as tints, shades, or tones.

Value scale a nine-step scale of neutral colors located on a perpendicular axis at the center of the color wheel. A chromatic value scale may be constructed from each hue and includes a base hue plus tints and shades mixed from white, black, and the base hue.

Tint colors mixed with white and located above medium (Value 5) on the value scale.

Shade colors mixed with black and located below medium (Value 5) on the value scale.

Tone colors mixed with grey.

Chroma the brightness of a color, determined by its purity as a result of the presence or absence of its complimentary color. *Intensity, brightness,* and *saturation* are frequently used as synonyms for *chroma.*

COLOR MIXING

Pure hues, as they appear on the perimeter of the color wheel, are seldom used in design. They are usually modified in some way. Colors may be combined with other hues, adjusted in value, or reduced in chroma, or all three components may be modified concurrently. A color may be created or altered in one of the following ways:

A new color may be created by mixing two or more existing hues.

A tint may be made by adding white to a color.

A shade may be mixed by adding black to a color.

A tone may be created by adding grey to a color.

A color may be reduced in chroma by adding its complementary color.

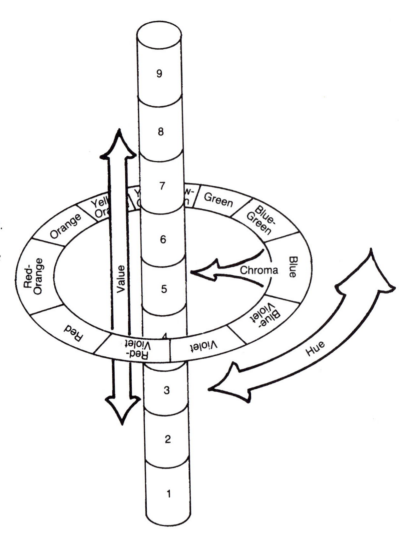

FIGURE 5–5

Color mixing can be visualized as three-dimensional movement. A change in hue will move a color around the perimeter of the color wheel, a change in chroma will move a color toward the value scale, and a change in value will move a color up or down the value scale.

It is helpful to think of color mixing as three-dimensional movement (Figure 5–5): (1) a change in hue causes a color to move around the perimeter of the color wheel; (2) a change in value causes vertical movement up or down the value scale; and (3) a change in chroma causes movement toward the center of the color wheel.

In the construction of the color wheel, secondary hues were formed by mixing equal proportions of two adjacent primary colors. In this way, green was made by mixing yellow and blue pigment. Intermediate colors were mixed in a similar manner. Variations of secondary and intermediate colors are mixed by adjusting proportions of the base colors that are combined. In this manner, a color falling anywhere between two hues on the color wheel can be created. For instance, an infinite variety of red-violets can be mixed by increasing or decreasing the proportion of red. Similarly, a variety of yellow-orange hues can be mixed varying the proportion of either hue contributing to the mixture.

Other colors may be mixed by blending hues located in any other position on the color wheel. For instance, yellow-orange may be mixed with red-violet to create a brownish color, or yellow-orange may be mixed with green to create a chartreuse color. The specific color created is dependent not only on the choice of hues but also on the proportion of the colors contained in the mixture. Thus, a yellow-orange, red-violet mixture might be dominated by one hue or by the other. The mixture could be further modified by increasing the proportion of violet, red, or yellow in the base colors. This mixture of yellow-orange and red-violet would result in a new hue; however, the new color will be weaker in chroma than either of the base colors (Figure 5–6). Such reductions in chroma occur whenever two nonanalogous hues (hues not located next to each other on the color wheel) are mixed together. Further modifications of chroma can be caused by adding a small amount of a hue that is close to the complement of the

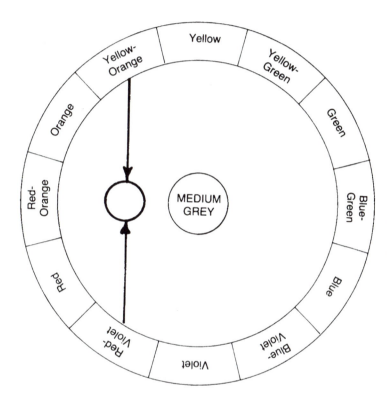

FIGURE 5–6
Mixing nonanalogous colors will result in a reduction of chroma that brings the new color closer to medium grey than either of the starting colors.

new color. In this case, blue-green would be the appropriate complement (Figure 5-7). Large additions of the complementary color will totally neutralize the mixture and result in a muddy, neutral color.

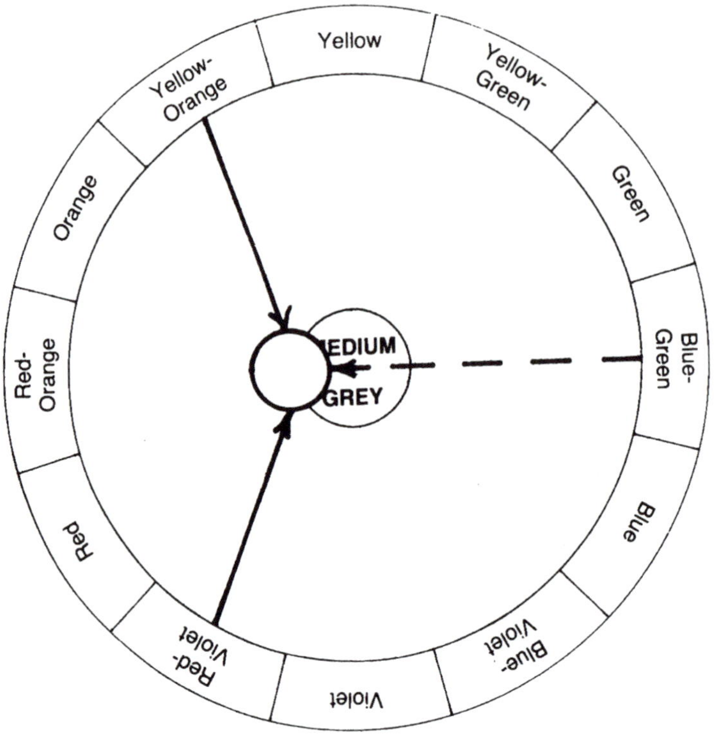

FIGURE 5-7
Adding the complement of the new color created by combining the two nonanalogous hues will further reduce the chroma of the new color.

In addition to modifying chroma, an alteration of value occurs when nonanalogous hues are mixed together. It is apparent in Figure C-4 that yellow-orange has a fairly high natural value and that the value of red-violet is lower. When these hues are mixed together, the inherent value of yellow-orange is reduced in the new color, and the value of red-violet is raised. In other words, a mixture of yellow-orange and red-violet results in a new color with both a weaker chroma and a different value than either of the base colors contributing to the mixture. This principle of color mixing is true for all combinations of nonanalogous hues.

Creating a tint, shade, or tone is a much more direct process than mixing hues or adjusting chroma. Any color can be made into a tint by adding white or may be made into a shade by adding black to the base color. Mixtures of tones are dependent on the addition of both black and white to a color. The quality of a tone created in this manner is dependent on the proportions of white, black, and the base hue. A greater proportion of any one variable will dominate the new color.

TRADITIONAL COLOR PALETTES

The hues on the color wheel and the neutrals on the value scale can be combined to create several thousand different colors; therefore, it would seem that anyone mixing paints should only need 14 colors to accomplish the work: the three primary, three secondary, and six intermediate colors, plus black and white. Yet designer's paintboxes and studio paint rooms seem to be crammed with tubes, bins, and buckets of pigments. Over 30 colors of scene paint are available. This broad range of pigments is available for three reasons: (1) to allow the artist to devote the greatest amount of energy to applying paints rather than mixing them, (2) to make common colors handily available in large quantities, and (3) to make strong colors available. It is not mandatory that all theatres stock all 30 colors of scene paint or that they should all be used in a design. The practitioner must exercise control of the palette to achieve desired effects.

Based on principles of harmony, contrast, and variety, a number of traditional color palettes have emerged. These should be considered only as guides by the artist. Production concepts, theatrical effects, technical limitations, and ever-changing audience taste should dictate the use of color, not traditions or rules.

Monochromatic Color Palette

A design may contain a multitude of colors, like a Harlequin costume, or may be limited to a single color, like a sepia photograph. The Harlequin is polychromatic (multicolored); the photograph is monochromatic (one color). A monochromatic palette may be used effectively by the scene or costume designer; the artist then uses tints, tones, and shades to create the design. Variety is achieved by manipulating line, form, texture, mass, and light rather than color. The design is automatically unified in color. From one point of view, a monochromatic palette is the easiest and safest utilization of color. From another point of view, a single-color design requires highly creative use of line, form, mass, and texture to avoid tedium.

Analogous Color Palette

Closely related to monochromatic use of color is the palette of analogous colors. This approach expands the single color of a monochromatic palette to include the hues located to the right and left of a base hue on the color wheel.

An analogous color palette constructed around blue might include all variations of blue-violet and blue-green. In practical terms, a broader palette of analogous colors might extend from blue-green through violet. Using all variations of tints, tones, and shades, an almost infinite selection of colors is available to the designer to provide visual interest. For instance, a medium-value, strong-chroma violet piping might be used as trim on a high-value, weak-chroma blue-green dress decorated with low-value, high-chroma blue-violet flowers. Differences in hue, value, and chroma provide variety; the presence of blue in each color provides unity. The designer, however, must carefully control value and chroma if the desired effect is harmony. Should the designer wish to create an effect of dissonance, the strength of all chromas might be increased, but the costume would then appear garish.

Straight-Complement Color Palette

An alternative method to using colors related by proximity is using colors related by distance. Designs may be arranged around a palette of opposite or complementary colors such as green/red or yellow/violet. This does not mean that precise opposites must be used. A near-complement can be as effective as a direct complement. It is easy to imagine the discordant effects possible with such palettes; however, harmonious designs resulting in beautiful, lively effects can be created. The use of complementary colors usually requires one of the two colors to be dominant in chroma and value; the second color should be of weaker chroma but cover a larger area. Extreme care must be taken to select the appropriate value and chroma when using a palette of opposites. The designer must be further cautioned that lighting colors may significantly affect the appearance of one or both hues when they are separated by such great distance on the color wheel.

Split-Complement Color Palette

A split-complement palette offers greater variety than the straight-complement palette. The split-complement palette utilizes a base hue and the colors on each side of the complement of the base color; for instance, green with red-orange and red-violet (Figure 5–8). The same cautions for obtaining balance by controlling chroma and value apply here as with a straight-complement palette. With both the split and straight-complement palettes, a more balanced and harmonious design is more likely to be achieved when the stronger purer colors are used in the form of accents, such as molding or ornaments on sets or trim and accessories on costumes. This does not mean that in a yellow, red-violet, blue-violet split-complement palette that yellow must be re-

FIGURE 5–8
Split-complement color palette consists of a base hue and the colors on either side of the complement of the base hue.

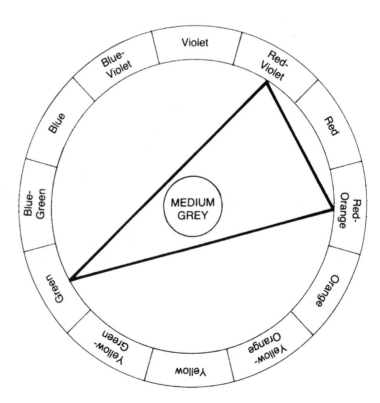

stricted to doorknobs and window frames. Instead, a tint, tone, or shade of yellow might be used to paint the major areas of the setting but their value and chroma must not be allowed to become too strong. The two violets could be used as accent colors. Alternatively, the violets could be subdued for use as the base color in the set and the yellow pigment at full chroma restricted to use as an accent color.

Color-Triad Palette

The greatest variety may be achieved by using a color triad. This palette uses colors equally spaced around the color wheel (Figure 5–9). A primary triad includes red, blue, and yellow; another example of a triad is blue-violet, yellow-green, and red-orange. A harmonious design in each of the triads requires one of the three hues to be selected as the key color, which is available throughout its entire range of chroma and value. The other two colors are used at reduced chroma, which may be adjusted through tints, tones, and shades. The result will be a harmonious and exciting design. In contrast, a discordant and garish effect might be purposely created for a surrealistic or expressionistic production by using all three colors of the triad in pure form and in equal proportions.

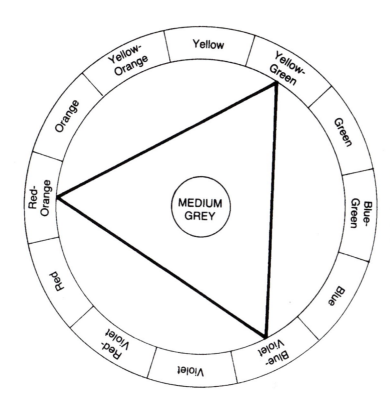

FIGURE 5–9
The color-triad palette consists of three hues equally spaced around the perimeter of the color wheel.

Although these are traditional palettes that have been found to yield harmonious compositions in art, the designer must be reminded that they do not imply rigid rules to be observed at all times. These palettes simply provide traditional guidelines for safe color choices. In the performing arts, production concepts, characterizations, and lighting may dictate a conscious deviation from these guidelines.

COLOR PERCEPTION

Although a knowledge of the vocabulary and technology of color is important, it only serves to prepare for the task of manipulating color in a design. The choices that must be made are dependent on some understanding of the human perception of color.

The way we see color is a physical phenomenon dependent on light, pigment, and vision. People also respond to color as a psychological phenomenon. It is known, for instance, that colors communicate and sometimes cause a sense of warmth or cold, vitality, happiness, depression, melancholy, joy, anger, or tension. Colors also have a specific psychological meaning: red warns, white is pure, black represents death. Extensive research continues to be done in this area of psychology. For the designer, an awareness of these meanings can help determine appropriate color choices. These choices, however, should be made with further understanding not only of the technology of color but also of the effects of color perception.

Seen against a neutral background, a color seems to have inherent characteristics that are identifiable in terms of hue, value, and chroma. That same color is perceived differently when placed against a chromatic background. A color may be pleasant and soft or harsh and sharp, depending on its surroundings. In different environments, a color may jump out of the picture or recede into it; it may appear luminous, misty, glossy, metallic, transparent, or dull. It is the relationship of the color to its surroundings that causes these variations in appearance. The designer must be conscious of this effect, because it contributes not only to the selection of hue but to the determination of chroma and value. The effect can be described with some specificity in relation to warm and cool colors.

Warm and Cool Colors

Colors that have a red or yellow quality communicate a sense of warmth, and colors that have a blue or green characteristic communicate a sense of coolness, when either color group is seen against a neutral background. Any warm color, such as red-orange, appears warmer when placed against a cool background such as green; however, that same red-orange will appear cooler when placed against a warm background such as red (Figure C–7). The color does not actually change; only its appearance changes as the color is moved from background to background. This change in "apparent temperature" is a characteristic of color perception.

Color Perspective

In perspective drawing, objects in the distance appear smaller on the page than objects in the foreground. Distance also affects color. Objects in the distance appear more neutral—greyer—than objects close to the observer. This neutralization of color in the distance is called **color perspective**.

The contrast between the color of an object and the color of its surroundings contributes to perspective effects. For instance, a square of yellow on a light background will appear significantly larger when moved to a dark background (Figure C–8). There is no physical change in the size of the yellow square, only a change in perception by the observer. Also, in the first instance, the high-value, strong-chroma yellow square seems to remain fixed on the light background. Against the dark background, the yellow square seems to advance or jump off the surface. In contrast, a black square seen against a deep-violet background appears to remain fixed on the surface; but when the black square is moved to a yellow background, the black area seems to recede into the surface, creating a deep hole (Figure C–9).

In the theatre, these effects play a part in the selection of values and chroma for any element of a production. The challenge is to select appropriate colors and avoid creating "holes," distorting dimensions, or causing the loss of perspective relationships.

CONCLUSION

The use of color is a relative matter. An understanding of how colors are created and the interrelationships of the components of color can facilitate work on a production. Rules of harmony, contrast, and color mixing should be considered as guides to the use of color. Ultimately the designer must determine the appropriate combinations based on the effects desired. Success in reaching these goals is dependent on good taste and solid technical knowledge.

CHAPTER 6

Props and Set Dressings

INTRODUCTION

Next to the actor, properties and set dressings are among the most important physical elements on the stage. These are the objects actors use during the performance: the furniture they sit on, the articles they carry and handle, and the objects that decorate the space. Whether the play takes place in an apartment in Manhattan or a forest in Argonne, there will be props that contribute to the action and help complete the stage picture.

The importance of props and set dressings can be exemplified by incidents in daily life. When an apartment is rented, there is nothing in it to identify what the new tenant is like. The walls are bare, the furniture is absent, and there is not even a toothbrush to indicate anything about who lives there. The moment the first box is carried into the apartment, the space begins to reflect the character of its new occupant. The period, style, and condition of the furniture, lamps, pictures for the walls, rugs, kitchen utensils, even the quality of the moving boxes are personal choices that help describe the person moving in and complete the apartment—or, on the stage, the appearance of the setting. These details give the space personality and make it credible as a real place.

In addition to set dressings, actors carry, wear, and use articles that complete their character. An actor may smoke a pipe, twirl a pencil, or carry a riding crop. These personal articles help explain who a character is; how the actor uses these things helps the audience understand what the character is like.

Some props may be absolutely essential personal items, such as a sword for Hamlet, or they may be necessary hand props, such as the linguini thrown into the kitchen in *The Odd Couple*. They might be important articles that complete the stage picture and inform the audience about a situation, such as the stepladder, paint buckets, and drop cloths required at the opening of *Barefoot in the Park*. On the other hand, props might do nothing more than decorate the space to give it a sense of actuality, such as farm implements and hay bales in *Oklahoma* or glass and ceramic knickknacks on the mantel in *Hedda Gabler*. All of these items, whether required by the script or added to the production to complete the stage picture, contribute to the credibility of the play. They must be appropriate to the action, period, place, and style of production, and they must be sufficiently durable to withstand the rigors of rehearsal and performance.

Since they bear this level of importance to the production, props should be given time, energy, and enthusiasm to produce appropriate results. Often the task is as monumental as constructing the setting. The work always requires careful planning and creative thinking.

WHAT PROPS ARE NEEDED?

The **properties master** along with the props crew is responsible for identifying, procuring, and caring for the props for a production—and for the safe return of any borrowed articles following the close of the show. The work begins by compiling a **props list**, which identifies the properties and set dressings needed, along with descriptions of what they look like and when and how they are used. The list is developed from three sources: the script, the director, and the scenic design. Many scripts include a props list at the back of the text. This list may be a summary of notes by the playwright or a list from a previous production; it should be treated only as a guide to what was done once before or might be done for this production. The list is a suggestion—not a list of requirements. In addition, most texts contain a description of each setting. A careful reading of those descriptions, the text as a whole, and the list at the back of the script will provide an initial props list to which articles may be added as a result of the scenic design and rehearsals with the actors. As rehearsals progress, the quantity, nature, and specific requirements of props for a show become more clearly defined.

It is very important that the historical period and theatrical style of the show are defined early in the production process. This is usually determined by the script and the design idea, but other factors should contribute to this decision. A knowledge of the properties available in storage can simplify the choice. If the theatre happens to have an extensive stock of Victorian furniture, assigning a play to that period is practical; however, if there is no Victorian furniture in stock and the region has few antique stores, another style of furnishing would be a better choice. Sometimes it is possible to build fairly simple stylized furniture for a play (Figure 6–1). This might be a solution for Greek or even medieval plays.

FIGURE 6–1

Homemade stylized furniture constructed from plywood for a production of The Imaginary Invalid. *(Courtesy Theatre UNI, University of Northern Iowa)*

It is also important to know in advance how properties will be used during the performance. If something is simply to hang on the wall, concern about its value is a little less significant than if it is going to be handled by actors. The props master must know if an upholstered sofa is going to be walked on or if a chair is to be kicked or thrown; he or she should be informed when weapons will actually be involved in battles. This knowledge makes it easier to find appropriate pieces for the production and can reduce embarrassment later should something that was borrowed become damaged. In other words, very specific information is needed by the properties crew. If a sofa is called for, what period should it be? What color? How long must it be? Should it be old and worn? New? Will it be walked on? Slept on? Jumped over? Spilled on? If the props list calls for a pen, should it be a contemporary ballpoint pen? Fountain pen? Quill pen? Must it write? Is it carried by an actor? Where is it carried? Should it have a screw top? Click point? Have engraved advertising? Look cheap? Look expensive? Be a specific color?

The final step in the preparation for finding or making props is some research into the nature of the things sought. The props crew should be directed to or given some photographs, drawings, or paintings of specific items so they have a clear understanding as to what is needed. This documentation will also help on the phone as questions are exchanged about the period and style of an item.

WHERE TO BEGIN

Once the props list has been made and the requirements for each piece defined, it is necessary to determine if the items already exist in storage. Does the theatre own the exact thing or something close that can be modified to meet the requirements of the props list? Any item that is similar to something specified should be examined:

Can it be used as is?
Can it be used with practical modification, such as paint?
Can it be adapted for use by reconstruction?
Is it too valuable to be modified?

If the piece is acceptable or can be reasonably modified, it can be checked off the search list and put on the work list. At this point, it is worthwhile to write a brief summary of the work planned for that item on a 3" × 5" card and attach it to the prop. This note will help organize the work and crews.

After the storage areas have been checked, it is time to begin a strategy to deal with the props remaining on the list. Three options exist for each item: (1) if the object cannot be found in stock, it might be possible to borrow it; (2) if budget allows, the article might be rented or purchased; or (3) if the item cannot be found anywhere or budget prohibits renting or purchasing it, a facsimile might be constructed.

Borrowing, renting, and purchasing begin with the same initial step: finding the items. The search process for props is the work of a detective. It often requires some very creative thinking to figure out who might possess a Samurai sword, a fireplace screen, or a bust of

Plato. The easiest solution is to try another local theatre—they may have the very thing needed in storage. If not, the best reference to begin searching for props is the Yellow Pages of a telephone directory. Learning to use this book is important. No matter how small the community, there are always local and distant businesses, clubs, and public and private organizations listed in hundreds of classifications. Begin to use the book by looking in the index of categories. Look for the most logical headings and then expand the search to reasonable and even extreme alternatives. Some versatility is required. It is unlikely in all but the largest cities that a listing will advertise exactly what is sought. This initial search is to identify any potential sources that should be telephoned. The individual, business, or club may not have what is sought, but if asked, someone there might have another idea where to look or may know someone who might have what is needed. Whether or not the person or business called is able to help, it is important to be courteous on the phone and thank the speaker for his or her time.

Following is an example of a logical progression that might be used to find a Samurai sword by working through the categories in the phone book.

Classifications

1. Swords
2. Weapons
3. Armor
4. Military supplies
5. Cutlery
6. Specialty stores
   a. Oriental
   b. Oriental grocery stores
   c. Novelty shops
   d. Theatrical equipment and supplies
   e. Display supplies and services
7. Travel agents
8. Clubs and organizations
   a. Veterans' and military organizations
      (1) Veterans of Foreign Wars (VFW)
      (2) American Legion
      (3) Amvets
   b. Fraternal clubs
9. Museums
   a. Historical museums
   b. National museums
10. Restaurants
11. Self-defense schools
12. Military reserve units
13. Recruiting officers
14. Foreign embassies
15. Display departments of larger stores
16. Photographers

In each case, if an organization is found in a category, it should be contacted. After identifying himself or herself as a member of the theatre, the caller should ask: (1) "Do you have any Samurai swords?" (2) "Do you or does anyone there know who might have a Samurai sword or where I might call to find out about them?"

Once an item is found, it may be purchased if it is within budget. When asked, some merchants are willing to give a discount as high as 25 percent to theatres. Although it is fair to ask for a discount, it may not be possible for the store to give one because of store policy or economic conditions.

Sometimes it is possible to borrow things. Persuading an individual or a merchant to loan something of value requires courtesy and tact. The following guidelines are helpful to preserve good, long-term rapport with sources.

1. Select the specific items desired before requesting to borrow anything.

2. Keep a set of alternatives in mind in case a source is willing to loan items but the specific choices are not available.

3. If borrowing from a store, seek permission from the owner or manager; if possible, speak directly to this person rather than being interpreted through a clerk. If borrowing from an individual, seek permission from the actual owner of the article.

4. Do not ask to borrow something unless it really is needed.

5. Only someone with authority to borrow should negotiate for a loan and acceptance of responsibility for the borrowed item.

6. It is imperative to be honest with the person from whom something is borrowed. Let the owner know about the likelihood of damage, the care that will be given the item, and the responsibility for damage and loss that will be assumed by the theatre.

7. Set absolute dates and times for the pick-up and return of the articles, and meet those obligations.

8. Complete a loan agreement.

9. Offer some kind of compensation for the courtesy of the loan. This may be complimentary tickets or acknowledgment in the program, or both.

Should a business or an individual agree to loan something for use as a prop, a number of things should be done.

1. A formal loan agreement should be prepared by the representative of the theatre borrowing the item and signed by the person making the loan. The loan agreement should indicate the following:

    a. The condition of the object at the time loaned, noting all scrapes, scratches, dents, flaws, and any other damage. These should be listed and pointed out to the owner. The owner should agree to their presence at the time of the loan.

    b. The current value of the item—as agreed on by the owner and the borrower. (This will become the basis for repayment in the event of loss or damage.)

c. Who shall be responsible for transportation of the item.

d. Place at which the article will be used.

e. Name and telephone number of the person making the loan.

f. Name and telephone number of the person borrowing the item as a representative of the theatre.

g. Date (and time) the item is to be returned.

h. A space should be provided on the form to acknowledge return of the item with a statement of the condition in which it was returned. This should be written in a positive way that encourages inspection but discourages complaints. A copy of this receipt should be given to the person making the loan and should be kept on file in the event of a claim of damage.

2. A specific time and date should be established to pick up the article.

3. The theatre should offer an acknowledgment in the program to the organization or individual making the loan. Program credit should be given *only* with permission of the person or business being acknowledged. There are times when an individual or business may prefer not to be acknowledged. As an alternative, a pair of complimentary tickets may be offered. If a great number of tickets are given away, it can be quite costly to the theatre; however, it may be the most persuasive means to obtain a needed prop. Complimentary tickets should be given in pairs; giving away single tickets seems cheap. However, it is reasonable to limit the dates that complimentary tickets may be used. For instance, if the theatre usually sells out Saturday nights, offer complimentary tickets for the Thursday or Friday performances, but do not make the Saturday evening tickets available.

4. Establish a definite return date and time in the loan agreement and keep that commitment.

5. Arrange security for any borrowed items.

6. Should anything borrowed become lost or damaged, accept responsibility and immediately contact the owner to arrange payment or replacement.

Should it be necessary to borrow extremely valuable items, a temporary rider to the insurance policy for the school or theatre can be obtained. This coverage is usually inexpensive and (if the program administrator agrees) easy to obtain. It provides assurance to the owner and financial security for the theatre.

Never, under any circumstances, borrow something that is irreplaceable. This includes one-of-a-kind objects and things that have great sentimental value to the owner.

A borrowed object must be treated with great care. Borrowing means that the theatre is taking *complete and absolute* responsibility for property that belongs to someone else. If it is not possible to protect these things from damage or theft, they should not be borrowed. Some people truly enjoy lending things to a theatre; others feel an obligation to help out. That desire to help and that sense of obligation will cease if property is abused, damaged, or lost.

After borrowed props are returned as promised, the final action in a borrowing procedure should be a thank you letter from the theatre to each person or business who loaned something for the production.

Since stores need their inventory on hand to make sales, it is sometimes difficult to persuade them to loan goods for use as stage props; however, if they can be assured that the theatre will take responsibility for any damage, a store might be willing to rent some articles for a small fee. This allows the store to make a little money while still helping the theatre out at a low cost.

If the props for a show can be borrowed, rented, or purchased, the task of the props master is eased significantly, for the work is then limited to caring for the items obtained and returning them in good condition at the end of the production. The likelihood of borrowing all of the props for any show is slim. Ultimately, some things must be built because they cannot be found, or owners are unwilling to loan or rent them, or the use to which a borrowed article might be subjected will be too abusive. As a result, there are almost always things that must be manufactured or modified for a show. Whether it is something as simple as a 1965 Manhattan phone book or as challenging as a Russian samovar, the props crew will need to turn trash into treasures. Half of this task is the clever use of materials; the other half is well executed finishing and painting processes, which are described in Chapter 4.

The appearance of what finally reaches the stage is often a result of what is available rather then what is desired. These, it is hoped, are pragmatic choices dictated by time, budget, and energy. Compromise should be possible without damaging the appearance of the show as a whole. This requires dedication by the props crew and flexibility by the director and designer.

CONSTRUCTING PROPS

Props Material

Props are constructed from everything! In addition to standard construction and craft materials, cereal boxes, artificial leaves, swatches of fabric, garden hose, kitchen funnels, juice cans, paintbrushes, or anything else may find its way into a prop. Most of the materials described in Chapters 3 and 4 may be used for properties construction from wood, white glue, and muslin to carpet roller tubes, Styrofoam, and panel adhesive. The choice of specific materials depends on the final shape needed and the way in which an article is to be used. Roughly handled items require the use of sturdier materials and construction techniques; something that simply hangs on the wall can be made from more delicate materials.

Although anything may be used to make props, there are some materials that are especially handy. Note, however, that many of these substances bear significant health hazards. *CAUTION:* **Always read and follow the instructions and safety information on labels.**

Sculpting and Construction Materials

Some of the most common craft materials are old standbys for the props maker. Included in this group are clay, plaster of paris, illustration board, felt, burlap, cheesecloth, and muslin. These materials may be used independently or combined with others.

Clay is essentially earth mixed with water. It is used in pottery and sculpting because it is easily molded, maintains its shape, takes glazes well, and becomes very hard when properly fired in a kiln. For the props maker this is an excellent material to make molds and for sculpting. In both instances, it can be worked and reworked until the desired design is achieved. Although it should be dried, glazed, and fired for permanency, it is possible to use unfired clay objects on stage. After the clay has dried, it will accept most artist or scene paints and can be painted effectively. The advantages of clay are that it is readily available, moderately easy to work, hazard free, and relatively inexpensive. Its disadvantages are that it is extremely heavy, has a long drying time, and is fragile and will crumble unless fired. The best use of clay is as a mold for casting or a form for modeling papier-mâché, celastic, felt, and other materials.

Another group of modeling materials available to the props maker consists of substitutes for both clay and papier-mâché. Sold under brand names such as **Celluclay**, this modeling material can be sculpted like clay, allowed to dry, and then cut, drilled, and sanded like wood. It weighs less than clay and dries without baking to a very hard surface that exceeds the strength of papier-mâché or unfired clay. It can be coated with scenic, artist, or household paints, wood stains, or commercial finishes such as varnish. This and similar products are sold at art, craft, and hobby stores as well as display and school supply companies.

Sculpt Or Coat is a water-soluble, nontoxic, nonflammable plastic that can be used as an adhesive or protective coating for almost any material, including fabrics, plastics, glass, ceramics, woods, or metals. It also can be applied in sufficient density to make fabrics and almost any other materials into modeling or sculpting mediums. The cream can be diluted for use as a transparent coating to which a colorant can be added, if desired. The coating dries to a hard, mar-resistant finish. At its highest concentration, Sculpt Or Coat can be used with fabrics, felt, carpet, or foam rubber that may be sculpted into rocks, armor, masks, architectural moldings, tree bark, props, set pieces, or costume trim. With sufficient treatment, the completed forms can even be walked on or sat on. A rock sculpted from carpet or foam rubber might be finished by adding mulch and sawdust to final layers of coating to create a mossy effect. Once the cream has dried, it will accept most paints used for scenic production. The material is nontoxic, safe to the skin, nonflammable, and requires only water for clean-up. It is an especially safe modeling compound and adhesive for the theatre.

Plaster of paris is a casting material. It can be poured into a mold for a positive form or used to make negative molds of faces, statues, or most other objects. The negative cast can be used as is or modified with clay to reproduce the articles in plaster, papier-mâché, fiberglass, or plastic. The material is easy to work with, sets quickly, and produces greatly detailed impressions. Cured plaster can be coated with almost any kind of finish, including all water-base and enamel paints. There are a few cautions when working with plaster of paris. Anything that is cast must first be coated with a release agent such as petroleum jelly to allow the hardened plaster to be removed. Without the coating, the plaster will adhere to the object. When a casting is made, the means of removal must be planned so that hardened plaster does not hook around protrusions that will prevent removal or cause either the mold or the casting to break. This may require casting an object in two or more sections or carefully cutting the mold to remove it. Plaster generates a great deal of heat as it sets. If a thick cast is being made, enough heat may be generated to damage the model or cause the casting to crack. *CAUTION*: **Do not pour plaster down the drain—it blocks pipes! Allow any unused plaster to harden and then throw it in the trash.**

Drug stores and medical suppliers sell **plaster-impregnated gauze** in rolls for constructing casts for broken bones. It is fairly inexpensive and very easy to use. Strips of the gauze bandage are soaked in a bowl of warm water for a short period and then smoothed onto the object being cast. As the gauze is rubbed, the plaster smooths out and fills the surface. A minimum of three or four layers of plaster-impregnated gauze is needed to attain sufficient strength and additional reinforcement may be needed before using this as a mold.

Illustration board is available from art stores in light, medium, and heavy weights. It is a thin, sturdy, flexible, smooth cardboard that may be easily cut with a matte knife. It can be bent into tight curves or folded into angular shapes, and it may be stapled or glued to wooden or plastic forms. Illustration board is a wonderful material to use as a substitute for thin metal constructions. Any scenic or artist paint can be used with it.

Felt is a unique fabric. It is composed of wool fibers that are pressed together to make a cloth. It can be permanently molded with steam into specific shapes or coated with paints, glues, and polishes to change the characteristics of its surface. When cut, the material produces a smooth, finished edge. Felt is available in numerous colors and in different weights from very thin fabrics to extremely thick industrial felts. The thicker the material, the stronger it is for most props applications. Roll ends of industrial felt sometimes can be obtained from manufacturing plants; otherwise, the heaviest felt available should be used.

Celastic is a resin-impregnated, felt-like material that is applied like papier-mâché and dries to an extremely hard substance. Strips of celastic are torn or cut from the roll, dipped in acetone to activate the resin, and then applied to a prepared mold. As the acetone evaporates, the fabric becomes very hard. Usually two or three layers of celastic are needed to attain sufficient strength. This material is only available from theatrical suppliers. *CAUTION*: **Acetone is a very dangerous chemical. It has a flash point of 0° Centigrade, badly irritates skin, and produces a toxic vapor that is damaging to the tissues of the lungs. Because of these hazards, rubber gloves must be worn, use of a rubber apron is encouraged, and a vapor mask is required, as well as very good ventilation in the work area.**

Fiberglass is a casting and modeling system composed of a glass-fiber fabric and a liquid plastic resin. The fabric serves as a reinforcing web within the cured plastic resin. The materials in combination are so strong that boats and car bodies are manufactured from them. It is available from auto and boat repair shops and craft stores. These materials may be used in combination in shallow molds, draped over an armature, or wrapped around objects to give them strength. *CAUTION*: **Read warning statements carefully! Avoid prolonged contact, wear protective clothing—including gloves, apron, face mask, and breathing protection—and work only in a well-ventilated atmosphere.**

Casting resin is similar to the resin used to fabricate fiberglass. It is designed to produce a crystal-clear casting that may be plain, colored with special dyes, filled with glitter, or have three-dimensional objects suspended in it. The finished form can be glued, screwed, drilled, sawed, and sanded. A variety of resins are available from craft stores and some hardware stores. *CAUTION*: **Read warning statements carefully! Avoid prolonged contact, wear protective clothing—including gloves, apron, face mask, and breathing protection—and work only in a well-ventilated atmosphere.**

Foam-in-place plastics may be purchased in small quantities from hardware stores. This material is sold for use as an insulation in walls around electrical outlets. Larger packages of the material may be purchased from some craft stores, insulation contractors, and boat-repair businesses. The foams are usually two-part systems that must be poured or mixed together in precise proportions. *Improper mixing can be dangerous.* The foam can be allowed to form freely to make rocks or other amorphous objects or it can be placed in a mold lined with plastic sheeting or protected with a release agent to reproduce specific forms. *CAUTION*: **Vigorously adhere to mixing instructions! Most of the foams produce toxic gases and significant heat during the expansion process. Adequate ventilation is required in the work area, and molds must not restrict escape of gases. The liquid material is dangerous to the skin and eyes. Protective clothing, including gloves, apron, and face mask, must be worn; a respirator is encouraged; and good ventilation is required.**

Adhesives

There are numerous adhesives that are especially helpful to the props maker. The handiest and most common is white glue, the same adhesive that is used throughout the scenery construction process. This binder can be used straight from the container or diluted for spreading, or other materials may be added to change its composition.

Phlex-Glu is an adhesive made especially for the theatre. It looks the same as white glue and behaves in a similar manner; however, a plasticizer may be added to it which makes the dried glue both flexible and water repellent. Once Phlex-Glu has dried, it adheres permanently to most materials and fabrics. It can be used as a strong, flexible binder, as a preparatory coating for future finishing work, or as a flexible gloss finish on fabric, plastics, and standard construction materials. Other than being difficult to wash off after it has dried, there appear to be no hazards associated with this material.

Hot-melt glue is one of the handiest adhesives available for properties work. It quickly adheres to most surfaces and can be peeled off most materials without causing damage. The adhesive is a solid stick that is pushed into a hot-melt glue gun in which it is melted. The molten glue is puddled on one of the surfaces being joined and the materials are pressed together and held until the glue cools. The hot-melt glue becomes an intermediate layer that causes the adhesion. The glue may be used to temporarily tack materials or objects in place; attach glass, fabric, or ceramic props to furniture; seam fabrics; or bond almost any materials together that won't melt. It can also be applied as three-dimensional trim to decorate set pieces such as jewelry boxes. Both hot-melt glue and hot-melt glue guns are sold at hardware stores and craft shops. The only hazard associated with this binder is the likelihood of being burned by the hot glue or the nozzle of the glue gun.

Rubber cement is another handy glue that often can be used as a temporary or permanent adhesive. It is especially handy when joining two nonporous materials such as glass or plastic. This thick liquid is coated onto one surface, spread around, and then covered with the second material to create a temporary bond. If a permanent connection is sought, the glue is coated onto both surfaces, allowed to dry, and then the two coated surfaces are carefully pressed together. The advantage to rubber cement is that it stays entirely on the surface of most materials and usually can be rubbed off where not desired without causing damage to the original surface. It can be used with paper, fabric, ceramics, glass, wood, and some plastics; however, the solvent in rubber cement may also dissolve some plastics.

Epoxy is a two-part binder. This expensive adhesive is usually sold in small tubes at the hardware store. An equal amount of material is released from each tube and then stirred together. As soon as the materials begin to mix, they also begin to harden, so it is imperative that work with epoxy is performed quickly. Epoxy is especially handy to glue nonporous materials together, such as glass or ceramics. The mixed adhesive is spread onto one surface of the materials to be joined, the materials are brought together, wiggled around a bit, separated, and then reattached and held firmly until the adhesive is set. It is important to dry the adhesive under pressure until the glue is fully set. When properly mixed, applied, and allowed to dry thoroughly, this is an extremely strong binder. *CAUTION*: **Eye contact and ingestion are extremely dangerous, and prolonged contact with the skin must be avoided; it is very difficult to remove the dried adhesive from anything—including skin.** Once dry, the adhesive presents no hazards.

The construction industry uses many different kinds of **spray cements** in aerosol cans. These are manufactured by companies such as 3M and Bostik to perform very specific tasks. Each spray cement should be tested carefully to ensure that it will not damage the materials being joined. Spray cements are generally very strong and very permanent. *CAUTION*: **Labels must be read carefully to determine the safety requirements of each product; most are highly flammable and contain a solvent that requires good ventilation to prevent toxic accumulations.**

Tapes

Tape is a handy material for almost any kind of work. The props maker can use it for anything from simple packaging to implying leather wrapping on the handle of a knife. There are special tapes for specific applications, ranging from masking tape to aid painters, to sports tape for athletes, to duct tape for the construction industry. Tapes are sold by type, width, and length at various quality levels.

Masking tape was originally designed for the painter to protect areas or temporarily define lines of demarcation between colors. It is made of paper that is coated with a moderate adhesive on one side and wax on the other side. The adhesive must be strong enough to form a temporary bond but should permit release without significant damage to the surface it is protecting. The quality of adhesive varies; better masking tape has a stronger adhesive and is preferred for props construction. Masking tape is available in widths as narrow as ¼" and as wide as 2". Rolls are usually 60 yards long. It is sometimes available in a nonwaxed variety and in black. Masking tape should not be confused with drafting tape, which looks exactly like it but is made with a weaker adhesive.

Duct tape is a wide grey fabric tape used in the construction industry to assemble heating ducts. The tape has a very strong fabric base and an adhesive that is designed for a warm atmosphere. Its width, strength, and ability to accept acrylic paints makes duct tape useful for many props. However, it has three flaws: (1) the tape is not water resistant; (2) it leaves a difficult-to-remove gummy residue on most surfaces, especially if the tape is left in place for a long time; and (3) the tape does not work very well in cold atmospheres. In addition to the grey variety, duct tape is available in black and chrome.

Gaffer's tape is an expensive fabric tape that looks exactly the same as duct tape except it does not have a glossy finish. It has better adhesion qualities—it will stick to almost anything—but does not leave a gummy residue in the same way as duct tape. Gaffer's tape is available in grey and black in 2" × 60 yard rolls.

Foam construction tape is available from hardware stores and lumberyards. This thin, flexible, double-faced foam tape has a strong adhesive on both sides. The adhesive is so effective that it often exceeds the strength of the materials being joined and is almost impossible to remove. It may be used to adhere heavier objects to walls or to attach set dressings to furniture. The tape should first be tested on a safe area of finished materials to see if it will damage the surfaces being attached. This tape is sometimes sold as a foam mounting tape to hang pictures.

Other Common Props Materials

The artificial flower section of any discount store is always a popular hunting ground for propsmaking supplies. In addition to an enormous assortment of plastic and fabric flowers, it is possible to find geometric Styrofoam shapes, floral tape, armatures for wreaths, bouquet decorations, ribbons, artificial vases, inexpensive stoneware, and a host of other products that may be used. If there is access to a floral wholesale company or if it is possible to find a display store, many of these and other materials that are especially handy for the manufacture of props can be found.

Three-dimensional trim is very important to many props. Finding appropriate materials for that purpose can sometimes be difficult. One of the handiest materials currently available is **ethafoam rod**, or **backer rod**. This is a flexible, grey plastic foam that is used in the construction industry to fill gaps in preparation for caulking. Backer rod is available in diameters from ¼" to 2" on long coils and in greater diameters in 8'-0" lengths. It may be cut in half or quarters and used as a flexible molding around curves or it may be wrapped around a paper towel roller to give the impression of a complex lathe-turned spindle. The rod may be attached with hot-melt glue, panel adhesive, staples, or nails. It resists most paints, so a prime coat of Phlex-Glu or gesso is required. Vinyl acrylic paints work best on it.

Other flexible three-dimensional trims can be made with string, rope, wire, plastic, or rubber hose. Trims can also be created from such common things as pencils, plastic and paper cups, silverware, plates, screws, thumbtacks, upholstery tacks, cabinet knobs, bolts, nuts, washers, buttons, old keys, and plastic spoons and forks. In addition, craft stores offer geometric foam shapes, wooden macramé balls and beads, glass and stone decorations, large and small pipe cleaners, metallic foils, glitter, candle molds, and hundreds of other shapes that might be usable. All materials should be tested with the adhesives and paints planned for them before they are used to make something.

Surface Preparation

Often, the props maker constructs an object from one material but must paint it to make it appear as a significantly different material. Good surface preparation facilitates this painting. A number of standard materials and techniques can be used for this purpose.

1. Sculpt Or Coat can be brushed over the surface or the object can be dipped in Sculpt Or Coat and allowed to dry. Colorant or textures added to this coating produces an excellent base for painting.

2. White glue or Phlex-Glu can be used to apply toilet paper, paper towels, cheesecloth, or muslin for a smooth or slightly textured surface.

3. Plaster of paris can be applied to smooth out coarse textures such as Styrofoam. The plaster may be brushed on in two coats or an object may be dipped in the material. Should either process yield imperfections, the plaster can be lightly smoothed with fine (120-grit) sandpaper.

4. Wood filler such as Durham's Water Putty can be applied as a thick coating on coarse textures as well. This is a quick-drying material that forms a harder surface than plaster of paris and does not generate heat while drying. A surface can be coated with the wood filler, allowed to dry, and then sanded. Three-dimensional textures such as wood grains can be scraped into the wood filler as it dries. A different three-dimensional textural effect can be created by applying the filler over net or another coarse fabric and then removing the fabric while the filler is drying.

5. Acrylic gesso (pronounced *JES-so*) is a plaster-like opaque liquid used to prepare surfaces for artist acrylic paints. It can be brushed onto almost all materials in one or two coats and dries quickly to a very smooth finish. If necessary, dried gesso can be sanded. Acrylic artist colors can be mixed with the gesso to produce a colored prime coat.

PROPERTIES TECHNIQUES

Since the props and set dressings needed for production are so varied, it is impossible to give specific instructions on how to build every lantern, knife, or table that may appear on a props list. This section provides instructions that explain processes for individual projects that can be adapted to make other props. *These solutions are examples*—and indeed, they are only one method of actually constructing each of the props. Careful note should be taken of the materials, equipment, and processes used and especially the safety precautions stated.

Papier-Mâché

Papier-mâché is the process of constructing a form in a mold or on an armature by building up layers of paper saturated with wheat paste. A mold may be cast with plaster of paris, Celluclay, or other modeling materials, or an **armature**, an interior frame that gives shape and strength to the structure, may be made from wood and chicken wire, clay, lightbulbs, geometric foam shapes, or any other material that gives form and strength to the finished object. When modeling is completed, the armature may remain part of the object, may be partially cut away, or it might be entirely removed from the structure.

Example: To Make a Large Witch's Cauldron

Materials List	Equipment List
½ sheet ¾" plywood	Drill
6d box nails	Yardstick
Chicken wire	Saber saw
Staples	Framing square
Wheat paste, white glue, or Sculpt Or Coat	Hammer
Newspaper	Staple gun
Shellac	Paint brush
Black paint	
Silver or white spray paint	
Ethafoam rod or garden hose	

1. Lay out the armature. Draw a line 1'-0" from each edge of a piece of ¾" × 2'-0" × 2'-0" plywood. Drill a ³⁄₁₆" diameter hole at the 1", 10½", and 12½" marks on a yardstick. Slip a 6d nail through the hole at 1" and drive it partially into the plywood where the two lines intersect. Place the point of a pencil in one of the other holes and draw a circle, using the yardstick as the compass and the nail as the center point. Put the pencil in the other hole and draw another circle. Remove the nail and yardstick. Draw a line across the board ½" from one edge of the plywood.

2. Cut out the large circle and flatten one side by cutting on the line ½" from the edge of the board (Figure 6–2A). Cut out the small interior circle. Trace this pattern onto another sheet of ¾" plywood and cut it out again.

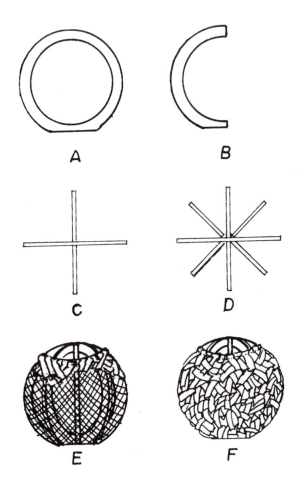

FIGURE 6–2
To build a papier-mache cauldron, (A) cut a circle to the appropriate diameter and flatten one side by cutting off a portion. (B) Cut six more half-circles. (C) Attach two half-circles to the whole circle. (D) Attach the remaining half circles to the whole circle. (E) Cover the form with chicken wire. (F) Apply at least 3 three-layer coats of paper to the form.

A   B

C   D

E   F

3. Cut the first pattern in half on the centerline (Figure 6–2B). Using the cut halves as a guide, draw four additional half-circles on scrap plywood. The new layouts do not have to form complete circles; they simply must be large enough for the pieces to fit in any direction. Cut out the additional half-circles. There should be a total of one whole circle with a flat edge and six half circles, each with a flat edge.

4. With the flat sides down, attach one half-circle to the side of the full circle at the centerline. Attach another half-circle on the other side of the full circle at the centerline (Figure 6–2C). There should now be four ribs 90° apart. Attach each of the remaining half-circles at the centerline evenly spaced around the center point (Figure 6–2D).

5. Place a mark 8" from the centerline down the edge of each rib. Staple chicken wire below this mark around the ribs carefully to form a smooth ball (Figure 6–2E). It will be necessary to cut V-shaped sections out of the wire near the top and bottom edges to form it smoothly. Use the cut ends of the chicken wire to weave it back together.

6. Using garden hose or ethafoam rod, attach a "lip" around the top edge of the wire where it stops 8" below the top of the ribs.

7. Make about a quart of wheat paste. Tear 25 or 30 pages of newspaper into 2" wide strips. Dip a few strips of newspaper into the paste and allow them to become thoroughly saturated. Apply a layer of strips around the perimeter of the lip at the top of the cauldron. Continue applying saturated newspaper strips over the outside of the chicken wire, working from the top toward the bottom (Figure 6–2F). Place the paste-saturated newspaper randomly in three layers. Allow the pasted structure to dry thoroughly. Drying time can be reduced by placing the cauldron in front of a fan.

8. After the first three layers have dried, tear shorter, narrower strips of newspaper and add an additional three layers of paper in the same manner. Once again, allow the paste to dry thoroughly.

9. Finally, using even smaller pieces of newspaper, add three more layers of pasted newspaper and once again allow the work to dry thoroughly. Alternate: Cut triangle sections of jute or foam-backed carpet to fit the shape of the cauldron. Staple the carpet in place with the backing facing out. Brush Sculpt Or Coat over the entire surface and allow to dry. Apply several additional layers of Sculpt Or Coat to the outside of the form. After the final layer has hardened, coat the inside of the cauldron with Sculpt Or Coat as well. Finally, apply a final layer of Sculpt Or Coat with black or grey colorant added. Allow to dry before proceeding with finishing processes.

10. Use a handsaw or saber saw to cut out the sections of ribs that cross the opening at the top of the cauldron.

11. Be sure that the wheat paste, white glue, or Sculpt Or Coat is thoroughly dry and then paint both the inside and outside of the cauldron with shellac. The shellac will improve the painting surface and will protect the wheat paste from rodents. Paint the cauldron flat black and allow it to dry. Using white or silver aerosol, spray a mist of paint into the air *above* the cauldron—not at the cauldron, above it! Allow the mist to drift down and settle on the black paint. This will put a slight highlight on the paint and give it the appearance of metallic gloss.

Any kind of paper can be used for this process. Newspaper is preferred because it tears well, holds the paste well, is readily available, and is free. The basic technique of constructing an armature and layering material over it can be used with muslin and white glue, Sculpt Or Coat and fabric or paper, celastic, or even fiberglass to build any variety of objects.

Fiberglass

Working with fiberglass requires fiberglass fabric, polyester resin, a properly prepared mold, release agent, safety equipment, and a well-ventilated work area.

Two kinds of **fiberglass fabric** are available. Woven mat in various weights is the strongest form of fabric and is used as the base for most construction; a chopped strand mat is used for complex and highly detailed structures. During fabrication, the glass fabric is saturated with **polyester resin**. This is a thick liquid that is mixed with a catalyst that causes it to harden. The proportion of hardener to resin is critical and mixing instructions must be followed carefully. As soon as the hardener is added to the resin, chemical action begins to occur. Selected materials may be added to the resin to change its color or develop special finishes. Additives that may be used include dyes, polyester pigments, and metal fillers such as bronzing powder. Depending on the specific composition of the resin and hardener, the presence of additives, and the temperature of the working atmosphere, initial hardening can occur within 30 minutes although complete curing takes longer. *CAUTION:* **This material must be used only in adequate ventilation. In addition, most resins and hardeners are highly flammable, as are their vapors. Avoid flame and high temperatures when working with the resin. Wear safety equipment, including protective gloves, a vinyl apron, face mask, and respirator.**

Fiberglass is usually fabricated in a mold. All molds must be coated with a release agent to permit separation of the resin from the mold. The release agent may be a paste wax such as Trewax or a spray specially formulated for this use.

Example: To Mold a Fiberglass Helmet

Materials List	*Equipment List*
Rubber ball	Scissors
Trims	Bucket
Newspaper	Stir sticks
Wheat paste	Mixing cups
Plaster bandages	Disposable brush
Mold release	Rubber gloves
Polyester resin	Chemical apron
Shredded fiberglass mat	Face mask
Steel wool	Respirator
Rub-N-Buff	

1. Find a rubber ball or some other form that is the hat size needed and decorate it with three-dimensional trim. Rope, string, costume jewels, clay, pebbles, or any other appropriate material may be used.

2. Make a plaster mold of the decorated form. Clean and heavily coat the inside of the mold with a release agent.

3. Prepare approximately one cup of polyester resin according to the mixing instructions on the container. *Follow the instructions precisely!*

Brush the resin in an even layer inside the mold and allow it to begin curing; this is called the **gel coat**. Once the resin has become tacky, mix a second batch without colorants or fillers and apply another coat of resin inside the mold. Lay a piece of fiberglass mat on a plastic drop cloth and thoroughly coat it with clear resin. Immediately press the glass mat into the wet resin, making sure the mat gets into every crevice and there are no air bubbles caught under the fabric. Special rollers may be used to force the mat in place and drive out any entrapped air. The mat should appear translucent when it is fully saturated with the resin.

4. Apply at least two additional layers of fiberglass mat, being sure that the fabric is fully saturated with resin and no air bubbles are trapped in the form.

5. After the fiberglass and resin have thoroughly hardened, remove the helmet from the mold. Spray the helmet with silver, bronze, or gold metallic paint and add touches of silver Rub-N-Buff, a burnishing compound available from craft, art, and hobby shops, to give dimension to the surface. Use additional polyester resin to glue costume jewels or other trim to the helmet.

Casting Resin

Casting resin is relatively easy to use for the theatre. It is simply mixed with its hardener and any additives such as dyes, pigments, metallic powders, or glitter, and then poured into a prepared mold. Once it is removed from the mold it may be sawed, drilled, or sanded with any power tool. Commercial molds may be purchased or molds may be made from clay, wax, Celluclay, plaster of paris or papier-mâché. Different resin-hardener formulations are used for thin and for thick castings. The appropriate resin should be used for each application to achieve the greatest strength and proper curing. In addition, the resin may be extended by adding **micro-balloons**. These are opaque, hollow glass beads that increase the mass but reduce the weight of cast forms and make them easier to cut, drill, and sand. ***CAUTION:*** **Casting resins must be used only in adequate ventilation. The resin and hardeners are highly flammable, as are their vapors. Avoid flame and high temperatures, and wear safety equipment, including protective gloves, a chemical apron, face mask, and respirator when working with this material!**

Example: To Cast a Glass Bust

Materials List	*Equipment List*
Plaster bandages	Scissors
Petroleum jelly	Pan of water
Plaster of paris	Mixing cups
Casting resin	Stir stick
Tape	

1. Make the mold by taking a plaster cast of an existing bust or the head and upper torso of someone. Be sure to use petroleum jelly as a mold release. Rather than casting entirely with plaster of paris, wrap plaster-impregnated bandages around the model. After the bandages have hardened, very carefully cut the cast in half from side to side along the ear lines and remove the sections from the model. Partially fill a cardboard carton with plaster of paris and gently press each section of the bandage mold into the wet plaster, being careful not to distort the molds. Allow the plaster to harden. This will add a great deal of strength to the molds when the casting resin is poured into them. Clean and thoroughly treat the molds with mold-release agent.

2. Following directions carefully, mix a sufficient quantity of resin to fill one of the molds and gently pour the liquid into it so no air bubbles become embedded. Mix the resin and fill the other mold. Allow the resin to harden. It will dry clear.

3. After the resin has thoroughly cured, remove the forms from the molds. Mix another small amount of resin and coat one of the flat joining surfaces with it. Press the two halves together and slide them around so the wet resin covers all of both surfaces. Be careful not to capture any air in the joint. Wipe away any excess resin. Place the halves on a piece of aluminum foil and carefully align the parts. Use wire or string to hold the parts in alignment while the resin hardens.

Felt

Another material that may be used for molding as well as many other effects is felt. It is moderately inexpensive and easily obtained from most fabric and craft stores.

Example: Make a Leather Saddle Bag from Felt

Materials List	*Equipment List*
Heavy brown felt	Paint brush
Plastic drop cloth	Scissors
Sheet of plywood	
Phlex-Glu or white glue	
Black and cordovan paste wax shoe polish	
Muslin	
Brown shoelaces	

1. Obtain the thickest piece of brown felt possible. Be sure that it is large enough for the saddle bag, keeping in mind that the material will shrink when it is moistened.

2. Wrap a clear plastic drop cloth tightly around a sheet of plywood and staple it in place. Using a hot air gun or a hair dryer, shrink the plastic until it is smooth by blowing hot air over the surface in continually moving circular patterns.

3. Thoroughly coat one side of the felt with undiluted Phlex-Glu or white glue. Wrinkle the fabric by balling it up tightly, then open it and spread the saturated felt on the plastic drop cloth; do not smooth it out too tightly since the wrinkles will give the sense of aging needed for old leather. If this were to be new leather, it would not be wrinkled but would be smoothed out flat on the plastic. Allow the glue to dry overnight. If the felt was thoroughly saturated, it might take even longer to dry.

4. After the felt has dried thoroughly, peel it off the drop cloth. All parts in contact with the plastic will have a shiny surface. Apply a coat of oxblood or cordovan paste wax shoe polish and black shoe polish randomly to the glued side of the felt. Buff the polish to a shine.

5. Draw the saddle bag pattern on the material and cut it out. If greater strength is desired, cut the same pattern from a piece of muslin and sew the two pieces of fabric together.

6. Punch holes along the seams and sew the fabric together with dark brown shoelaces.

Wood

Example: To Make a Sword from Wood

Materials List	*Equipment List*
3/4" plywood	Saber saw
Shellac, white glue, or Sculpt Or Coat	Belt sander with 50 or 80 grit paper
Chrome duct tape (or silver spray paint)	Hot-melt glue gun
Antique gold spray paint	
1/4" thick foam rubber	
Masking tape	
Cotton rope (clothesline)	
Hot-melt glue	
Cordovan shoe polish	

1. Find a drawing or photograph of the sword desired and draw its outline on 3/4" AD plywood. Cut out the sword with a saber saw or band saw.

2. Mark the longitudinal centerline of the blade (Figure 6–3A); this will be the blade's thickest part. The edges should taper to no less

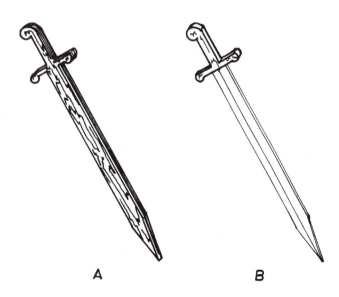

FIGURE 6–3
To make a sword, (A) cut the sword from a piece of 3/4" plywood. (B) Sand the sword to the appropriate taper and then trim it with chrome tape and other decorations.

A   B

239

than $\frac{1}{8}$" thick so they will not break easily. Using a belt sander with 80 grit paper, sand all sides of the blade to form the tapered edges of the sword. This may take quite a while.

3. Apply a coat of shellac, white glue, or Sculpt Or Coat to the entire sword. After this sealant has dried, spray the blade with silver spray paint. As an alternative, apply chrome auto body tape or chrome duct tape to the blade (Figure 6–3B). Make sure that the tape is very smooth. If more than one piece of tape is used, joints between pieces should only occur in logical places such as the edge of the blade or the high point on the V of the blade.

4. Paint the handle with antique gold spray paint. Wrap the grip with a thin layer of foam rubber, then neatly wind masking tape over the rubber in an overlapping spiral. Wrap one turn of $\frac{1}{4}$" cotton clothesline around each end of the handle and attach it with hot-melt glue. Coat the masking tape with brown or cordovan shoe polish and buff it dry. Add any desired costume jewels or trim.

If it is desirable, a metal sword can be manufactured by grinding flat steel into the appropriate shape and then polishing it with finer grinding stones until an actual sword has been made. The handle can be steel built up with wood, tape, and trims as described above. Pikes, halberds, and spears can be made in a similar manner.

Example: To Make a Scabbard

Materials List	*Equipment List*
$\frac{1}{8}$" hardboard	Saber saw
$\frac{1}{2}$" plywood	Pop riveter
White glue	
Masking tape	
Cordovan shoe polish	
$\frac{1}{8}$" pop rivet	
Strap	

1. Trace the outline of the blade of the sword that will be carried in the scabbard onto a piece of $\frac{1}{2}$" plywood. Thicker plywood may be needed if the maximum thickness of the blade is greater than $\frac{3}{8}$". Enlarge the pattern by $\frac{1}{2}$" on all edges.

2. Cut out the plywood and two pieces of $\frac{1}{8}$" hardboard on the outer line. Draw another line $\frac{3}{8}$" in from the edge of the plywood only and cut out the middle of only the $\frac{1}{2}$" plywood (Figure 6-4).

3. Placing white glue between each layer, make a sandwich of $\frac{1}{8}$" hardboard, the $\frac{1}{2}$" cut-out piece of plywood, and the remaining $\frac{1}{8}$" piece of hardboard. Tack these pieces together with some very small nails, brads, or staples and allow the glue to dry.

4. Wrap the scabbard from top to bottom with $\frac{3}{4}$" wide masking tape in an overlapping spiral pattern. Coat the tape with dark brown or cordovan paste-wax shoe polish and buff it dry.

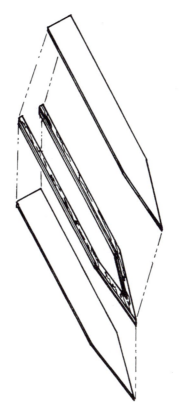

FIGURE 6–4
A scabbard can be made from a plywood core and two pieces of ⅛" hardboard cut to shape.

5. Make a loop of leather or fabric that will fit over a belt. Attach the loop of fabric to the top of the scabbard with a small pop rivet. Add decorative trim as desired. Insert the sword.

Example: To Make a Primitive Burning Torch

Materials List	Equipment List
1 2 × 2 × 2'-6"	Saw
Scrap board	Sandpaper
Plaster of paris	Mixing buckets
8d nail	
Modeling compound	
Sterno	

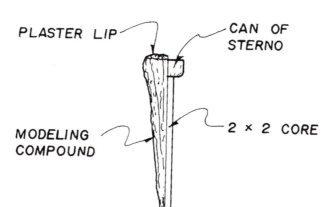

PLASTER LIP

CAN OF STERNO

MODELING COMPOUND

2 × 2 CORE

FIGURE 6–5
A primitive torch can be built around a core of 2 × 2. It is then molded with a modeling compound. Sterno is used for the flame.

1. Cut a piece of 2 × 2 approximately 2'-6" long. Round the edges and sand it smooth. A large dowel or a broom handle could be substituted for the 2 × 2. Drive an 8d nail through any board into the end of the 2 × 2. Clamp or nail the board to a table.

2. Mix a batch of Celluclay or similar modeling compound. Form the modeling compound around the 2 × 2 from a narrow handle at the bottom tapering in a cone to a 3" diameter at the top.

3. Center a can of **Sterno**, solid alcohol that is used under chafing dishes, on the very top of the 2 × 2 and bring the modeling compound tightly around the can to ¼" below its top edge. Allow the modeling compound to dry thoroughly.

4. Mix a small amount of plaster of paris and form it around the top edge of the Sterno can. Do not let the plaster overlap the top of the can. Blend some of the plaster down onto the dried modeling compound. Allow the plaster to dry.

5. Paint the torch as desired. Tree bark or a similar effect is appropriate.

To use the torch, open the can of Sterno and sprinkle in a dash of salt. The salt makes the flame more visible. Ignite the flame with a match. To put out the flame, snuff it with a damp (not wet) cloth; then tightly cover the can. When the Sterno is expended, pry the old can out and slip in a new can with a little hot-melt glue on the bottom to hold it in place.

Example: To Make a Silver Candelabra

Materials List	*Equipment List*
1" × 16" dowel rod	Saw
Scrap board	Matte knife
8d nail	Hot-melt glue gun
8 ounce drinking cup	
6" diameter paper plate	
Plaster of paris	
16 or 32 ounce drinking cup	
Masking tape	
Candle stub	
1/4" clothesline	
1/8" sash cord	
Tiny plastic leaves	
Hot-melt glue	
White glue	
Silver spray paint	

1. Cut a piece of 1" diameter dowel rod 16" long. Be sure that both ends are perfectly square. Sand the rod very smooth. Drive an 8d nail through a board into one end of the rod and nail or clamp the board to a table or work bench.

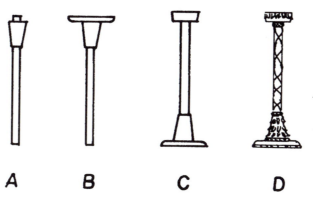

FIGURE 6–6
To make a silver candelabra, (A and B) make the base from a paper cup and a paper plate filled with plaster of paris. (C) Make the candle cup from a portion of a paper cup filled with plaster of paris. (D) Decorate the assembly with hot-melt glue, twine, small leaves and other appropriate trims and jewels.

2. Cut a hole large enough for the dowel rod to pass through in the bottom of a 6- or 8-ounce drinking cup and at the exact center of a 6" diameter paper plate. Slip the cup over the end of the dowel rod until ½" of the rod extends beyond the top of the cup (Figure 6–6A). Put a ring of tape around the bottom of the cup to hold it in place.

3. Fill the paper cup with plaster of paris, and then slip the paper plate onto the dowel rod so that the bottom of the plate is against the lip of the cup. Fill the paper plate with plaster of paris also (Figure 6–6B). Allow the plaster to harden.

4. Pull the nail attaching the dowel rod to the board. Turn the assembly over so that it rests on the plaster-filled plate. Find a large drinking cup with a 2½" to 3" diameter bottom. Cut 1" of the bottom off the cup. Cut a hole large enough for the dowel rod to pass through at the exact center of the cup bottom and slide it right-side-up ½" onto the dowel rod (Figure 6–6C). Wrap a piece of tape around the bottom of the cup to hold it in place. Fill the cup two-thirds full with plaster of paris. Cut off 1½" of the bottom end of the size candle to be used in this holder. Coat it with petroleum jelly and center it in the plaster-filled cup bottom. After the plaster has set but is not yet completely hardened, work the candle segment out of the cup.

5. After the plaster has fully dried, remove the tape holding the top and bottom drinking cups in place and sand off any plaster spills.

6. Use hot-melt glue to attach the trim. Wrap a ring of ¼" cotton clothesline around the bottom of the paper plate, another where the plate meets the small drinking cup, a third where the small drinking cup meets the dowel rod, and finally where the rod meets the bottom of the large drinking cup (Figure 6–6D).

7. Wrap ⅛" sash cord or thick twine in a spiral pattern around the center section of the rod in each direction. Apply tiny plastic leaves in a pattern to the sides of each of the drinking cups and around the flat surface of the candle holder. Apply an even pattern of flutes around the perimeter of the small and large drinking cups with hot-melt glue.

8. Coat the entire assembly with undiluted white glue or gesso, allow it to dry, and then spray the candlestick with silver or gold paint and burnish with Rub N Buff.

Example: To Make an Ancient Metallic Chandelier

Materials List	*Equipment List*
1 24" × 24" ³/₄" AD plywood	Saber saw
3 ¹/₂" screw eyes	Matte knife
Medium-weight illustration board	Staple gun
Staples	
Black paint	
Chain	
Candles	

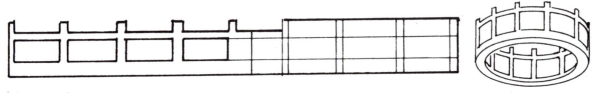

FIGURE 6–7

To make a medieval metal chandelier, make the sides from illustration board and the base from ³/₄" plywood.

1. Cut a piece of ³/₄" AD plywood into a 24" diameter circle. Measure 2" in from the edge of the circle and cut out the center portion to leave a 24" diameter outer ring that is 2" wide.

2. Determine the circumference of this circle. The formula is diameter × pi (3.14) = circumference (24" × 3.14 = 75.36"). Select a starting point and place a mark at one-third points (every 25¹/₈") around the perimeter of the ring. Insert a screw eye at each mark on the D side of the plywood.

3. Cut strips of medium-weight illustration board 8" wide and of sufficient length to measure 75¹/₂" long (the circumference of the ring of the plywood circle) to encircle the ring. Lay out the pattern of the sides of the chandelier on the illustration board and cut it out with a matte knife (Figure 6-7). An easy pattern consists of a 2" wide band solidly around the bottom, a 3" wide space above that, followed by a 1" wide band. A 1" wide vertical strip the full 8" height of the illustration board should be placed 8¹/₄" on-center throughout the pattern.

4. Staple the illustration board to the sides of the plywood ring. Make sure the screw eyes are pointed up. Paint the ring and illustration board black. Any paint may be used, but be careful not to get the illustration board too wet.

5. Attach a light-weight chain 2'-0" long to each of the screw eyes. Attach the chains to the bottom link of a long chain that will rise from that point.

6. If desirable, pieces of ¹/₂" diameter conduit topped with miniature Christmas tree lights can be taped inside the illustration board or candles can be attached inside the perimeter of the chandelier at each of the verticals. The candles may *not* be lit.

Example: To Make an Electronics Console

Materials List	*Equipment List*
4" × 19" × ¼" hardboard	Handsaw
Silver spray paint	Hot-melt glue gun
¼", ½", and 1" dowel rods	
Black electrician's tape	
Hot-melt glue	
Felt-tip marker	

1. Cut a piece of ¼" hardboard 4" × 19". Paint it with silver spray paint. Two or three thin coats will do this best.

2. Cut pieces of various diameter dowel rods ½" long. Sand each piece smooth and paint it silver.

3. Use hot-melt glue to attach the painted pieces of dowel rod onto the hardboard panel console face, matching the pattern of knobs and buttons on actual electronics equipment. Where backlighted windows must occur, use black electrical tape carefully and smoothly laid in place.

4. Use a felt-tip pen or an enamel art pen to letter in names and marks by each group of controls.

For this prop to look appropriate on stage, it must not be placed next to real electronics equipment or a true metallic finish. The contrast will make the prop look fake.

Example: To Make an Ancient Leather-Bound Book

Materials List	*Equipment List*
(Old issues of *The Wall Street Journal*)	Matte knife
Strong tea	Scissors
1 6" × 6" × 17½" piece of muslin	Paint brush
White glue	
2 12" × 18" × ⅛" hardboard	
Vinyl fabric 20" × 28¼"	
Rubber cement	
Decorative fabric or paper	
India ink	

1. The finished book will measure 12" wide × 18" high and 2" thick. Use the inside pages of *The Wall Street Journal* or another newspaper that does not have any pictures to make the pages of the book. Cut a 2" thick stack of newspaper pages to 11½" × 17½". Spread the pages out and brush them on both sides with strong tea. Allow the paper to dry. This will stain the pages to make them look like old paper.

A.

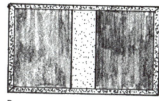

B.

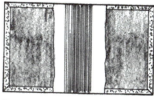

C.

FIGURE 6–8

To make an ancient-appearing book, (A) bind newspaper with muslin. (B) Construct a cover from hardboard and leather-looking vinyl. (C) Attach the newspaper stack to the cover. Trim as appropriate.

2. Restack the newspaper and coat one edge of the stack with undiluted white glue. Saturate a piece of muslin 6" wide by 17½" long with glue. Center the fabric over the glued edge of the stack of newspapers and allow it to dry (Figure 6–8A).

3. Cut two pieces of ⅛" hardboard 12" × 18". Cut a piece of leather-looking vinyl the width of the two covers plus the thickness of the binding, plus 2¼" (12" + 12" + 2" + 2¼" = 28¼") by the height of the covers plus 2" (18" + 2" = 20"). Draw a pencil line 1" in from each edge on the back (wrong side) of the vinyl.

4. Spread rubber cement or spray adhesive on one side of each hardboard cover. Place the covers on the pencil lines 1" from each edge of the fabric leaving a 2¼" gap between the pieces. Spread some additional glue on the 1" border around each piece of hardboard and neatly fold the material over the edge of the hardboard; trim inside the corners for a neat fit (Figure 6–8B).

5. Center the glued stack of newspapers over the gap between the hardboard covers and push the hardboard against either side of the stack. Glue the muslin flaps to the inside of the hardboard covers (Figure 6–8C).

6. Cut a piece of decorative fabric or paper to fit the inside cover on each side of the book and glue it in place.

7. Letter the back of the binding with black transfer letters, India ink, or gold ink.

Example: To Make a Manhattan Phone Book

Materials List	*Equipment List*
Old thick phone book	Matte knife
Flint paper	
Rubber cement	
Dry transfer letters	

1. Old phone books are often available from public libraries. Each year they should be contacted and asked for their discards to build a stock of phone books for historical purposes as well as for adaptation. Also, current telephone directories for other cities can be purchased from the telephone company. For contemporary plays, a Manhattan phone book from the current year is satisfactory; however, the style of phone books has changed so a production set in the 1960s or 1970s will need a different cover.

2. Obtain some white, grey, or yellow flint paper. **Flint paper** is a glossy paper similar to that used as a cover on telephone books; it is available from better art stores. Enamel paper from printers can also be used. If neither flint nor enamel paper is available, use a good-quality opaque paper in the proper color.

3. Cut the paper a few inches larger than the cover of any existing 3" or thicker phone book. Coat the existing cover and also the underside of the flint paper with rubber cement and allow it to dry.

4. After the cement has dried, smooth the paper into place. Once the two glued surfaces make contact they are almost impossible to separate. Trim the new cover even with the edges of the existing cover.

5. Using **dry transfer letters**, letters that are rubbed off a sheet of plastic onto the surface, apply the name *Manhattan* to the front cover and spine of the phone book. As an alternative, the title can be generated on a computer with a laser printer.

Example: To Make a Large Ornate Samovar

Materials List	*Equipment List*
Cake stand	Matte knife
2½ gallon round ice cream carton	Pop riveter
	Hot-melt glue gun
Plumber's plunger	Paint brush
Lamp shade finial	
1 × 4 block of wood	
Cabinet pulls	
Pop rivets	
1" ethafoam rod	
Hot-melt glue	
Small plastic leaves	
Toilet paper	
White glue	
Antique gold spray paint	
Brass Rub-N-Buff	

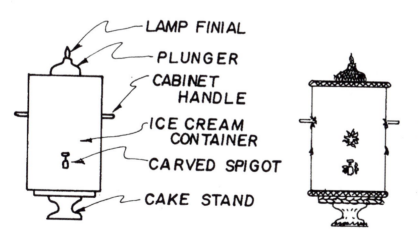

LAMP FINIAL
PLUNGER
CABINET HANDLE
ICE CREAM CONTAINER
CARVED SPIGOT
CAKE STAND

FIGURE 6–9
To make a samovar, assemble a variety of parts that create the proper look and then carefully decorate and paint the piece.

1. Make a spigot from a piece of wood cut into the proper profile and sanded into shape. Attach the spigot pointing up 4" below the top edge of a round 2½-gallon commercial ice cream container or tall narrow stock pot. To do this, install a screw from the inside of the container toward the outside into the back of the spigot. Put some panel adhesive or hot-melt glue on the back of the spigot as well.

2. Start with a plastic cake stand as a base. An inverted banana-split serving dish as well as a variety of other shapes can be used instead. Use hot-melt glue to attach the ice cream container upside down to the top of the stand so the spigot points down.

3. Attach the rubber portion of a plumber's plunger or a large kitchen funnel centered at the top of the ice cream container. Again, other plastic serving dishes or any other object of appropriate shape might be used in place of the plunger. Attach a finial from the top of a lamp shade, a small decorative cabinet pull, or some other small decorative knob on top of the plumber's plunger (Figure 6–9A).

4. Find a pair of small, matching cabinet handles. Using pop rivets, attach each handle at exactly the same location on either side of the ice cream container.

5. Encircle the top and bottom edges of the ice cream container with 1" ethafoam rod cut in half. Measure the length of ethafoam needed, lay it on the table, and simply draw a matte knife through it the long way. Glue the ethafoam in place with hot-melt glue or panel adhesive. Apply a consistent zigzag pattern of hot-melt glue or twine over the ethafoam rod.

6. Pull several small leaves off a plastic vine. Glue them in a pattern around the spigot where it attaches to the ice cream container. Attach an overlapping pattern of leaves around the base of the plumber's plunger and another pattern around the base of the cake plate. Add a small pattern of plastic flowers and leaves as decoration centered above the spigot and around each of the handles where they attach to the ice cream container. Arrange another pattern of leaves and blossoms centered on each side of the samovar below the handles (Figure 6–9B).

7. Cover the entire assembly with gesso or toilet paper and white glue. Allow it to dry thoroughly, and then paint the samovar with two or three thin coats of antique gold spray paint. Treat the raised texture of the samovar with brass or copper Rub-N-Buff.

Example: To Make a Colonial Wall Sconce

Materials List	*Equipment List*
1 1 × 2 × 6"	Saw
1 fluted 10" paper plate	Caulk gun
1/8" hardboard	
Empty thread spool	
Panel adhesive	
White glue	
Black spray paint	
Plastic parfait sundae glass	

FIGURE 6–10
To make a wall sconce, make the reflector from a paper plate and make the globe from a plastic ice cream sundae glass. The arm can be a piece of 1 × 2.

1. Cut a piece of wood 1 × 2 × 6" long. Sand it thoroughly. Staple the block of wood to a 10" paper plate. The fluted edges of the plate may face toward the block or away from it. Glue an empty thread spool centered near the end of the 1 × 2 block (Figure 6–10).

2. Cut a piece of 1/8" hardboard to fit inside the flat part of the plate. Glue the hardboard to the plate with panel adhesive.

3. Coat the entire assembly with white glue. When it is dry, spray it with flat black paint.

4. Using hot-melt glue or panel adhesive, attach a plastic parfait sundae glass centered on the thread spool. Melt the bottom of a candle and stand it up inside the parfait glass. Do not light it!

5. Attach the sconce to scenery by stapling around the edges of the plate to a stile in a flat or to another wooden surface.

Example: To Make a Lantern

Materials List

1   1 × 6 × 12"
1   1 × 4 × 9"
6d box or finish nails
White glue
Flat black paint
Flashlight
2   D-cell batteries
20" of #18 wire
Low-voltage toggle switch
Hot-melt glue
Frost gel or illustration board
Black electrician's tape
Small screw eye
Short, light chain

Equipment List

Saw

Hammer

Soldering gun

Hot-melt glue gun

Matte knife

Stapler

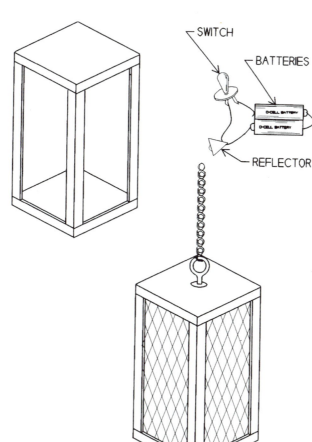

SWITCH

BATTERIES

REFLECTOR

FIGURE 6–11
Assemble a lantern from a wooden frame made from 1 × 1 and 1 × 6 for the top and bottom. Use plastic sheets to make "glass" sides. Build the wiring around the parts of a flashlight.

249

1. Cut two blocks of $1 \times 6 \times 5\frac{1}{2}$" long and rip four pieces of $1 \times 1 \times 9$" long from the 1×4. Using 6d box or finish nails and white glue, attach a 1×1 at each corner of the blocks to form a hollow rectangle with the 1×6 as ends and the 1×1s between them. Paint the assembly black (Figure 6–11).

2. Remove the reflector and socket from a flashlight. Tape two D-cell batteries together side by side facing opposite directions. Solder a 6" long piece of insulated (18 to 22 gauge) wire to the top of one battery, another to the bottom of the other battery, and then a short wire between the unattached top and bottom of both batteries.

3. Solder the unattached wire from the top of the battery to the base of the lightbulb socket. Solder the unattached wire from the bottom of the battery to the switch removed from the flashlight. Attach another wire to the other side of the switch and connect it to the side of the lightbulb socket. Flip the switch to make sure the light works.

4. Hot-melt glue the battery/light assembly inside the bottom of the lantern. Bundle the wires so they are out of the way but allow the switch to be accessible.

5. Cut four pieces of frost **gel**, light coloring media available from theatrical suppliers, $5\frac{1}{2}$" $\times 10\frac{1}{2}$". Glue or staple a piece of gel to each side of the lantern. Cover the staples and seams with black electrician's tape. If a pierced tin look is desired, the gel can be replaced with illustration board punched with an appropriate pattern and painted with black spray paint.

6. Insert a small screw eye at the exact center of the top of the lantern and attach a lightweight chain to it.

Example: To Make a Magic Wand

Materials List	*Equipment List*
$\frac{1}{2}$" dowel rod 24" long	Saw
$1\frac{1}{2}$" wooden macrame ball	Screwdriver
2" $\times$ #8 roundhead wood screw and flat washer	Drill
White glue	
Gold glitter	
Star mold	
Casting resin	

1. Cut a piece of $\frac{1}{2}$" diameter dowel rod 24" long. Attach a $1\frac{1}{2}$" wooden macramé ball to one end of the rod with a 2" $\times$ #8 roundhead wood screw (it may be necessary to use a washer to prevent the screw from going through the hole in the ball). Brush the rod and ball with white glue and then sprinkle gold glitter on it.

2. Obtain or make a star mold.

3. Mix a small batch of casting resin and add some gold glitter to it. Fill the mold with this mixture and allow the resin to cure.

4. Remove the star from the mold. Drill a $\frac{5}{8}$" diameter hole in the edge of the star. Slide the glitter-coated dowel rod into the hole and fill the void with a little bit of prepared casting resin. Allow the resin to harden.

Example: To Make an Elaborately Decorated Picture Frame of Any Size

Materials List

Hardboard

Hot-melt glue

$\frac{1}{8}$" sash cord

Plastic flowers and leaves

$\frac{1}{2}$" rope

$\frac{1}{4}$" rope

Uncooked pasta shapes

Gesso or toilet paper and
   white glue

Gold spray paint

Equipment List

Matte knife

Hot-melt glue gun

Paint brush

1. Cut a piece of hardboard to the exact size and shape needed. If the frame is to be quite large, $\frac{1}{4}$" thick material should be used; however, if it is a small or medium-sized frame, $\frac{1}{8}$" hardboard will be adequate.

2. At each corner, glue $\frac{1}{8}$" sash cord arranged in a coil.

3. Glue a plastic flower blossom at the center of each side of the frame. Tear some leaves from old plastic vines or flowers and assemble them in a pattern around each of the blossoms.

4. Glue $\frac{1}{2}$" rope all the way around the outside perimeter of the frame. Glue $\frac{1}{8}$" sash cord all the way around the inside perimeter of the frame.

5. Glue various kinds of uncooked pasta over all of the remaining surface of the hardboard.

6. Coat the entire assembly with gesso. Allow it to dry thoroughly. Paint the frame with gold spray paint.

Example: To Make a Cannon

Materials List

1   5'-0" carpet roller tube

1   6'-0" carpet roller tube

Panel adhesive

Tape

20"   1" ethafoam rod

1   6" diameter paper plate

Dope and muslin or wheat
   paste and newspaper

$\frac{1}{4}$" × 4'-0" × 4'-0"
   hardboard

2" × 3'-0" × 4'-0"
   Styrofoam

1   2 × 12 × 1'-6"

Equipment List

Saw

Drill with $\frac{1}{4}$" and 1" bit

Paint brush

Example: To Make a Cannon (continued)

White glue

8   3½" × 12 roundhead
    wood screws

1   1" × 48" dowel rod

1   ¼" × 36" dowel rod

Toilet paper

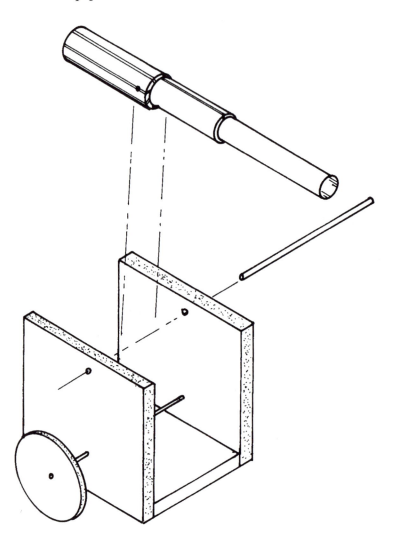

FIGURE 6–12

To build a cannon, assemble the barrel from carpet roller tube. The base and wheels can be manufactured from hardboard and plastic foam.

1. Cut a piece of carpet roller tube 5'-0" long, another 3'-0" long, and two pieces 1'-6" long. Cut the 3'-0" long piece into two long half-cylinders; cut both 1'-6" long pieces into four quarter-cylinders (Figure 6–12).

2. Using panel adhesive, glue the two 3'-0" long half-cylinders around one end of the 5'-0" long piece of tube; hold them in place with duct or masking tape. Glue as many pieces as needed of the 1'-6" long tube that was cut in quarters around the end of the 3'-0" sections; hold these in place with tape as well.

3. Wrap the narrow end of the barrel with 1" diameter ethafoam rod; use panel adhesive to hold it in place. If necessary, a roll of muslin or newspaper could be used or a sock could be stuffed to form this lip.

4. Glue a 6" diameter paper plate to the opposite end of the barrel. If desired, additional trim can be glued to the back of the paper plate.

5. Cover the barrel with three layers of papier-mâché, or paint the barrel with dope and apply wide muslin strips over the tube. Saturate the muslin with another coat of dope and allow it to dry. Trim off any excess fabric.

6. Cut four pieces of ¼" hardboard and two pieces of 2" thick Styrofoam 1'-6" × 1'-6". Cut four pieces of ¼" hardboard and two pieces of 2" thick Styrofoam into 12" diameter circles. Using panel adhesive, assemble each piece of foam between two layers of hardboard.

7. Draw a centerline on each of the square hardboard-and-foam sandwiches. Drill one 1" diameter hole on the centerline 3" down from the top and another 1" diameter hole 3" up from the bottom.

8. Cut a piece of 2 × 12 1'-6" long and sand it smooth. Using white glue and 3½" × #12 roundhead wood screws or drywall screws, attach the hardboard-and-foam panels to each side of the 2 × 12 to form a U with one hole just above the 2 × 12 and the other at the open top edge. Cover the entire U with white glue and toilet paper; allow it to dry thoroughly.

9. Drill a 1" diameter hole in the center of each hardboard-and-foam circle.

10. Cut a piece of 1" dowel rod 24¼" long. Drill ¼" holes all the way through the rod 1", 3¼" and 4¼" from each end. Cut six pieces of ¼" dowel rod 2½" long.

11. Slide the 1" dowel through one of the 12" discs, then through the bottom holes in the U and finally through the other 12" disc. The discs should be between the holes at 1" and 3¼" on the rod. The U should fall between the holes at 4¼". Put some white glue on each of the ¼" dowel rods and tap one into each ¼" hole.

12. Drill a 1" diameter hole all the way through the carpet tube 1'-8" from the back of the cannon barrel.

13. Cut a piece of 1" dowel rod 17" long. Drill a ¼" hole all the way through the dowel rod ½" and 5" in from each end. Cut four pieces of ¼" dowel rod 2½" long.

14. Slide the 1" dowel rod through the top hole on one side of the U. Hold the cannon barrel in place in the middle of the U and pass the rod through it and into the other side of the U. Center the rod and the cannon barrel. Put a little white glue on each of the ¼" dowel rods and tap them into each of the holes in the 1" dowel.

15. Paint the cannon black and allow it to dry. Spray some silver paint into the air *above* the cannon and allow the mist to fall onto it.

Easy and Fast Solutions

Coins

Alternative #1: Go to a construction site and find the knockouts from electrical boxes. File off any rough edges and then paint them silver or gold.

Alternative #2: Place a small piece of masking tape over the holes of various-size metal washers. Spray paint the coins silver or gold.

Alternative #3: Purchase some heavy tooling foil from an art or hobby store. Use a punch or scissors to cut the foil into round, square, or octagonal coins.

Books

Books on shelves are always attractive set dressings for interiors: they add color and visual interest. School libraries are sometimes willing to loan books for this use. However, books are very heavy so bookcases must be quite strong to support them or alternatives must be found.

Alternative #1: Remove and save the spine from all of the books. Define the area of the flat that is to be the bookshelf and paint it black. Frame that area if it were a three-dimensional bookshelf using appropriate moldings; then glue or nail painted 1 × 1s to the flat to look like the edges of the shelves. Use hot-melt glue to attach the spines of the books to the flat so it appears that the books are resting on the shelves.

Alternative #2: Remove the inside of each of the books and only keep the covers. Fill the space between the covers with pieces of plastic foam or small blocks of wood to give the books the proper thickness. Place these books on existing three-dimensional bookshelves.

Since actual books are destroyed for these solutions, it is best to purchase inexpensive books with attractive bindings from Goodwill stores or at rummage sales.

Parchment

Parchment can easily be made from good typing paper or onion-skin paper. If parchment scrolls are needed, they can be made from white shelving paper. To create the effect, brush very strong tea onto the paper. A more intense effect is created if the tea is allowed to puddle in places to create deeper and uneven staining. After the tea has dried, wrinkles can be removed by going over the paper with a warm iron. If the parchment and the message on it are ancient, letter the material before staining the paper with tea. If the parchment and message are new, treat the paper first and then letter the message.

Foaming Beer

Carefully remove the caps from real beer bottles, remove the contents, and clean the bottles. Refill the bottles with a mixture of ginger ale and root beer. Then carefully recap them. It may be necessary to crimp the caps with pliers. Just before the foaming beer is needed on stage, wrap a towel around the top of the bottle and shake it up. When the bottle is opened on stage it should fizz vigorously. Warm soda pop fizzes more than cold soda.

Champagne

Obtain empty champagne bottles, being sure to collect the corks as well. Thoroughly rinse out the bottles and refill them with good ginger ale. Force the cork back into each bottle. If necessary, the cork may be trimmed with a knife or sandpaper to get it to fit. Wrap the top with thin decorative foil. Shake the bottle vigorously before it is taken on stage to be opened.

Wine and Liquor

Food coloring is mixed with water to represent noncarbonated alcoholic beverages. It is important to get the correct color for each beverage mixed. Yellow food color with a few drops of red and a drop of blue makes excellent whiskey, scotch, and bourbon. Red food color with a drop of blue makes a good burgundy wine. White wine should have a slightly yellow tint to it. All of the colors should be checked under stage lighting.

Guns

Period weapons are always difficult to find for a production. The easiest and safest solution is to purchase and assemble hobby kits of reproduction weapons. Often these are available completely finished so the only task is assembly, and painting is unnecessary.

Inedible Food

Whether it is a Thanksgiving turkey or a ham sandwich, food can be a very demanding props problem. The easiest solution is to have as much food as possible in a show in covered containers. If the lid is never lifted no one in the audience will know that the mashed potatoes are actually sawdust. If the food must be exposed, very expensive artificial foods are available from display companies. Replacements can be carved from plastic foam or foam rubber, molded from papier-mâché, or made from soft sculptures of stuffed nylons. These must be well painted to be convincing. If there is no other solution, real food can be used instead of the artificial food. This is very expensive and can be quite smelly since it will spoil quickly due to the heat on stage.

Stored Food

Food in cabinets is always in containers so it is simply a matter of collecting cereal boxes, soup cans, and so on to place on the shelves. Variety can be added to this collection or a sense of historical period created by using home-canned goods. Glass canning jars can be filled with red ball fringe and some water to represent canned cherries. Green vegetables can be replicated with green ball fringe or shreds of green fabric and water. Pickles can be made from short pieces of garden hose. Mincemeat might be sawdust in a suspension of brown food color and water. Pickled pigs feet can be balls of pink socks. Dried meat such as jerky can be made from scraps of leather, vinyl, or felt. Freshly butchered meat can best be represented by wrapping a bundle of newspaper or fabric in butcher paper and tying it with string; adding just a touch of brown-red paint to suggest blood can be helpful. Preserves can be duplicated by coating the inside of a jar with an opaque orange, red, or deep purple paint. Bread in pans, milkshakes in glasses, and mounds of mashed potatoes can be made with foam-in-place plastic and just a little bit of paint; the shape of the foam food, the container that it is in, and additions of appropriate accessories such as a straw or a cherry are persuasive details. The opportunity for creativity with these solutions is virtually endless.

Edible Food

Food consumed by an actor must be mild in flavor, easy to chew and swallow, and must not clog the throat. Most beef can be represented by slightly moistening and compressing slices of dark bread; turkey may be slices of compressed white bread; and sliced ham can be made from compressed white bread cut to shape and a little food color brushed over it. A loaf of coarse dark bread can easily substitute for a meat loaf. Gravy can be made from a mix or by diluting chocolate pudding. A fancy sandwich need be nothing more than bread with margarine and lettuce. Whenever bread is used, put a little margarine on it to help the actor swallow. Nuts and popcorn are easy props to use; however, they often catch in the actor's throat. Small balls of moistened bread can be substituted for either of these snacks. Other foods that are easy to adapt to look like real food and that actors can usually swallow easily are mashed potatoes, pudding, gelatin dessert, and Cool-Whip.

SPECIAL EFFECTS

Many productions are enhanced by the addition of explosions, fog, smoke, and flame. Here are a few ways to achieve these effects.

Fog and Smoke

Fog and smoke are essentially the same effect. It is more a matter of how the effect is perceived than how it is made that determines whether the audience is watching a fire or a foggy night.

Commercial fog machines may be rented or purchased. Remote-control chemical foggers utilize an oil-based compound that is pressurized and heated to project a constant stream of fog. Projected directly from the machine, the fog tends to fill the air with a haze. If the stream of fog is passed over some dry ice as it comes out of the machine, the fog tends to stay closer to the floor for a more ground-hugging effect. The fog stays in the air for quite a while unless there is a draft or strong air currents that will dissipate the effect quickly. The fog may be directed to a specific location by shooting it into flexible dryer hose that carries it to the desired spot.

Movement of the fog can be aided with a blower box (Figure 6–13). Construct a wooden box that is one-third larger than the fog machine. Install a small squirrel-cage blower on the top or at one end and a 4" vent on the other. Place the fog machine inside the box, attach a dryer hose to the 4" vent, and turn on the fog and the blower. Fog will accumulate inside the box and will be blown along the hose to the set. This offers several advantages: (1) the fog machine is located out of the setting so it need not be hidden, (2) the machine can be easily reached for servicing in the event of a failure, and (3) the machine noise heard by the audience is minimized since the fogger can be placed in a remote location.

A low, rolling, ground-hugging fog is obtained with a dry-ice fogger. These fairly simple machines may be rented or purchased. They consist of a 30- or 55-gallon drum fitted with an electric water-heater element, a tight-fitting lid, and a squirrel-cage blower. Flexible dryer

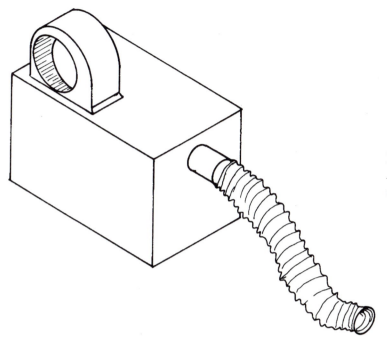

FIGURE 6–13
A blower box for a fog machine.

hose is run from the top of the drum to the set. To make fog, the drum is partially filled with water that is heated by the electric element. Dry ice is plunged into the hot water and boils to produce a fog that is blown out of the barrel into the dryer hose by the fan. This fog will stay low and close to the ground until it disperses. It dissipates quickly. The water cools rapidly and must reheat before another shot of fog is possible; this can take several hours. *CAUTION:* **If the water is allowed to get too hot, it will boil over when the dry ice is immersed in it and may cause severe burns.**

A slow, coiling smoke coming from a burning cigarette, a bubbling cauldron, or a smoking electrical outlet can be simulated by placing **sal ammoniac** on a pie plate and heating it on a hot plate. Once heated a $1/4$ teaspoon of the chemical will produce quite a lot of smoke. Sal ammoniac may be obtained from chemistry departments at schools and chemical supply companies.

Quick bursts of smoke or fog can be obtained from a carbon dioxide (CO_2) fire extinguisher. The shot from the extinguisher is very noisy and the fog dissipates quickly. If large amounts of fog are needed, it is practical to obtain large cylinders of the chemical from companies that supply industrial or hospital gases.

Small puffs of smoke can be made by filling a kitchen baster with unscented talcum powder and squeezing the bulb to blow the powder into the air.

Gun Shots

Unless an especially loud shot is needed, the effect of a gunshot can be created by placing the end of a 2'-0" long 1 × 6 under one foot and holding the other end of the board about 18" off of the floor. By putting pressure on the board with the foot and letting go, the board will slap the floor to make the cracking noise of a gunshot. The noise can be intensified by slapping the board on an unpadded platform raised off the floor. The sound can also be altered by using different size boards and varying the surface they strike.

Another way to simulate a gunshot sound is with a **starter pistol**, which can often be borrowed from an athletic department. These small pistols use blank ammunition. The end of the barrel is partially blocked so the paper wad from the pistol will break up. Starter pistols sound satisfactory in small theatres but sound like cap guns in large spaces. On stage, a starter pistol usually looks like a toy gun.

Real weapons are always dangerous on stage and should be avoided whenever possible. Any pistol or rifle capable of firing should be kept strictly under lock and key. When it is brought out for use, the barrel and chamber should be inspected by the props master and the person who carries the weapon. If the weapon is fired, it should be inspected by the person at whom it is fired as well. If a real weapon is fired on stage, it must be loaded with blank ammunition. All chambers should be filled with blanks just before the weapon is taken on stage and all chambers should be emptied as soon as the weapon is brought offstage after the last time it is fired. To avoid misfires, the weapon should be cleaned before the run of the production. *CAUTION:* **The paper wad that holds the gun powder charge in a blank cartridge is propelled from the end of the weapon upon discharge. The paper wad can penetrate flesh and bone within several feet of the weapon and the exploded gun powder can cause burns. Never aim a blank charge directly at someone on stage nor at the audience.**

Flame

Actual flame should be avoided on stage whenever possible. Not only is live flame dangerous because of all the flammables usually present on stage, but live flames distract the audience from the performance. Sometimes, however, real torches or candles are needed. In those situations, reasonable precautions should be taken to prevent a fire and preparations should be made in case a fire does start. Certified workable ABC (usable on all fires) fire extinguishers should be placed in each wing and all crew members trained in their use.

When torches or some other kind of open flame are being used, a "cool" fuel such as Sterno should be used. It should be lit just before the torch is carried on stage and smothered and capped as soon as it is brought off the stage. A little salt added to the Sterno will make the flame more visible. Candles must always be firmly seated in a weighted holder or in moist sand when they are used so they do not accidentally tip over. When possible, candles should be replaced with a battery-operated substitute. When actors smoke on stage, deep ashtrays should be filled with damp sand and shallow ashtrays should have a little bit of water in the bottom of them so actors can quickly stub out cigarettes.

Flashes

Flashes in the wings can be simulated with a single burst of a strobe light or with a flashbulb from a camera. Onstage flashes can be created with flash powder. **Flash powder** is a modified mixture of gun powder. It must be fired only from an acceptable container. Commercial flash pots can be purchased and should be used. **Flash paper** may also be used to create a quick effect. This is a treated tissue paper that will ignite at very low temperature. A single spark can set it off.

CONCLUSION

There are seemingly hundreds of props and special effects needed for production. The larger, more complex the show, the more furniture, hand props, set dressings, accessories, and special effects necessary. The nature of these articles is dictated by the period, style, and quality of the production. Careful planning when a play is selected and designed, as well as good organization and communication about the needs of the show, can ease the task of the props master.

The props master is a creative problem solver who devises schemes to find props and creates designs and invents solutions to manufacture articles. The solutions presented here should be used as guides to direct thinking about the process of invention and problem solving. In addition, there are a few good books listed in the Bibliography specifically on the subject of properties construction that will also be helpful for the props master.

When the props are appropriate for the play, they strengthen the dramatic effect of the performance and enhance credibility of the production. This is the goal of props for a production.

Bibliography

Adams, Jeanette T. *New Complete Woodworking Handbook* (Rev. Ed.). New York: Arco, 1975.

Association of Theatrical Artists and Craftspeople. *The New York Theatrical Source Book*. New York: Broadway Press, 1985.

Burris-Meyer, Harold, and E. C. Cole. *Scenery for the Theatre* (Rev. Ed.). Boston: Little, Brown, & Co., 1971.

Carter, Paul. *Backstage Handbook: An Illustrated Almanac of Technical Information*. New York: Broadway Press, 1988.

Clark, Stephen, and Daniel Lyman (Eds.). *The Complete Illustrated Tool Book*. New York: Galahad Books, 1974.

Clay, James H., and Daniel Krempel. *The Theatrical Image*. New York: McGraw-Hill, 1967.

Committee of Wire Rope Producers. *Wire Rope Users Manual* (2nd ed.). Washington, DC: Iron and Steel Institute, 1981.

Gillette, A. S., and J. Michael Gillette. *Stage Scenery: Its Construction and Rigging* (3rd ed.). New York: Harper and Row, 1981.

Glerum, Jay O. *Stage Rigging Handbook*. Carbondale, IL: Southern Illinois University Press, 1987.

Govier, Jacquie. *Create Your Own Stage Props*. Englewood Cliffs, NJ: Prentice Hall, 1984.

James, Thurston. *The Theatre Props Handbook*. Whitehall, VA: Betterway Publications, 1987.

McCloud, Kevin. *Decorative Style: The Most Original and Comprehensive Sourcebook of Styles, Treatments, Techniques and Materials*. New York: Simon and Schuster, 1990.

Marx, Ina Brousseau, Allen Marx, and Robert Marx. *Professional Painted Finishes*. New York: Watson-Guptill Publications, 1991.

Motley. *Theatre Props*. New York: Drama Book Specialists (Publishers), 1975.

Payne, Chris. *Furniture Finishing and Refinishing*. Menlo Park, CA: Lane Publishing, 1977.

Payne, Darwin Reid. *Design for the Stage: First Steps*. Carbondale, IL: Southern Illinois University Press, 1974.

Pecktal, Lynn. *Designing and Painting for the Theatre*. New York: Holt, Rinehart and Winston, 1975.

Pinnell, William H. *Theatrical Scene Painting: A Lesson Guide*. Carbondale, IL: Southern Illinois University Press, 1987.

Rossol, Miriam. *Stage Fright: Health & Safety in the Theatre*. New York: Allworth Press, 1991.

Sammler, Ben, and Don Harvey (Eds.). *The Technical Brief Collection:* New Haven: Yale School of Drama, 1992.

Stern, Lawrence. *Stage Management: A Guide of Practical Techniques* (2nd ed). Boston: Allyn and Bacon, 1982.

Sweet, Harvey. *The Complete Book of Drawing for the Theatre* (2nd ed.). Boston: Allyn and Bacon, 1995.

Sweet, Harvey. *Handbook of Scenery, Properties, and Lighting, Volume II: Lighting* (2nd ed.). Boston: Allyn and Bacon, 1995.

Theatre Crafts. *How-To: Volume One*. New York: Theatre Crafts Books, 1984.

Theatre Crafts. *Theatre Crafts Directory*. New York: Theatre Crafts and Lighting Dimensions, annually.

Index